GARY
BARLOW
THE BIOGRAPHY

JUSTIN LEWIS

JOHN BLAKE

Published by John Blake Publishing Ltd,
3 Bramber Court, 2 Bramber Road,
London W14 9PB, England

www.johnblakepublishing.co.uk

www.facebook.com/johnblakebooks ▪
twitter.com/jblakebooks ▪

First published in hardback in 2013
This edition published in 2014

ISBN: 978-1-78418-020-1

British Library Cataloguing-in-Publication Data:

A catalogue record for this book is available from the British Library.

Design by www.envydesign.co.uk

Printed and bound in Great Britain by CPI Group (UK) Ltd

1 3 5 7 9 10 8 6 4 2

Papers used by John Blake Publishing are natural, recyclable
products made from wood grown in sustainable forests.
The manufacturing processes conform to the environmental
regulations of the country of origin.

Every attempt has been made to contact the relevant copyright-holders,
but some were unobtainable. We would be grateful if the appropriate people
could contact us.

CONTENTS

CHAPTER 1

INTRODUCTION

In the autumn of 2005, a defunct and almost forgotten British pop group of the 1990s made a three-pronged comeback bid. They took part in a TV documentary in which they reminisced about their lives, released a greatest hits album and announced they would be going back on the road just one more time.

No one could have guessed what would happen next. Such was the public reaction that they decided to make an album of brand new material. Their first in over 10 years, it sold nearly three million copies in Britain alone. In the next few years, they would break all sorts of sales records for their recordings and concert tickets. Take That had achieved something that no other British band had ever done before: after a lengthy sabbatical, this major multi-million-selling group had returned to the spotlight, and were now even bigger. Not only were they bigger, they may even have been better. Sophisticated grown-up songs like 'Shine', 'Patience', 'Greatest Day' and 'Rule the World' put them back at the top of the charts. By 2010's *Progress*, their first album in 15 years to feature estranged member Robbie Williams, they were arguably making their boldest, most adventurous music yet. And music that still sold millions.

The sort of revival that Take That have experienced is not supposed to happen in pop music. The biggest-selling groups and artists are usually so 'of their time' that a comeback is, at best, a celebration of nostalgia. Few have the ability to almost entirely reinvent themselves a decade later. When a band is revived, it is not expected to stick around for very long. The usual drill is for them to reappear, run through their old hits one more time, collect the money, and start the car. It is most unlikely that the public wants to hear their new songs.

So how did Take That and their chief songwriter Gary Barlow put a line through so many of pop's rules in trumping their first career second time around? In *Time to Shine*, we'll examine how Gary developed from a teenage singer and organist on the club circuit, in and around his native Cheshire, to stardom in the 1990s as part of the five-piece boyband. As of early 2014, his sales figures were estimated at over 50 million albums, he had reached number one in the singles charts on 14 occasions (a record for a British artist, bettered only by the four members of the Beatles), and topped the album charts nine times. He had been a tireless charity campaigner, was a constant fixture on various TV shows (most obviously *The X Factor*) and regularly participated in royal occasions, including organising the pop concert for the

Queen's Diamond Jubilee celebrations in 2012. Soon afterwards, he was honoured with the Order of the British Empire. But, inevitably, Gary Barlow's biggest achievement continues to lie with Take That.

Take That – five handsome and good-humoured young men who had been thrown together in Manchester as the 'British New Kids On The Block', but who became friends in the process – made their original breakthrough in 1992. Good looks and charisma undoubtedly played a part in their appeal to millions of teenage girls, but there is no way they could have maintained this popularity for four years without memorable songs. While a handful of their hits were cover versions, the vast majority were Gary Barlow originals, including several of the 1990s' best-loved pop songs: 'Pray', 'Everything Changes', 'Never Forget', 'A Million Love Songs'. Above all, there was 'Back for Good', which on its release in spring 1995 became the UK's fastest-selling single for a decade.

Although the sudden departure of Robbie Williams in 1995 unbalanced relations within the group, and hastened its own demise only months later, Take That Mark I bowed out at the top. Gary struck out as a solo act, touted as a future George Michael, but found the going much harder on his own, especially when Robbie's own solo bid for stardom unexpectedly took off in a sensational fashion. By the turn of the 21st century, Gary's records were flopping, his shows were two-thirds full and his contract with his record company was terminated.

The troughs of Gary Barlow's story are as significant as its peaks. What really tests someone's character in the celebrity world is how they react to failure and oblivion, and, though

Gary undoubtedly found this hard, he continued to work diligently as a songwriter and producer, with the constant support of his family, friends and colleagues. Then again, even as a teenager, he was a driven, ambitious and hard-working individual. He may not have shone as a dancer, but his singing voice, musicianship, gift for original songwriting and stage presence were excellent credentials for when opportunity knocked with Take That in 1990.

Take That, by Gary's own admission, was not an equal partnership in the 1990s. Because he wrote the songs, he earned far more money than the others, and part of the agreement when they re-formed was that all the group members had a creative say. The second act of Take That (when the 'boyband' became a 'manband') is not only a leap forward musically, but it also introduced an atmosphere that was warmer and more relaxed all round.

Time to Shine is a story about talent and ambition but it's also about generosity, co-operation and understanding in the frequently cut-throat entertainment business. More than anything, it's about camaraderie. Robbie Williams once described their journey as 'five boys who needed to go through therapy, heal a little bit, forgive and be forgiven. Or else it was panto.' For Gary Barlow, the secret of Take That's success lay in their friendship: 'As long as our friendship is as close as it is, I think the world is our oyster.'

CHAPTER 2

PLUGGING IN

The singles charts can be a hotchpotch at the best of times, but in January 1971, they showed a pop scene with little obvious sense of direction. The glam rock trend of Slade, David Bowie and The Sweet was still a year away. The Beatles had broken up, although, with 'My Sweet Lord', George Harrison was their first former member to reach the number one spot in Britain. Rock groups such as Status Quo, T. Rex, Badfinger and The Kinks nestled alongside easy-listening favourites like Andy Williams, the Carpenters and Frank Sinatra, whose 'My Way' had been in the charts for the best part of two years. Then there were the singers who wrote their own songs and performed them, too: Gilbert O'Sullivan, Neil Diamond and a 23-year-old from Pinner in Middlesex who was making his chart debut. Reginald Kenneth Dwight, aka Elton John, was the pop world's hottest new star of 1971.

It was perhaps fitting that Gary William Barlow would become one of Elton John's biggest fans. Born the same week as 'Your Song' became Elton's first-ever hit, he made his debut at lunchtime on Wednesday, 20 January 1971 in Frodsham, in the north-west English county of Cheshire. His first home was in Ashton Drive, part of a council estate on the fringes of a village about to be given town status. Three miles north lay the town of Runcorn. The cities of Chester, Liverpool and Manchester were a little further away.

There was already an elder child in the Barlow household. Ian had been born three years previously in 1968. The pair would get along well as adults, but as kids they would sometimes clash. 'I hated him as a youngster,' a 25-year-old Gary admitted in 1996, 'but we get on so well now. He could be the real, upset, forgotten-about brother and he isn't: he's just so proud of what I do.'

The boys' dad was Colin, who worked as a project manager for a fertiliser company. The position often required him to work nights, and, with a second job at a farm in the late afternoons, he had no choice but to snatch a precious few hours of sleep during the mornings. After Gary started school, his mum Marjorie went back to work as a laboratory technician at a hospital in the nearby city of Chester.

Gary drew a strong work ethic from both his parents and, from an early age, assimilated it into his own life. He was never lectured about the importance of toil, but he could appreciate the effort and commitment of both of them. The extra income amassed by those extra hours meant that the Barlows could enjoy the occasional luxury. They bought a colour television at a time when by no means all 1970s families could afford one and their budget stretched to a holiday in Ibiza when Gary was five years old and Ian was eight. 'They're scrimpers and savers, my mum and dad,' commented Gary in 1996. 'They'll clear out the attic and do boot sales for the next four weeks.'

His obsession with music began early. The first toy to truly capture his imagination was a Fisher Price toy keyboard. In one way, it was hard to see where Gary's inspiration for music originated. It did not come from his mum or dad – neither of them played an instrument. But there were plenty of records in the house at Ashton Drive in the 70s, everything from the disco-pop of Boney M and the Bee Gees, to classics from The Beatles and the US record label Tamla Motown (home to the Supremes, Stevie Wonder, the Temptations, the Jackson Five and others). Meanwhile, the Griffiths family next door, whose children were older than the Barlows', owned all the latest chart singles.

When Gary was about six years old, the first single he owned was 'Living Next Door to Alice' by a then-popular group from Yorkshire called Smokie. Within two years, he was already practising his fantasy of being a pop icon, and had formed his first group – in the garage. A school friend called Tracey Oultram was also involved, although she conceded their instruments were a tad basic. 'We used upturned bins for drums,' she recalled, 'and my friend played the triangle. His mum always used to come in and tell him to shut up.'

Gary's early fascination with popular culture extended to cinematic blockbusters. The garden became the location for a special *Star Wars* remake starring Gary and Tracey. 'As we were kind of boyfriend/girlfriend at the time,' said Tracey, 'he asked if I'd be Princess Leia. His brother was Chewbacca. All I remember is Chewbacca jumping off the porch, trying to attack me, and Gary rescuing me with a kiss. I think I pretended to faint.'

It was 1980 when Gary began to buy and collect his own records at the age of nine. His first purchase was 'D.I.S.C.O.' by the French group Ottawan, but he soon became entranced by the emergence of Adam Ant. Each of Adam and the Ants' hit singles – 'Dog Eat Dog', 'Antmusic', 'Kings of the Wild Frontier' – was accompanied by a striking and unforgettable promotional video, fast becoming an effective way of selling pop music as three- or four-minute mini-films.

Adam Ant (born Stuart Goddard) was a colourful frontman, obsessive about constantly reinventing himself and dressing up in different guises: a pirate, a highwayman ('Stand and Deliver') and Prince Charming. Some of the videos featured guest stars, such as the British actress Diana Dors and (in the case of the 'Ant Rap' video) the Scottish singer Lulu.

At the end of March 1981, Gary attended Adam and the Ants' concert at Manchester Apollo. 'There was half a pirate ship on stage,' he marvelled to Q magazine many years later. 'I was an Antette. I had the stripy make-up, the full regalia.' It seemed more like a theatrical show than a gig. The Ants were playing their songs in a series of flamboyant costumes and with spectacular sets.

Within a year of that Manchester show, the Ants would be no more, although Adam would embark on a variable solo career. Like David Bowie and The Beatles before him, he seemed equally inspired by rock'n'roll and British variety. Adam seemed to be not just a survivor of punk rock but also heavily indebted to light entertainment. He loved the Sex Pistols but would also appear with Cannon and Ball on television, and at the Children's Royal Variety Performance. Though he acted the rebel, he could also reach out to the mainstream.

While sibling Ian preferred to stay in the background, Gary was a talkative child who after a while began longing for the limelight. One of his early passions outside music was for magic, and he was regularly glued to illusionist Paul Daniels' television show on Saturday nights. Before long, Gary had a magic act adequate enough to provide some entertainment for his dad Colin's pigeon club.

That same year, 1981, was the year that the Barlows moved house, but they continued to live in Frodsham. From their three-bedroom semi-detached house in Ashton Drive, they moved into a bungalow in London Road called 'Ravenscroft'.

At school, Gary would never truly shine academically, but at least there were music classes at Weaver Vale Primary School. Under the strict watch of a teacher called Mrs Bourne – 'Everyone was scared of her' – he and his classmates were given the chance to play some musical instruments, mostly of the percussive kind. 'When we were told we could play them,' he remembered, 'there would be a mad dash to get to the best ones first – no one wanted to be left with the triangle.'

In the summer of 1981, Weaver Vale Primary's new headmaster had the bright idea of staging a production of *Joseph and the Amazing Technicolor Dreamcoat*, written by Andrew Lloyd Webber and Tim Rice, which had first been performed as a musical in 1970. Ten-year-old Gary was determined to be a part of the school production, and so spent the whole of the summer holidays engrossed in the stage cast LP, trying to memorise every bar and every word. On returning to school in the autumn, he found his preparation had paid off; he was cast in the lead role of Joseph: 'Andrew Lloyd Webber and Tim Rice's musical is what got me started on stage, and I have to say I loved every second of it. The showman in me had emerged.'

Gary had been bitten by the stage bug and the concept of performing. Like every pop fan, he would sit down each week to watch *Top of the Pops* on television, a special rare treat to have music on TV in primetime. In the days before 24-hour music television, let alone the World Wide Web, pop music did not appear much as part of popular television. When it did, it was usually as a break in a variety show or comedy series, so the likes of *Top of the Pops* and Saturday-morning children's programmes like Noel Edmonds' *Multi-Coloured Swap Shop* and *Tiswas* (hosted by Chris Tarrant and Lenny Henry) were essential outlets for pop videos and performances.

Apart from Adam and the Ants, Gary's favourite groups of the time included Duran Duran and Spandau Ballet, key bands of the early 1980s New Romantic movement, in which the electronic influence of Kraftwerk was combined with disco, and the same sort of outrageous image and fashion displayed in the 1970s by David Bowie, Marc Bolan and Bryan Ferry's Roxy Music. It was a good time to be a fan of British pop. And then, in October 1981, Gary had some sort of musical epiphany. While watching *Top of the Pops* one Thursday night, he fell in love with the sound of 'Just Can't Get Enough', an early hit single for the Basildon synth-pop quartet Depeche Mode. He had never heard anything quite like it before. The very next day, he knew he wanted an electronic keyboard.

Christmas was still several weeks away, but his parents agreed to help him choose an instrument. They visited a music shop in Chester, where a helpful salesman guided them towards a Yamaha keyboard, specifically the PS-2 model. On Christmas Day, Gary plugged in the equipment, tried out a few seasonal carols and Scott Joplin's 'The Entertainer' (a must for any budding pianist). He was on his way, but, within three weeks, he felt he was already outgrowing the instrument. So it was back to Chester, and back to the same music shop, this time on the lookout for something that looked and sounded a bit more professional. The organ that Gary fell in love with, which comprised two keyboards and bass pedals for the feet, had a price tag of £500, a steep price, especially in the early 1980s. It seemed completely unaffordable, until dad Colin worked out that, because he had been working so hard, he had some spare holiday. He could sell back his holiday to the company. With the money raised from this, they could buy the keyboard. The Barlow work ethic had won out, yet again.

Gary's other hobby outside music in his formative years was karate. He had joined a club at the tender age of six, and became extremely proficient, but suffered a setback at the age of 12 when he broke one of his fingers. Soon afterwards, he found himself confronting a troublemaker at school who was trying to punch him. 'I blocked [the punch] with a karate move and broke his arm. I remember the sheer horror on everyone's face. I got suspended for two weeks, so that put an end to that.'

Other than that, though, Gary's secondary school days, spent at the comprehensive Frodsham High School, were uneventful. While his brother Ian had briefly entered a mildly rebellious phase in his teens – smoking and riding motorbikes with no crash helmet – Gary kept his head down and tried to stay out of mischief. According to one of the Barlows' neighbours, it was best he didn't get into trouble as, by then, his mum Marge was working at the same school as a lab technician.

Returning to musical matters, Gary knew that, in order to improve as an instrumentalist, he needed to have some extra tuition. So, in 1982, he began private lessons with an organ teacher called Chris Greenleaves, who lived nearby. It was Chris who taught him the J.S. Bach-inspired 1967 number one hit 'A Whiter Shade of Pale' by Procol Harum, which had a very distinctive organ melody. Soon, Gary was learning everything from TV themes like *Hill Street Blues* and *Fame*, to hits old and new by singer-songwriters Neil Diamond, Billy Joel and Lionel Richie.

Gary was becoming a versatile musician, and, as he grew more confident in replicating the songs of others, he gradually became aware of song structure. How a song fitted together, how a verse built up towards a strong chorus, how the bridge, middle-eight and instrumental break slotted in, and so on. These lessons were invaluable training for when he began to write his own songs. In his words, 'I became aware of their DNA.'

CHAPTER 3

CUE, GARY!

In the winter of 1984, 13-year-old Gary Barlow found out about a local talent competition. His mum Marjorie had spotted an advert in the local newspaper, the *Chester Observer*, which was organising a Club Act of the Year contest in conjunction with the Greenall Whitley brewery. Gary applied and, on 15 March, he showed up at the Labour Party Club in Connah's Quay, just over the Welsh border in Clwyd. He didn't just play the organ and sing during his 15-minute set, which included a rendition of 'A Whiter Shade of Pale'. On his mum's advice, he also talked in between songs, and even put in a joke or two. It wasn't exactly Gary at Carnegie Hall, but it was a start.

Before the club secretary Norman Hill announced the results of the contest, he approached Gary for a quiet word. The lad had been placed third, but he was offered the chance to work as a regular at the club on Saturday nights during the spring. His duties would be to play well-loved oldies to the clientele, people who in stark contrast to the Take That fans 10 years later were unlikely to be screaming for more. Actually, they wouldn't even necessarily be *listening*. His first task was to try to persuade them to do that.

In 2001, the workingmen's club scene would be satirised by Peter Kay, Dave Spikey and Neil Fitzmaurice, the writers of a very popular Channel 4 sitcom. 'Because we've all seen *Phoenix Nights*,' Gary said, 'we've a bit more insight into how those clubs used to be. It really was that bad, every one of those characters is in every club. But I wasn't laughing at all back then. I was fascinated by how it all worked and I took in all the best bits and made my own show, eventually.'

The juvenile entertainer 'Gary', billed at this point with no surname, studied everything at the Labour Club carefully. He watched the other acts, but also the audience – how they responded, if they were interested, whether they were bored. He was quietly learning how to build an act, and how to inspire the crowds to react to it. Soon, he had developed a regular set. 'A Whiter Shade of Pale' from Chris Greenleaves' organ lessons was part of it, as was 'I Will Survive', the Gloria Gaynor disco classic.

The teenager instinctively knew that chart music, the music he himself was enjoying, was not necessarily the taste of the older audience who would be in a club on a Saturday night waiting for the bingo or a headlining act, so he tailored his act accordingly. To begin with, he struggled. Attempts to break up the music with illusions or even jokes from stand-ups he'd seen on TV didn't really work. Taking requests was a more effective idea. Then, one night, a member of the sparse gathering at the bar asked if he knew an Everly Brothers' number from the 1950s called 'All I Have to Do is Dream'. It was the kind of song few teenagers in the 1980s would have known, but Gary assured the man that he knew it. The man then asked if he could sing it, with Gary acting as accompanist. An 'open mic' night every Saturday was born, a common practice in clubs as a way for members of the audience to participate, if they so wished. In a way, it was karaoke before the arrival of karaoke in Britain.

Gary had three musical heroes in his teens. One was the frontman and songwriter with Wham!, which had begun as a white funk duo but by 1984 crossed over into straight pop: 'I remember the first time I saw George Michael, I couldn't stop looking at him. Stars like that have charisma all around them.' He was intrigued that Michael could be a massive teen star, then simultaneously release solo singles (the million-selling 'Careless Whisper' in 1984 was his first), which gained him greater respect, and even bigger sales. In turn, Michael was a huge fan of Elton John, who had become internationally famous in the 1970s after a spell as an anonymous session musician, and Gary felt the same way about him.

Gary's club act was clearly not cutting-edge, but instead catered to those with more middle-of-the-road tastes. 'We used to see him play gigs at clubs,' one school friend told the *Daily Mirror* a decade later, 'and we thought he would be a star like Barry Manilow – because of the songs he sang.' In fact, Manilow was Gary's third musical hero of the time. He loved his middle-of-the-road but impeccably professional act performed to sell-out concert venues all over the world. Barry

Manilow had enjoyed many hits, including 'Mandy', 'Copacabana' and 'Could It Be Magic'. He was not what Britain's teenagers were listening to, but a more mature demographic couldn't get enough of him.

Soon, Gary's club commitments increased to three nights a week – Friday and Sunday, as well as Saturday. He roped in a friend from school, Heather Woodall, to form a musical double act called Karisma. They had already known each other for a couple of years and would for a time be boyfriend and girlfriend. 'He was a real showman,' Heather told the *News of the World* in 1996. 'If we were watching a boring TV programme he would switch it off and start entertaining me and his mum. He would ask which songs we wanted to hear and play like he was a jukebox.'

Karisma, with organist Gary sharing vocal duties with Heather, entered another talent competition in May 1985 called Starmaker 85. Their set included 'Flashdance (What A Feeling)', the Carpenters' 'Top of the World' and, bringing things bang up to date, 'I Know Him So Well', a recent number one for Elaine Paige and Barbara Dickson. They failed to reach the finals, but were awarded £100 in the 'Act Showing Greatest Potential' category. Furthermore, the contest organiser Mike Bain secured plenty of other bookings for Karisma around the area: in nearby Runcorn, the Wirral, even Liverpool and a Widnes club called Frenchies. All the while, they were earning enough for Gary to buy more sophisticated technical equipment: an amplifier, speakers and microphones, as well as a better keyboard. Even so, the Yamaha DX7 organ cost well over £1,000 – Marge had to buy it on her credit card, and it took Gary more than a year to pay her back.

So, was he aware that he was going to be famous? Certainly, he was preparing for a music career by investing in proper musical hardware, and he was playing a few nights a week. Heather later remembered that he used to practise signing his autograph too. All the same, to *feel* successful seemed sufficient for now. 'I thought I'd struck gold,' he later said. 'It was wonderful training, and I was making a lot of money for a schoolboy.'

Sometimes his ambition would get the better of him, though. By his own admission, the double act with Heather dissolved when Mike Bain asked Gary to do a booking in Austria – but solo. Though the date never went ahead, it caused a rift between the pair's parents (Heather's parents had paid for one of Gary's keyboards along the way) and, although they stayed friends for a time, Karisma were effectively over as a duo. Gary later confessed that his drive to be successful and famous had a negative effect on his personality: 'I thought I deserved to be famous. I wasn't a nice teenager, I wanted to be better than everyone else.'

At the end of 1985, Chris Greenlcaves told Gary he was leaving his spot as the resident organist at a British Legion club in the Runcorn suburb of Halton. The teenager auditioned and got the job, but had to reveal how young he was. At 14, he didn't even have a National Insurance number. The solution was for him to be paid a bit less, and that way he would avoid paying tax and National Insurance.

At Halton Legion Club, Gary backed singers and occasionally strippers. Before long, he was one-third of the resident music act there, with singer Chris Harrison and a drummer by the name of John Tedford.

There is rarely one and only one big break in any entertainer or musician's life. Usually, there are several. Each step along the road to success is significant. In 1986, Gary's secondary school music teacher Mrs Nelson told him about a TV competition for secondary schools called *A Song for Christmas*. It was a spin-off from the Birmingham-based lunchtime magazine show *Pebble Mill at One*, and asked for pupils to write their own seasonal carols. Gary's attempt was entitled 'Let's Pray for Christmas' and, to his and Mrs Nelson's delight, his effort (representing Frodsham High) was placed in the finals, to be televised by the BBC in the days leading up to Yuletide. In preparation, he and his teacher visited a recording studio in north London, where the contest's musical director Robert Howes recorded the song with some 30 musicians and backing singers.

On Christmas Eve 1986, the *Song for Christmas* final, hosted by Phillip Schofield, was broadcast on BBC1. Surrounded by fake snow and gaudy decorations, and dressed in a pink jumper and grey slacks, Gary sang 'Let's Pray for Christmas'. The carol, dedicated to his nan, came second. It was beaten by a Catholic school from Wales, whose headmaster was heard to mutter, 'He won't win – his song is theologically unsound. One minute he's in the manger, then he's talking about tinsel.'

The judging panel comprised Aled Jones, then a 15-year-old star choirboy, Mike Batt (a versatile songwriter and producer but still known above all for being the man behind the Wombles' hits of the 70s) and Bucks Fizz member Shelley Preston. Playing Simon Cowell as panel chairman was a kindlier Peter Skellern, best known to pop fans for his early

1970s hit 'You're A Lady'. Skellern could see Gary's potential in mixing sacred with secular: 'First-rate. For those who tire of the more traditional carol, this is a very good alternative. Although we don't judge the performance, we thought Gary's delivery of it was tremendous.'

Frodsham's second placing in *A Song for Christmas* made Gary think that perhaps he had a talent for writing original songs. This was his final year at school – he was due to leave after his O-levels in the summer of 1987 – and he was already seeing if he could take all the influences from the many songs he had learned to cover in cabaret and create his own work. 'Let's Pray for Christmas' was an early foray into songwriting and, in landing his school a TV spot, Gary's potential was there for all to see.

After the contest, Gary kept in contact with Robert Howes, who encouraged him to keep sending him tapes of his songs. It gave him a perspective on his songwriting capabilities and on his performance. His club work was becoming more and more lucrative, and invaluable in dealing with audiences, but he needed a more professional reaction to his songs. Robert gave him plenty of feedback. He was especially taken with a ballad Gary had penned and recorded at home, heavily influenced by the work of Lionel Richie and Neil Diamond, but with its own identity. It was called '1 Million Love Songs Later'. His nan and his mum Marge liked it too, but few at this stage could have imagined how big a smash hit it would eventually become – under a slightly different title.

CHAPTER 4

THE HUMAN JUKEBOX

G ary Barlow had come second in *A Song for Christmas*, but in 1987, his last year at Frodsham High School, he would go one better. Another original song of his which represented the school, 'Now We're Gone', won the National Schools Make Music Competition, sponsored by EMI. Part of the prize was to record the winning song at Abbey Road Studios in London, home to so many classic hits, including the many Beatles recordings of the 1960s.

Sixteen-year-old Gary left school that summer. 1987 was the last year of O-level examinations before they were replaced by GCSEs. Gary had taken music O-level a year early, and now added four more passes – but maybe he didn't need that many academic qualifications anyway. Financially, he was raking it in – singing and performing in clubs six nights of the week, and earning up to £450 per week. And he was quite the entrepreneur, trying to persuade punters to buy audio cassettes of his material, on electronic organ and drum machine, including his covers of Chris de Burgh's 'Lady in Red' and Simon & Garfunkel's 'Bridge Over Troubled Water'. Sometimes he would succeed; these would soon become collectors' items. One family friend was given a few tapes in 1989 with the promise: 'Lock them up, they'll be worth a lot of money.' In 1996, the friend cashed in at Christie's, where the recordings fetched £15,000.

Gary was still in touch with Robert Howes from *A Song for Christmas*. On Howes' advice, and with the help of his contacts book, Gary started sending out his demo tapes to the music publishers and record companies of London. He would arrange a meeting, and travel down by train from Cheshire to the capital. Hoping to look official and professional, he would turn up in a suit but the reaction was often deathly, and occasionally humiliating. At one appointment, at a publisher called Rocket Publishing (part of a company owned by his hero Elton John), an executive's response was to stand up in silence, hurl Gary's tape out of an open window and say: 'Don't ever bring your songs in here again.' Solace of a kind came on his long journey back home – he heard the moving Peter Gabriel and Kate Bush duet 'Don't Give Up'. Experiences such as this only made him more determined.

Back at Halton Social Club, Gary and his drummer John Tedford continued to provide the entertainment, and helped back many famous visiting comics, from Bob Monkhouse to Ken Dodd – the latter notorious for his marathon stand-up routines lasting several hours. Gary and John formed their own duo for a time, Stax, and entered the *Runcorn Weekly*

News and Greenall Whitley Act of the Year contest again. They won, the first time Gary had been placed first, and scooped a prize of £500.

He still kept an eye on the charts, which by 1987 were dominated by the high-energy, dance-pop of writer-producer trio Mike Stock, Matt Aitken and Pete Waterman. Though they had many critics, who decried their output as samey and formulaic, their work would be undeniably popular for the rest of the 1980s. Artists they nurtured included Mel and Kim, Kylie Minogue, Jason Donovan and Sonia. For a time, their biggest name of all was a white soul singer who, like Gary Barlow, hailed from the north-west. 'I was really, really jealous of Rick Astley,' admitted Gary, nearly 10 years later. 'He used to come from round my way. I wanted to be him.' Astley's vocal style, itself influenced by American soul singers like Luther Vandross, and the studio sound of Stock Aitken Waterman (all clattering rhythms and catchy synth hooks), led to a string of hits for him, including the best-seller of 1987, 'Never Gonna Give You Up'. It would convince Gary, for now, that manufactured pop was the way forward if he was to get noticed as a singer-songwriter.

At the same time, he worked hard at making his cabaret act more energetic. Never a dance whiz, he at least began to inject more movement into his performance. He had the advantage over more mature performers when adding to his repertoire a song like Michael Jackson's 'The Way You Make Me Feel': 'I'd do a bit of a routine to it. None of these 40-year-old singers could do that – they'd be out of breath bending to one knee.'

Where he had once been ferried to clubs and bars by his mum and dad, as soon as Gary passed his driving test, he bought a car, and so could provide his own transport. Rather than opt for a BMW, he invested more modestly, in a diesel Ford. One night he could be as far away as Blackpool, on another in Wigan, or closer to home in Halton, where he would still be playing weekend shows. The club money was excellent – he was now making more than his brother Ian (on a government Youth Training building scheme) and even his dad. Colin expressed some concern about whether his younger son should concentrate on finding 'a proper job', perhaps out of nervousness about the precarious world of showbiz.

But no one could claim Gary lacked commitment or determination to make it in the music game. It wasn't just the money, or the long hours. His bedroom at the London Road bungalow was so crammed with recording equipment and musical instruments that there was no longer space for a bed. For three years, he slept on the living-room sofa.

He remained convinced that he might be able to make it as a pop musician. By 1989, he had begun to feel trapped by the club circuit. He had been doing it for five years in all, including three and a half years at Halton British Legion Club: 'I'd been on the club scene too long. I was 18, going on 58. At that time, I was quite bitter – bit of a chip on my shoulder.' In June, he left the Halton club, and, though he continued at venues on Merseyside and Lancashire, he could attract bookings much further afield, sometimes in Yorkshire, and occasionally as far south as Essex. For a time, he tried to join a group, a rock band based in Chester called Passion, but found it difficult to commit to their schedule as he was already heavily booked with his own club commitments. It was a frustrating time in a way – most of his audience was more than twice his own age.

'I was desperate to get into pop,' he later told the *Daily Mirror*. 'I tried everything I could to get a break.'

Then, in the summer of 1989, a local agent called Barry Wooley from the Leo Agency approached him after a gig about a recording project down in Nottingham. It was a remake of 'Love is in the Air', a pop-disco hit first recorded in the late 1970s by the New Zealander John Paul Young. Once in the studio, Gary laid down a vocal, only to be told that a satisfactory lead vocal already existed, but, because the original singer was unavailable for the video shoot, he was asked to appear instead, under the pseudonym of 'Kurtis Rush'. 'Love is in the Air' was never released, either as a record or a video, but one of the younger dancers, an 18-year-old called Dawn, would later become a major part of Gary's life.

While 'Love is in the Air' was never going to be Gary's big break, he did at least receive a fanatical national write-up at the close of 1989. He had entered yet another talent contest, this time sponsored by the *Manchester Evening News*, called 'Search for a Star'. A few years earlier, the contest had discovered a teenage vocal sensation from Rochdale called Lisa Stansfield, and, as the 1989 contest took place, she had just been number one in the national charts with 'All Around the World'.

'Search for a Star' 1989 took place in December at a Salford club called The Willows Variety Centre. Gary finished the contest in third place, but, when *The Stage* reviewed the show in its final issue of the year, it paid tribute to his potential: 'Totally at ease on stage, this enthusiastic 18-year-old has special charisma, putting over his self-penned material with vocal power and visual charm, and throwing in some fabulous footwork. The search was for a star, and here was one in the making.' The article also mentioned that the Leo Agency had given Gary a special award as the finalist with the 'best long-term prospects'.

As the 1990s dawned, the future was looking bright for Gary Barlow.

CHAPTER 5

NIGEL

At the turn of the 1990s, the big teen sensation to arrive in Britain was a five-piece boyband from the United States called New Kids On The Block. After several major hits in the US, they were launched internationally, with their lives soon exhaustively documented in the UK teen press, in magazines like *Smash Hits* and *Number One*. Teenage girls screamed wherever they went. By November 1989, they were at number one in Britain with a single called 'You Got It (The Right Stuff)', a success swiftly emulated by its follow-up, 'Hangin' Tough'. Their image was a safe version of 'attitude' and 'street cred', ideal for an audience of children and young teenagers, though rock critics inevitably hated them on account of their manufactured nature.

Watching the inexorable rise of New Kids On The Block with great interest was a Manchester-based entertainment agent in his early 30s called Nigel Martin-Smith. He noticed that they had broken through in a comprehensive way that the British boybands of the late 1980s like Brother Beyond and Big Fun had failed to do. A trio called Bros had been the biggest teen act in the UK, but their songs were variable and, after they became a duo in 1989, their appeal (and especially their record sales) began to wane. Part of the problem lay with the fanbase. Anyone outside that obsessive group was unlikely to buy a Bros or a Big Fun record because the songs were mostly not strong enough.

Nigel had an idea. Why didn't he try to manufacture a British equivalent of New Kids? Their very sudden impact on the pop scene suggested that youngsters were more than happy to embrace a boyband again, with the same sort of feverish devotion as past groups such as The Osmonds in the 1970s, and Duran Duran and Wham! in the 1980s. He quite enjoyed New Kids' music, but was less keen on their public persona. 'I couldn't help but feel how obnoxious they were,' he told the *Daily Mirror* in 1993. 'I was sure I could form a Northern band which could create an equally big stir, but be charming, friendly and down-to-earth at the same time.'

Nigel had been running agencies in Manchester like Nidge's throughout the 1980s, usually representing models or actors. Occasionally, one of his clients would appear in the TV serials made in the north-west, such as Granada Television's long-running *Coronation Street*. Then, in 1988, he joined forces with another Manchester-based agent, Debra Burns, who had run a model agency, to form a company called the Boss Agency. The following year, 1989, one of its clients, a singer called Damian, managed a freak hit single in the shape of a cover of 'Time Warp' from *The Rocky Horror Show*. It got into the Top 10, Nigel's first major chart hit as a manager.

For his British New Kids, Nigel dreamed of a group that would please and excite, but not shock their target audience, the sort of lads 'that girls could take home to their mums for tea'. He wanted a lot of control too. 'I didn't want any of that nonsense about needing six months off for "my creativity",' he would bluntly tell *The Sunday Times* in 1994. Annual leave would be just two weeks. The members of the group would be accompanied by minders at all times in public, band members would avoid interviews that had not been previously organised, and would need to be committed to the group, its values and its career. The relationship between manager and group would act as an employment contract, with Nigel having the final say on who could interview his clients, as well as where these interviews would appear, and how photographs of the lads could be used. 'I knew if they took control it was doomed to failure,' he told *The Sunday Times*.

After Nigel placed an advertisement for his new boyband project in the regional press, he was approached by a dancer that he had already met backstage at *The Hitman and Her*, an ITV show Damian had performed on the previous summer. Jason Orange, born 10 July 1970, had been resident on the series since its inception in 1988, as a low-budget mix of nightclub culture and end-of-the-pier entertainment. Hosts Pete Waterman and Michaela Strachan introduced audience participation in the form of daft games and linked the floor-filling music from various clubs, usually in the North of England. It was not hip (these were not trendy warehouse rave parties), but it regularly attracted a million viewers – no mean feat for a programme broadcast on Saturday nights at two in the morning.

Before *The Hitman and Her*, Jason had been one of Manchester's breakdancing kings as a teenager, entertaining passers-by in the city's shopping areas. At home in Wythenshawe, he had painstakingly practised his routines in front of a mirror. He was one of six boys (one of whom was his twin brother), all raised as Mormons, but he renounced the faith in his teens.

Like Jason, Howard Donald, born in Droylsden on 28 April 1968, had also been in a breakdancing posse (in his case called the RDS Royals). Something else they had in common was that they had both been on government Youth Training Schemes after leaving school. Whereas Jason had trained to be a painter and decorator, Howard was spray-painting cars for £140 a week. Neither of them had musical training, nor indeed had they shown a keen interest in being in a band of any kind when their dance duo Street Beat approached Nigel Martin-Smith in early 1990. Howard liked the idea of being a club DJ, playing techno records. Jason, meanwhile, just wanted to enjoy himself, and be 'young and daft'. All the same, both contacted the manager at his Manchester offices with a very clear message: 'We want to extend our career.'

Another who got in touch with the Boss Agency was Mark Owen, who hailed from Oldham. Born on 27 January 1972, he dreamed of playing professional football in his teens and was promising enough to land trials with Huddersfield Town, Manchester United and Rochdale, but, sadly, he got no further. Instead, he worked at Barclays Bank, although Nigel later spun the myth that he had formed a duo with Gary called

The Cutest Rush – a name not a million miles from the 'Kurtis Rush' that Gary had been in 1989.

After *The Stage* had given his 'Search for a Star' performance such a good review at Christmas, Gary began 1990 by contacting lots of agencies and management companies whose contact details appeared in the classifieds at the back of the paper. For some, he enclosed a photograph, a short biography and a demo tape of songs, but, when he contacted Manchester's Boss Agency, he omitted to enclose the cassette as they seemed to favour actors and models – but he reasoned that maybe he could get one or two TV walk-on parts. When Boss replied, he was on the verge of accepting a job working on a cruise-ship for 12 months. Instead, he went to see Nigel, who seemed indifferent towards the notion of having a songwriter on board. After all, it wasn't as if New Kids On The Block wrote their own stuff. 'I gave him a demo tape,' said Gary, 'and I could tell he wasn't really interested in the idea of original songs – he just put it to one side on his desk.' Then again, the name New Kids On The Block meant nothing to Gary: 'I'd never heard of them before – I was out of touch because of playing in the clubs.' His tastes were still based in the 70s and 80s, adult-orientated pop songs like 'Africa' by Toto, Billy Joel's 'Piano Man' and Chicago's 'Hard Habit to Break'.

It was Nigel Martin-Smith himself who decided which of a shortlist of eight would be whittled down to the group he required, but he had in mind a quartet rather than a quintet: 'I originally wanted it to be a four-piece band. The reason I started out with five was because I thought one of them would be bound to drop out, get a job in Tesco's, or get married.'

His fifth potential member for the still-unnamed group was a 16-year-old youth from Stoke-on-Trent. He showed the others a photograph. 'This picture looked like a 14-year-old school kid, and I was a bit unsure,' was Gary's memory. Nigel told them, 'His name's Robbie and he's got a really good voice.'

Robert Peter Williams was born on 13 February 1974. His dad, Peter Conway, was an entertainer in the northern clubs and, during childhood, Robbie would accompany him around the country's seaside theatres in the summertime. 'I gave him the confidence to go a bit mad, take a few risks, though I did not know how far it would go,' Robbie's dad said of him in 1999. 'I knew he would be an entertainer – it could have been as an actor, a comedian or dancer. It just happened to be pop.'

After their parents' divorce in 1976, Robbie and his sister Sally were raised mostly by their mum Janet, who worked as a drugs counsellor.

During his schooldays, Robbie vowed that one day he would make it as a Hollywood icon. At eight, he trod the boards as the Artful Dodger in a junior school production of *Oliver!* But while he was good at sport, and enjoyed performing, he did not shine academically. He longed to work as an actor or teach drama. His one job would be working as a double-glazing salesman and he didn't last long as he tended to tell the customers how bad the product was! Then, one day in 1990, his mum happened to hear Nigel Martin-Smith on the radio, talking about his British New Kids' wheeze. She decided to write to him, pretending to be writing as Robbie, and the teen was invited to an audition. When the result came through, in August 1990, it was on the same day as his GCSE results. Robbie had passed one: a poor D grade for English

Literature. He may have flunked his exams, but he was in the group. 'I ran upstairs,' he later recalled, 'threw the window open and shouted: "I'm going to be famous!"'

Robbie was the last to join Take That. He later recalled his audition and the first time he ever met Gary: 'There was this guy sat there with really untrendy Adidas bottoms on, massive converse trainers, a stupid spiky haircut – and I'm not dissing him here, I mean it lovingly. He's got his legs crossed, with his hands on his knee and this bloody leather briefcase, which had song sheets for crap cabaret songs in it. I looked at him and I was told, "This is Gary Barlow. He's a professional club singer and he's going to make this group happen."'

Gary's first impression on meeting Robbie, still then only 16 years old, was that 'he was one of those precocious school kids who danced outrageously and was dead cheeky, but quite a likeable young lad'.

Nigel Martin-Smith may have thought of the quintet as a British New Kids, but they visibly did not share his ethos. 'They're very good at what they do,' was Robbie's ironic but diplomatic answer during a TV interview when almost everyone else was stuck for words. All were fond of music, but Robbie liked hip-hop, Howard was a techno fan, Jason also enjoyed some dance music as well as a bit of Pink Floyd, while Mark preferred indie-rock. Only Gary truly had a mainstream pop career in mind, but, even though Nigel had signed him up first, he still saw him as part of the five. He argued that it was too early for Gary to make it alone. In 1996, Gary would remember: 'He told me, "It's too early for you to be a solo artist. It would be better to have a foil around you and eventually leave the band."' But when would that be? Few could have guessed how long it would take, even fewer that here was a massively successful pop act of the future.

In the autumn of 1990, contracts were signed between manager and group members. Because some of the group were so young – Robbie was 16 – parents were encouraged to attend the meetings. At 19, Gary was older, but, all the same, his mum Marge came along. All they needed now was a name for the group. Nigel suggested Kick It, to much amusement. Finally, Take That was agreed upon. 'I gave them a list of the things they had to do, and not to do,' said Nigel later, 'and we shook hands on the deal.' Everyone agreed, and signed.

There were those, like Debra Burns, Nigel Martin-Smith's then business partner at Boss, who saw potential. Take That may have had variable experience as entertainers, and may not have been good enough as individuals to be stars, yet, when united, somehow they complemented each other. 'As individuals,' she would tell *The Sunday Times*, 'they all had that certain quality you look for when you are assessing ability. Together, they were a magical combination.'

Jason in particular felt a kinship with the others, perhaps because he related their closeness to the upbringing he had experienced with his five siblings: 'I think I have an insight into male group dynamics because of the way I was raised with my brothers.'

All the same, fine-tuning that rapport and streamlining those strengths would take time, especially when it came to things like TV interviews – interacting, reacting, not interrupting each other too much. Not only did they have to create and perfect their own individual personas, but they also had to work on how they inter-related. By the time they were stars, they were wisecracking types who could finish each other's sentences and indulge in silliness. But they had to learn fast. Early television interviews demonstrate with almost unflinching cruelty how unformed they still were: awkward pauses after admittedly terrible questions, saved only by Robbie's ebullient wit (though he would later put it down to sheer 'overconfidence') and Gary's serious level of ambition.

But, then again, it was hard to come up with great questions given the group had not even released a record yet. They were constantly asked their opinion of New Kids On The Block, and how they had all met; there was little else to discuss. They did laugh together, but, as Jason would later observe, 'It was a laugh that didn't go all the way to your belly. Not ungenuine, but a little bit hollow. There was always that thing of "we've been put together, we're not mates".'

'We went into the band from school with no real knowledge,' Mark reflected. 'We worked hard to get there and what we learned in that band we took on with us. It was like going into the Army or to college to learn a craft.'

Howard's parents were mystified that he could leave his trade in favour of a precarious position in a pop group, where the odds of stardom were tiny. He himself may have enjoyed the hedonism of dancing, but he also admitted: 'Never in a million years did I think I would do something like this.' In the end, he reasoned it was an adventure: 'I just thought I'd go with the flow, see what happens.'

Gary Barlow had taken some persuading to join Take That. There was the matter of his wobbly dancing abilities, but he also had doubts about his bandmates' prospects. What exactly were they bringing to the table? 'For the first few months,' he later admitted with some guilt, 'I had no real respect for the guys because they were dancers and actors.' Still, Nigel reassured him that he would be able to sing his own creations, with the others as backing singers and dancers. Gary caved in, and agreed to join, partly for that reason, but also for the simple fact that the experience could be fun. He had, after all, missed out on some of his adolescence. While his new professional friends had at least had a relatively normal adolescence, since the age of 13, Gary had been juggling school, club work and recording demos, and in recent times had hardly had a night off. Maybe it was time, in his words, to 'share and enjoy'.

'It had been a lonely old life, you know? Driving myself around those clubs in my Ford Orion. In a way,' he summed up, 'I had missed out.'

CHAPTER 6

JELLY,
YOU SAY?

In the closing months of 1990, after signing a contract with Nigel Martin-Smith, Take That started appearing on television. Because of Nigel's contacts in the Manchester area, they soon got a few bookings, and not just *The Hitman and Her*. The independent company that made *Hitman* for Granada, Clear Idea, also made a children's programme called *Cool Cube* for the satellite channel BSB. A Saturday-afternoon magazine show made at Granada's studios, its production team included a 19-year-old researcher called Zoe Ball. The group sang a cover version of Billy Ocean's 'Get Outta My Dreams, Get Into My Car', and debuted 'Girl', a Barlow original song, which was trailed as the first Take That single in early 1991. But, although Gary and co-vocalist Ian Wilson (member of the Manchester pop group Sad Café) would record the vocal parts for 'Girl' at a studio in Cheadle Hulme

– with the other four Thatters looking on – the song would never be officially released, not as a single, nor a B-side, nor even as an album track.

Demo tapes of 'Girl', plus 'Waiting Around' and the jewel of Gary's original repertoire from 1986, now with the shorter title of 'A Million Love Songs', were dispatched to various record labels – Jive, Debut, Polydor – but not one of them bit, not even Jive who had agreed to release 'Time Warp' by Damian, and earned Nigel a gold disc. Despite Nigel's *Hitman* connection, Stock Aitken Waterman weren't interested either. Nor was a 31-year-old called Simon Cowell, who was then running IQ Records, home to Top 10 hit singles in 1991 by Sonia and Dina Carroll.

Cowell had his own very clear idea of what constituted perfect pop music: 'It's a combination of good production, a great song and an artist who is appealing to TV.' He uttered those words in 1992, only months after he had dismissed Gary Barlow and Take That with the words that would soon come back to haunt him: 'Fire the fat one and I'll sign the band.' (This rejection would become part of Take That folklore, but, while Gary recognised it as a good story, he denied its accuracy. 'He gets quoted saying it, but I've asked him and it's not true.')

Meanwhile, Take That had started touring a 20-minute act, usually comprising the three songs from their demo tape, plus covers of The Rolling Stones' 'Get Off Of My Cloud' and 'Can't Stop the Music' by The Village People. Preparation had been frantic. Nigel and the rest of the Boss staff threw the boys at stylists, vocal coaches, dance teachers and choreographers, before packing them off on a whistle-stop tour of gay clubs across the North of England. Before long, they would be performing at under-18s discos as well.

The first-ever Take That gig took place at a Huddersfield nightspot called Flicks, with about 30 people in attendance. Gigs like this all over the country were a baptism of fire for the group, always with the risk of being hit by beer cans from disgruntled club-goers. That is, if anyone turned up in the first place. 'I literally had to *beg* clubs to hire them,' one promoter later said. 'Their concert fee then was between £25 and £50, which just about covered their petrol money to gigs. They started charging £100 per performance and thought they'd really hit the jackpot.' In truth, though, this took a while to happen. The early days of Take That would keep any ego in check. 'We started off in half-empty clubs. It was heart-breaking,' recalled Howard.

1991 was a directionless year for pop music in Britain. This is not to say that no 'important' records were being made (think Primal Scream, Nirvana, My Bloody Valentine, Massive Attack), but the mainstream chart pop scene was unfocused. The teen magazine *Smash Hits*, crammed with posters, irreverent humour, lyrics to chart hits and interviews, had been so popular throughout the 1980s that, from 1988, its readers' poll (The *Smash Hits* Poll Winners' Party) was broadcast on TV. But in the early 1990s, it struggled to find cover stars with staying power: icons with good songs but also magnetic and engaging personalities. Finding both was tough.

Though they still seemed a draw with young audiences, America's New Kids On The Block were selling fewer records, and there seemed to be no obvious successor with major teen appeal. Superficial pop fads came and went, like the white rapper

Vanilla Ice and 19-year-old British singer Chesney Hawkes, but the biggest-selling hits of 1991 were themes from blockbuster movies, old songs featured in TV adverts, and tie-ins from cartoons (*The Simpsons*) and from charity events (Comic Relief). The top-selling singles act of the year was The KLF, a brilliant but deliberately faceless dance project from two frustrated artist/musicians in their 30s. While the dance scene produced numerous fine records, the artists mostly lacked a strong identity, which was essential for video and TV appearances.

Teen pop has never been fashionable in serious rock music circles, but it might be argued that the transitory, temporary nature of chart pop is its strength. Rock can be pretentious and long-winded. Pop can be superficial and ephemeral, but its strength is in the here and now. 'Pop is of the moment, like a newspaper, only better,' was the view of Pet Shop Boys' Neil Tennant, himself a *Smash Hits* writer from 1982 to 1985. 'It doesn't aim to have lasting quality, whereas rock aims to be part of a body of work, and to last. You can't ask where a good pop group will be in five years' time because they'll have broken up.' Admittedly, some of the acts-to-watch of 1991 were lucky to manage five months in the spotlight.

As the charts were besieged by more and more dance acts (leading *Top of the Pops* to relaunch in the autumn of 1991, demanding vocalists sing live rather than mime), *Smash Hits* chose to award space to film stars, TV icons and fashion figures. A computer games page was introduced. The teenagers of the early 1980s (indeed, like Gary Barlow) had been music-obsessed but, a decade later, music had to share the attention of teenagers with television, cinema, fashion, computer games and so on. Jason Priestley from *Beverly Hills,*

90210, movie actor Christian Slater and children's TV host Phillip Schofield were as likely to adorn a teen's wall as Jordan Knight from New Kids.

Whenever the biggest teen act in Britain is not a homegrown one, this creates obvious problems. The records can be heard and bought, the videos may be seen and, if you're lucky, they'll visit the UK for promotional duties and perhaps even an arena concert. But it's not quite the same as having your favourite artist or group living in your own country. They're more likely to be available for TV interviews, will probably gig more often – and you might even get to see them in real life!

Nigel Martin-Smith had tried in vain to convince a major record label to sign Take That, but, despite the group gaining a following at under-18s discos all over the North of England, there were still no takers – at least not yet. 'A mistake the majors made was they never saw a performance,' Martin-Smith told music industry paper *Music Week*, 'and saw the girls screaming at them.' In the absence of any offers, there was no choice but to set up a record label of his own, and so Dance UK Records was born in order to release the first Take That single in July 1991.

'Waiting Around', with Gary Barlow offering up his best Rick Astley impersonation, was the flip side of Take That's debut single. On the A-side was a new Gary song, 'Do What U Like' – simple but catchy dance pop. But they still needed a video. Nigel hired the services of the *Cool Cube* producer, Ro Newton. Previously a journalist and broadcaster for BBC Radio 1 and BBC2's *Whistle Test* series, Newton was given a brief to make a three-minute clip that would get people talking. The result, made on 21 June 1991, would be five lads who began the clip in leather jackets and codpieces, and ended it wrestling in jelly. When the promo was exhumed for the *Take That & Party* compilation video, buyers were warned on the sleeve, 'Do not view if you are offended by bare bottoms.'

The deliberately provocative 'Do What U Like' video was aired just once on television: on *The Hitman and Her* in the early hours of Sunday, 14 July 1991, one week before the single was released. A 'cleaner' version – with no bare buttocks and a bit less jelly – was made for daytime television, so that they had a chance of some TV appearances watched by children. One programme that expressed interest was *The 8.15 from Manchester*, a live Saturday-morning show on BBC Television. The programme's researcher, Ruth Shimmin, had in fact been present at the video shoot. When she reported back to her bosses at the BBC and suggested Take That for the show, she received some 'good-natured flak', but, as she would later note, their appearance inspired a flock of devotees that already seemed to outnumber more established teen acts: 'There were more fans outside the building than when Bros appeared.'

On 3 August, Take That appeared on *The 8.15 from Manchester*. The other pop guests in the studio that morning were Blur, then promoting one of their less memorable singles ('Bang') at a time when their initial burst of acclaim was beginning to sour. 'We were all moody and hungover and "Who are these prancing puppet doinks?"' remembered bassist Alex James many years later. 'But they were all really smiley and soft and wide-eyed, and irresistibly pleasant.'

Gary, who confessed that he could be 'square' at times, felt rather uncomfortable with the nudity in the cheekier 'Do

What U Like' video. On the other hand, he knew that it was an attention-grabbing way to arrive on the pop scene, and he took the opportunity to bemoan the state of the 1991 Top 20: 'It's very safe, intit? We're here to bring some sex back into pop.' Like Frankie Goes To Hollywood eight years earlier, Take That had made their initial impact with a rude video that couldn't be played on *Top of the Pops*.

In early July 1991, New Kids On The Block had announced in the pages of *Smash Hits* that they were 'splitting up for five months' in order to pursue their own solo projects. This was the moment for Take That to make their move, and, on 10 July, the magazine launched them with a profile headlined 'THE MOST HANDSOME GROUP IN POP'. Reference was made to Gary's appearance a decade earlier in *Joseph and the Amazing Technicolor Dreamcoat*, a neat link to Jason Donovan's same leading role in the West End (and number one with 'Any Dream Will Do'). The group featured in three consecutive issues of *Smash Hits* that summer, but comparisons were not made between them and New Kids. Instead, they were likened to a cross between the London Boys (high-energy pop-dance duo) and the Chippendales (American troupe of dancers/strippers). Singles reviewer Kenny Thomas, a chart presence at the time, proclaimed them to be 'much better' than Big Fun. None of these reference points was remotely hip, though they were probably already better than Big Fun. 'There were all these faceless rave acts,' said Gary, 'and suddenly it was like, "Shit, here comes a band, and they're not bad looking! Give them the front cover."'

'Do What U Like' was released on 22 July 1991. It reached number 82 in the charts and promptly vanished. 'We thought we'd had our 15 minutes of fame,' Gary later commented, if 'number 82' can be called 'fame'. The failure of the single was put down to 'distribution problems' – in other words, practically no one could find it in the shops. What became apparent was that Take That needed a proper record deal with a major label. National television appearances and the pop press were all very well, but it was no use if no one could find the records.

Fortunately, Simon Cowell, who had refused to sign them at IQ Records, directed the group to RCA Records. It transpired that Nick Raymonde, who worked at RCA's Artist & Repertoire (A&R) department, had been reading all the *Smash Hits* coverage over the summer. His label urgently needed a big pop act. There had not really been one since Rick Astley in the late 1980s, and its other significant name, Eurythmics, had now split up.

In September 1991, Take That visited RCA's offices in London and signed on the dotted line. The following day, Gary signed a second contract, this time with Virgin Music Publishing, for his catalogue of original songs. It was a startling moment for him: 'All of a sudden, there was £150,000 in my bank account.' He felt in good company – at just 20 years of age, he was with the same music publisher as Seal and Terence Trent D'Arby. From the early days of Take That, it would mean that Gary would be its wealthiest member.

It was a busy autumn for Take That. In October, their first single for a major label was released. 'Promises' was by no means given universal support, but the song had its fans in radioland. One was Simon Bates, then host of BBC Radio 1's morning show. 'I always knew Take That would make it,' he crowed a year later, 'ever since my producer Fergus Dudley handed me "Promises" and said, "Take a listen." I played it, and I loved it.'

In the run-up to its release, Take That landed several further television appearances, mostly aimed at a young audience, like ITV's *Motormouth* and *Disney Club* (both transmitted at weekends). The bandmates appeared on *What's That Noise?*, a BBC programme hosted by Craig Charles that booked all sorts of musical guests, from orchestras to thrash-metal bands. They squeezed into afternoon TV's *Broom Cupboard* with Andi Peters and quacking gonk sidekick, Edd the Duck. Terry Wogan's chat show in the evening also gave them a spot. They were present, too, on the BBC's flagship Saturday-morning magazine *Going Live!* with Phillip Schofield and Sarah Greene, a big shop window for up-and-coming pop stars. A slot on *Going Live!* could prove as invaluable as one on *Top of the Pops*, with the added bonus that viewers would not only enjoy a song or video, but could also communicate with the group members themselves. Take That, even early on, seemed to engage brilliantly and easily with their young fans, answering questions and taking phone calls with the utmost professionalism and courtesy, yet with humour and charm, too.

What's more, *Smash Hits* magazine continued to back the new group. In October, in the run-up to its annual readers' poll, they sneaked Take That into the Best British Group category shortlist of 10, alongside EMF, Pet Shop Boys, The Cure, Bros, Carter USM, Deacon Blue, Wet Wet Wet, OMD and fellow newcomers Right Said Fred. Take That had only issued one single and it had flopped, so wasn't this kind of recognition a bit premature? It didn't seem to matter. The readers *liked* these newcomers, and, when the results appeared, Take That had come fourth, behind winners EMF, Bros and Right Said Fred. (When the celebrities filled in their poll entry forms, Blur fondly remembered Take That from their *8.15 from Manchester* meeting and voted them Best Dance Act.) But, as if to underline that no teen heroes can ever be universally popular, they were simultaneously voted fourth in the *Worst* Group category.

'Promises', with 'Do What U Like' revived for the B-side, was released on 11 November 1991. It was produced by Pete Hammond, an associate of Stock Aitken Waterman's Hit Factory. 'Definitely one to watch,' encouraged *Music Week*, but it was overshadowed by 'Black or White', the first new Michael Jackson material in four years and an obvious number one hit. In comparison, 'Promises' lay at number 38, its peak position. In truth, even the pop press felt lukewarm towards it. *Smash Hits* called it little more than 'a nimble-toed frolic with some tweety keyboard'. But at least it got them the magazine's front cover, the first of many, even if the headline ('Fame at last!!!') was a tad premature.

Meanwhile, as Christmas loomed, Take That went into the studio with producer Duncan Bridgeman, hitherto behind hits for Transvision Vamp, to record tracks for their debut LP. Songwriter Gary was learning plenty about the business of composing and having his own writing style. Anyone creative is likely to ape and copy in their early days, but you always had to be careful. With one song, 'Satisfied', it became clear to Bridgeman that the chorus bore an uncanny resemblance to a New Kids On The Block hit entitled 'Call It What You Want'.

Gary would remember the producer sensibly offering advice to change it and make it sufficiently different: 'Don't be daft – people will think you're just ripping off New Kids!' It was one thing to look or act like New Kids, but not to write the same tune. And it was sound advice: the last thing Gary needed was for successful songwriters to accuse him of plagiarism.

The record industry was now aware of Take That, and their campaign to rescue British pop music. As Bros announced their split in late 1991, their manager Tom Watkins had a new protégé: a Londoner called Tony Mortimer, who had plenty of songs but didn't have the voice. Watkins encouraged Mortimer to recruit people who could sing, and form a group based on the template of (the now ailing) New Kids On The Block. Sound familiar? They were given the name East 17 to reflect the postcode of their Walthamstow background, but it was only after signing their record deal that they were played a Take That video. 'We [were] told: "This is your competition",' recalled Mortimer, 20 years after being played 'Do What U Like'. 'It was some guys on the floor getting covered in jelly and wearing leather. And we were like, "OK, the market's ours if that's our competition!"'

CHAPTER 7

IT ONLY TAKES
A MINUTE

The first fruits of the Bridgeman sessions were made public in January 1992 with the third Take That single. 'Once You've Tasted Love' was yet another Barlow original, and, for this one, RCA ensured that there were plenty of attractions in the packaging of the record. A picture disc of the 12" version would become a collector's item, as did a fold-out calendar with the 7" single – the sort of extras the most committed fans would lap up. Unfortunately, the song was not one of Gary's best. It was flat in the verses and didn't improve much in the chorus. Radio 1 ignored it. Not even *Smash Hits* liked it much. 'Predictable, uninteresting and about as funky as a cauliflower,' sighed its singles reviewer.

The public seemed to agree. To the huge disappointment of both group and record label, 'Once You've Tasted Love' fared no better than number 47. RCA had delayed the release of the album until they could produce a major hit, but producing that hit seemed increasingly unlikely. 'We talked very seriously about splitting up around that time,' Gary remembered. 'We just couldn't break through. We couldn't get our records played on the radio and, no matter what we did, we weren't getting anywhere.'

Nigel Martin-Smith's solution to this setback was simple: he doubled their work rate. Between February and June 1992, they embarked on a hectic schedule that could include up to four gigs a day: first a school, next an evening matinee, then an under-18s club, and lastly a late-night showing at an over-18s club. It was an exhausting experience. 'We were absolutely fucked,' Howard said years later. 'We were doing four 35-minute shows a day – it was more than we do in concerts now.'

At the heart of all this promotion was a big idea of Nigel's: a tour of schools and nightclubs for under-18s called The Big Schools/Safe Sex Tour. Organised in conjunction with the Family Planning Association, it aimed to educate teenagers about the importance of safe sex and contraception, and the risks of unwanted pregnancy and sexually transmitted diseases. The lads would perform a few numbers and then hand out literature about safe sex to the audiences. It seemed the teens could relate to this new pop group on such subjects far more easily than if a parent or teacher had been addressing them. 'It worked brilliantly,' remembered Gary. 'The pupils really opened up to us. I felt really good when the kids were asking our opinions and advice about sex, AIDS, drugs and smoking.'

An estimated 60,000 youngsters saw Take That on this tour. It was a last-ditch attempt to break the band, but, while it was draining work, Gary mostly enjoyed the experience, checking in and out of a long succession of B&Bs around the country. He also discovered that sharing and making sacrifices and compromises (something he'd rarely had to do before now, by his own admission) was a good thing: 'I was quite a bold, selfish person at that time. And there was a bit of snobbery as well, because I was the musical one. But I grew to love these four people.'

In other words, relations between five very different young men were gelling. They were getting used to each other's constant company. What they had in common was being in a band, but like a comedy double-act, which relies on the personality differences, they used their distinctive qualities to push themselves. 'We learned how to be close,' explained Jason Orange, 'without having to go to a football match to do it, or having to go to the pub to get pissed to do it.'

There had been a lot of musical chairs at RCA Records in the spring of 1992. A new managing director, 31-year-old Jeremy Marsh, had been appointed. Hugh Goldsmith, the publishing director of *Sky* magazine, was poached by Marsh to be the label's head of marketing. Then, in May, Marsh also hired the man who had signed Gary Barlow to a publishing deal at Virgin Music. Mike McCormack was now RCA's A&R director. After Eurythmics split, singer Annie Lennox's debut album, *Diva*, would be the label's biggest album of 1992, but not far behind would be the five lads from Manchester. Jeremy Marsh was aware of Take That's potential, or at least of their manager's ambition: 'Nigel was clear from day one that this band were going to be, quote, "global superstars", or at the very least huge at home.'

The Take That album recorded at the end of 1991 with Duncan Bridgeman remained unreleased. None of their first three singles had really broken through, and so the group urgently needed a hit to make the album commercially viable. They were unlikely to sell many copies without a major hit in the singles chart and so there were further recording sessions with other producers, notably Ian Levine.

Levine, formerly resident DJ at London's legendary gay club Heaven, had produced soul acts such as the Supremes and the Temptations in the USA during the 1980s. 'I learned working with those Motown acts that you can't get a 17-year-old shop girl from Sheffield to go out and buy records by a 50-something soul group – she can't relate to it. But if you take the exact same music, that clean-cut soul with high bright harmonies, and lay it on a teenage boys' group, it works.'

Just before he produced Take That, Levine had worked with British vocal group The Pasadenas on the old 1970s soul hit 'I'm Doing Fine Now'. But the sessions that would produce three subsequent Take That hits – 'I Found Heaven', 'A Million Love Songs' and 'Could It Be Magic' – were stormy ones, and even verged on comical. The studio owner had three 'Dulux dogs', as Gary called them: 'One of these dogs decided to have a shit on the studio floor, and guess who stepped straight in it? Robbie!'

Gary was becoming frustrated by the wishes of producers. He knew how he wanted Take That's records to sound. Nigel would later insist that Levine's presence made precious little difference to the fortunes of Take That, 'and I can play you the original demos to prove it'. Gary sarcastically told Q magazine, with a snigger, how important Levine had supposedly been to the rise of his group: 'Just remember Ian Levine made this band. Don't ever forget that.'

Before anything from the Levine sessions was released to the public, a fourth Take That single was issued. It came out the same day (25 May 1992) as their appearance on the Children's Royal Variety Performance, the first of many royal engagements for the group. 'One of my ambitions was always to perform in front of royalty,' Gary told *Smash Hits*, 'so when we performed in front of Princess Margaret...[!] She was great. She said to us, "Well done. I heard lots of screams from the young girls."' Quite by chance, backstage, he also bumped into Dawn again, one of the dancers from the 'Kurtis Rush' video shoot, later to become so important in his life.

'It Only Takes a Minute', recorded at Nigel's insistence, was a far more familiar song than any of Take That's previous singles – mainly because it was a cover version. Dating from 1975, it had been a disco hit by the American group Tavares, although it also reached the Top 10 in the UK in the summer of 1976 when covered in a novelty version by One Hundred Ton & A Feather. For the new version, Take That had teamed up with producer Nigel Wright, whose credits included the jazz-funk group Shakatak and – yikes – Timmy Mallett's Bombalurina.

The group's frantic work schedule, racing around the country for three months, seemed to have paid off. With a video shot at a London boxing gym, 'It Only Takes a Minute' rescued Take That from pop's dumper. It entered the charts at number 16, making it easily their biggest hit so far. The bandmates learned of their breakthrough at a London restaurant called La Reserve. 'All the fans were waiting outside, crying,' Mark Owen commented. 'It was one of the best moments of my life. We felt like we'd really cracked it.'

'It Only Takes a Minute', which *Smash Hits* described as sounding 'exactly like the Village People', saved Take That's bacon. Even when it was a hit, Gary admitted the group had been on borrowed time, with their three previous singles all underperforming. 'We talked very seriously about splitting up before that song came out,' he confessed. 'We would not have been able to carry on if it had been a flop – we'd have been a laughing stock.' Fortunately, the familiarity of the song and the group's popularity with young record buyers meant that the bandmates would not have to return to dead-end jobs and obscurity.

Gary later confirmed that just having a hit gained an artist more music industry credibility: 'When this got to be a hit, suddenly a lot of people from our record company found time to be a lot more interested in us. Opinions about which trousers we should wear, and stuff. When you're stuck at number 54 in the charts, no one cares about your trousers.' Within weeks, Take That had become a priority act for RCA, although whether they were yet actually credible was a moot point. 'Pop music wasn't fashionable and people in the business treated us like lepers,' said its songwriter. 'We were accused of having no talent. I remember the first time we did *Top of the Pops* the camera crew were having bets about whether we could even sing, but that just spurred me on. I was determined to prove them wrong.'

It was nice to have a hit, but it couldn't have escaped the group's attention that it wasn't with a Gary Barlow original song. Some consider a cover version by a new act to be an easy option, and the charts of summer 1992 seemed determined to recreate the 1970s: revamps of hits like 'Please Don't Go', 'Hang On In There, Baby', 'Rock Your Baby', 'Baker Street' and many others. Erasure stayed at number one for a month with an EP of Abba covers. 'It Only Takes a Minute' would peak at number seven, but it was yet another old song, and, when the charts are full of covers, it suggests that pop music has no fresh ideas. What didn't help was that, in a UK recession, singles sales were poor, the lowest since 1972.

Take That were by no means home and dry, but no one in the media had a bad word to say about them. Future *Heat* editor Mark Frith was then working at *Smash Hits*. He was bowled over by the group's charm when they came into the office to make tea for the staff. 'They are lovely, lovely people,' he reminisced to the *Observer* in 2008. 'Unaffected. Ordinary. I remember Mark and Gary walking round the office with pieces of paper with everyone's milk and sugar requirements noted down. It was great tea, proper northern tea.'

Though he had sung lead on all their singles to date, Gary promised that other members of the group would eventually have their three minutes in the spotlight singing the top line. Privately, though, as he would later reveal, he was desperate to be recognised as a songwriter. Asked about his own taste in music, he cited as favourites the upmarket pop soul of Simply Red and Lisa Stansfield, and the teenage singer-songwriter Tanita Tikaram, who had established herself as a hit songwriter aged only 17 with hits like 'Twist in My Sobriety' and 'Good Tradition'. Gary Barlow was a more mature 21 years old by the time he reached the Top 10, but he was still one of the more youthful pop scribes around.

The next Take That single, 'I Found Heaven', wasn't a cover, nor was it a Gary song. The work of Ian Levine, who composed it with the soul singer Billy Griffin, it followed 'It Only Takes a Minute' into the Top 20, but failed to progress beyond number 15. It is not the most fondly remembered of the group's singles. In a 1995 *Smash Hits* magazine poll of its readers, it was voted their least favourite Take That single (in fact, just one reader nominated it as their favourite). As for Gary Barlow's verdict, he pulled no punches. 'Definitely the worst record Take That ever made,' he proclaimed in 1997. 'Crap song, rotten singing and production.'

At least it took Take That beyond one-hit-wonder status, though, and it meant their debut album could finally come out. *Take That & Party* (which contained all five of their singles to date) was finally released on 24 August 1992. From a Radio 1 Roadshow at Alton Towers to the foyers of TV studios, fans everywhere had screamed at them. Thousands turned up to meet the group members at record stores to have copies of the album signed in person, events that became chaotic and even bordered on the hazardous. A homecoming signing in Manchester attracted 5,000 people, and the only way the group could escape to safety was to disguise themselves as policemen, to blend in with the officers who had been drafted in to cope with the madness.

As accomplished and polished and upbeat as *Take That & Party* was, few who heard it could have imagined how much bigger the group would get. Heard now, it's a ragbag of styles, and lacks cohesiveness. But it was good enough, and the fans loved it. 'Zippy, eventful and cleanly put together,' said *Smash Hits*, while the adult rock monthly *Q* predicted that this 'likeable wisp of an album will enliven large parts of many young lives for a few months' and 'be fondly remembered in later life'. The only slip-up – and how could the critic have known this at the time? – came with the prediction that 'it will almost certainly do better than any of its successors'.

The album entered the charts at number five, a strong start (if outsold by two other new releases – a Kylie Minogue greatest hits package and the British rock band Thunder), but sank like a stone in the few weeks afterwards, suggesting that only the most dedicated fans were likely to bother with such a thing as a Take That album. Even so, such fans were a godsend during this uncertain time. One relieved RCA executive, present at a London venue where the group performed a PA in front of a shrieking crowd, said of their music: 'It's not what most of us would listen to at home, but they love it.'

In fact at this early stage some industry pundits weren't at all convinced. Producer Pete Waterman, founder of PWL and host of *The Hitman and Her* on late-night TV, didn't believe the group that his TV show had helped to break in the very early days had staying power. 'It's the records that count,' he told *Music Week* in September 1992. 'You won't win if you are all image and no songs, like Take That.' In addition, Waterman suspected that the group's album had appeared prematurely. 'The golden rule,' he insisted, 'is never to release a pop album until it has three or four hit singles.' In fact, Take That had released five singles so far, but only two reached the Top 20. Who knew that their next single would propel them into the big league?

The contrast between 'I Found Heaven' and its follow-up could hardly have been greater. 'A Million Love Songs', released at the end of September 1992, was perhaps *the* crucial Take That single and Gary Barlow song in terms of receiving respect and recognition. Gary later described it as 'the song that made people think Take That are *not* just a pop band'. Written when he was just 15, it was probably the highlight of his demo tape. Now this big ballad showed there might be more to the band than fluffy dance-pop and, in the case of 'It Only Takes a Minute', a throwback to the 70s. Yet releasing 'A Million Love Songs' was a risk. 'Our record company were convinced it would be the kiss of death if we released the song,' Gary told the *Daily Mirror*. 'It was a ballad and up till then we had been known as a band that made hot dance sounds. But we had faith in it and wanted it out. There were a lot of rows but in the end we got our way.'

The CD single version was given a special subtitle: 'The Love Songs EP', as if to underline that Take That were about songs, not just dancing. It felt satisfying to Gary in particular when the song climbed to number seven. 'It Only Takes a Minute' had peaked in the same position, but that was a familiar song; this was new and original. It became massively popular with radio, and Radio 1 DJ Simon Bates predicted great things for Gary, via a special mention in his *Daily Mirror* newspaper column: 'I predict that Gary Barlow will be named Composer of the Year at the Ivor Novello Awards for writing "A Million Love Songs". A previous winner was George Michael. The same dazzling success awaits Take That.'

Not quite everyone agreed, though. In *Smash Hits*, comedian Rob Newman, then part of television's *The Mary Whitehouse Experience*, dubbed it 'a love song by numbers' and 'the work of Satan'.

Lyrically, 'A Million Love Songs' is quite callow. Gary conceded that, because he wrote it in his mid-teens, it had quite an innocent lyric. It was written from the perspective of someone who at the time had experienced a far more profound relationship with pop than with lovers: he was in love with pop, in love with love songs. But he also explained it was about denial: 'The message here is that I've written love song after love song in my life, but I still can't say "I love you".'

Criticisms about the manufactured nature of Take That would persist, but they were gradually being taken more seriously. Gary would later insist that, although Nigel Martin-Smith's input in the early days had been invaluable to help get the boys noticed, the group themselves deserved more credit for their emergence as a credible pop act. 'Nigel earned this reputation as a Svengali manager,' he commented in 1996, 'but we were the ones to take the music to a different domain. Nigel was only ever involved with the creative side of the band in the early days.' In other words, the very earliest singles, and the connection with a major record label. 'A Million Love Songs' represented a major step forward for Take That, evidence that they might not just be a flash in the pan, and might even last to a second album.

The next test was for the group to shine as a live act. Twenty-minute club sets, where they performed to backing tapes, were one thing, but late 1992 saw them hit the road for their first full tour of the UK. 'They have better songs than Bros, are hunkier than New Kids On The Block, and more dynamic than Jason Donovan,' enthused one report of the first date, at Newcastle City Hall. Even after that show, they were unable to go to bed, as fans staying at the same hotel had set off the fire alarms. Endless tales of obsessive fandom abounded, and the group even had some famous fans in the pop world; Dannii Minogue and Neil Tennant and Chris Lowe from Pet Shop Boys showed up at the London dates.

Take That may have been built around the musical talents of Gary Barlow, but the others (hired for dancing ability, personality and aesthetic appeal) were getting plenty of attention from the fans – to the extent that the songsmith could feel left out. It was an ego-bruising experience to be 'the fat one photographers pushed out of the way to get to Robbie and Mark'. 'I'm the odd one out,' he would later admit. 'I'd go out on stage and everyone would be screaming and waving banners saying, "Mark! Fuck Me!" or "Jason! Show Us Your Bum!" or "Howard! Meet Us Backstage!" and "Robbie! Blow Us A Kiss!" Then there'd be, "Gary! We Love Your Music!"'

The official line reported to the press was that Take That were well-behaved lads. To some in their inner circle, it could be a different story. Alex Kadis, a journalist who became the editor of their fan club magazine, regularly went on the road with them. In 2000, she remembered the night on this first tour when they had just played a venue in York: 'Everyone had downed a formidable quantity of Depth Charges (a large shot of vodka sunk into a half-pint glass filled with snakebite, down in one, instant brain damage) and danced the night away in varying stages of undress at a nightclub. After several multicoloured hiccups on the way back to the hotel, I left Gary Barlow comatose and face down on his bed with his trousers round his ankles, bare bottom raised. I know I should have called my photographer. I know I should have published. But, well, I kind of liked him.'

And that was the *well-behaved* member of the group.

Touring could be hectic pressure. Mark described being on tour as being 'like *Groundhog Day*', in which every day seemed to be exactly the same. All that distinguished certain days could be illness and the feeling of being rundown. On one European tour, Jason had to be injected in his bottom to ease the pain from sprained limbs, Gary's heavy cold spread to the rest of the group, and Howard had chronic food poisoning. Yet the show still had to go on.

In less than a year, Gary, Robbie, Mark, Jason and Howard had already become famous beyond their wildest dreams, but they had sacrificed many things in their lives. They had little time off from recording, live work and promotional work. 'We all lost our girlfriends within weeks of getting our first hit,' claimed Mark in September 1992. 'They got fed up with constantly waiting around.' Gary insisted that they were '100 per cent committed to our careers' and sighed that 'Unfortunately it leaves little time for girlfriends.'

In fact, the 'no girlfriends' rule had been part of the original agreement with Nigel. Howard, the senior member of the group, found it especially hard to heed. 'I fall in love very deeply,' he explained. 'If I was to meet a girl, I would never find out if she was the right one because I wouldn't be able to spend enough time with her.'

Gary, however, felt that Nigel's rule must be followed – at least in terms of steady relationships. 'He didn't mind us making love – he didn't want us to be monks – but he reasoned that, if we fell madly in love, the group would start to take second place to our girlfriends. If we want careers, we must keep our minds on the job. We'll all have relationships once day, but it won't be easy because a girl could like us because of *what* we are rather than *who* we are.'

For Robbie, who was still a teenager, the rule forbidding long-term relationships held little water: 'I have never had a steady girlfriend. The longest I have ever been out with anybody is three weeks. Long-term relationships are not me.'

Even when Nigel's two-year rule ended (in late 1993), the group would decide to extend it anyway. 'It is hard for us,' Gary commented, 'but we know it will make sense.'

Others in the group would, however, grow broody. 'A lot of our friends have babies now,' Jason would explain, 'and we can't help but put ourselves in that position. Fatherhood is another thing that will have to be put on the back burner.'

Nigel had very specific reasons for demanding the 'no relationships' rule. A ban on romance was the key, he believed, to maintaining their appeal with a young audience, who could fantasise about the availability of their idols. 'Romance is a very powerful force,' he argued. 'Some people said it wasn't natural or they must be gay, but I stand by what I did. You can't tour the world with steady girlfriends in tow, because first the girls fall out, then the boys fall out over the girls, and, before you know where you are, you've not got a band. And I'd tell them, look at what happened to The Beatles with that Yoko Ono.'

For now, Take That would behave impeccably, at least when in front of the reporters and photographers. 'We get plenty of offers,' Robbie said of their fanbase, 'but we'd never consider fooling around.' It was emphasised in the media that, once a gig was over, the group members would immediately head back to the hotel, and to bed alone. To be seen as unattached undoubtedly helped the group maintain their popularity – in February 1993, they were said to have received some 57,000 cards for Valentine's Day.

By late 1992, the Take That tour (known as 'The Party Tour') and the success of 'A Million Love Songs' meant that the *Take That & Party* album had begun to sell again. It would eventually reach number two. At the start of December, the group won seven awards at the *Smash Hits* Poll Winners' Party, including Best Group in the World, Best Single (for 'A Million Love Songs'), Best Album (for *Take That & Party*) and even Best Video (for 'I Found Heaven', which had been shot on the Isle of Wight). That same month, a *Take That & Party* video compilation (including the 'naughty' version of 'Do What U Like') became the best-selling music VHS for the festive season. It sold well enough to reach the overall Top 10 video charts, racked alongside blockbusters like *Terminator 2*, Walt Disney's *Cinderella* and *Batman Returns*.

Live, on record and on video, Take That had joined the big league.

CHAPTER 8

NUMBER ONE

Take That enjoyed a blinding 1992. They began it as poster boys without a hit record, and ended it as Britain's top pop group. Previously, their Christmas single, 'Could It Be Magic', had only been available on the CD format of *Take That & Party*, which at the time was a much more expensive format for fans than vinyl or cassette. Remixed for single release, it was an up-tempo remake of Barry Manilow's highly charged 1973 ballad, but the kernel of the song dated back a lot further: to the 1830s and Frédéric Chopin's 'Prelude No. 20 in C Minor' for solo piano.

Despite a remarkable facility for writing catchy tunes, Barry Manilow (who began his career as the arranger and musical director for Bette Midler) had often been scoffed at by pop fans. As we have seen, the teenage Gary idolised Manilow, up to a point: 'He was my hero till I was 16 years old, and I suddenly thought, Hang on a minute, you're not getting any girlfriends. So I moved on to Lionel Richie.'

The lead vocal on Take That's remake of 'Could It Be Magic' was not by Gary, but by 18-year-old Robbie. It was their biggest hit to date, peaking at number three just after Christmas. In February 1993, it won the BRIT Award for the Best British Single – significantly a category decided by the general public rather than the record industry.

Around the same time, the bandmates were most unlucky to miss the number one spot with 'Why Can't I Wake Up With You?', which was trumped by the Dutch pop-techno duo 2 Unlimited and 'No Limit'. 'Why Can't I Wake Up With You?' had originally appeared on *Take That & Party* but was now rejuvenated with the help of the production team who had worked with Boyz II Men, the American vocal group of whom Gary was a big fan. As radically different as the latest version of the song was, the album had now spawned eight tracks as singles, and it was high time for some new material.

The first half of 1993 found Take That visiting international climes, where their records had started to sell: western Europe (France, Germany, Holland, Spain), and then to the Far East – where, in Japan, they found some particularly persistent fans mirroring their hotel bookings and first-class bullet train travel, just to try to catch a glimpse of the lads. They also made two promotional trips to North America, where they expressed wonder at New York City, and dismay at Niagara Falls. 'It surprised us,' remarked Gary. 'It was one of the tackiest places we'd ever seen. Really commercial.' Despite all the jet setting, they missed their homeland, though. 'Seeing the world is a wonderful experience,' said Gary, 'but it makes me appreciate just how much I love Britain – it's the best.'

Already, there was talk about Gary's songwriting talent and how he had the potential to fly as a solo act. He could be a slightly reluctant bystander of the group, quieter than the others in band interviews. In light of the huge attention given to them, he admitted to feeling uncertain about his place in the band, and about his future. 'I know I can probably go on after the group and earn a lot of money from it, but I don't know what I want, really. I always wanted this and, now I've got it, it's just not like I wanted it to be. But,' he emphasised, 'I am happy.'

In June 1993, Gary found his composing skills in demand for a different medium. He was asked to write a theme tune for the BBC pop magazine show *The O Zone*, on which Take That so often featured in their own right. '*The O Zone* has been behind Take That from day one,' said Nicki Chapman, who handled the group's TV promotion duties. 'The programme is a perfect placing for the band.' In a big departure from Take That's usual style, the instrumental piece was titled 'Banoffee Pie', seemingly for no other reason than 'I had just made some, which we were all eating and it seemed as good a name as any'.

At the same time, some old promotional photographs of Gary (dating from 1990) were being used for an advertising campaign in teen magazines for a brand of chewing gum called Stimorol. The images had featured in specialist grocery trade publications, but, with Gary's newfound fame, it was a perfect opportunity to resurrect them for a campaign for a new audience. 'Gary was chosen because he had pop star looks,' explained a spokesman from Stimorol, adding, 'even though he wasn't one at the time.' Gary himself admitted he'd agreed to appear in the ads even though he had no fondness for chewing gum.

Finally, on 5 July 1993, a brand-new Take That single (the group's ninth) was released. Such was their following that they could have put out almost anything as a single and been guaranteed a number one hit, but it was arguably their strongest song so far. Even before it arrived in the shops, 'Pray' had notched up a staggering 120,000 advance orders. Those were the days when singles still traditionally climbed up the charts to their highest position, rather than entered at their peak. Before 'Pray', only 30 songs in the 40-year history of the singles chart had entered at the number one spot.

'Pray' was Take That's first number one hit, staying at the top of the charts for a month. Like the re-recording of 'Why Can't I Wake Up With You?', the song showed a heavy influence of the R&B swingbeat which had been especially popular in the USA. It was a style of music Take That would integrate more and more into their sound over their next two albums. The single's video was shot in Mexico, after which the quintet had performed three songs at the Acapulco Festival.

There was little time to celebrate the success of 'Pray' as a summer arena tour of Britain was lined up, beginning in Manchester on 20 July. It was on this tour that the broadsheet newspapers, not just the popular tabloid press and the teen magazines, started to take a keen interest in Take That. *The Times*' Alan Jackson wondered if they could survive the onslaught of boyband rivals like East 17, and even newer competitors like Worlds Apart, Let Loose and Bad Boys Inc.

(the latter overseen by one Ian Levine). Observing 'lead singer Gary Barlow's relative unease at being the object of such unconditional schoolgirl love', Jackson concluded that he 'may eventually develop his talent in a similar way as did George Michael, post-Wham!'. For the time being, though, Take That could console themselves with being 'an inoffensive update of late-Seventies pop-soul and lots of energetic, coded sexuality'.

Admittedly, it's hard to write about what music sounds like when you can hardly hear it through the noise of the crowd. 'I gave Take That an evening,' began one critic's faux-complaint of the Wembley Arena date, 'and they gave me tinnitus.' The crowds waved banners begging for kisses and far more (sample slogan: 'Point your erections in our directions'), and the lads played up to the lust-fuelled requests, opting for costume changes on stage behind translucent screens. Here was a group who, in one climactic dance routine, dropped their trousers to expose flesh-coloured undies and a different letter on each cheek – a tactic that worked well when it spelled out the group's name, but was perhaps more controversial when they did the same thing at a charity gig to spell the word CHILDLINE. Gary Barlow was unrepentant about it: 'We wanted to give ChildLine the maximum amount of publicity, and we felt that this was a great fun way of doing it. We knew that would keep the word in every fan's mind.'

As well as 'Pray', most of the *Take That & Party* album was given a live outing on the summer tour, together with a medley of past American soul classics. Each of the group had a solo spot in this section as the work of the Temptations, James Brown and The Four Tops was addressed and acclaimed (Gary sang lead on a cover of the 1984 Temptations' hit, 'Treat Her Like a Lady'), before the five reunited for 'I'll Be There', first a success for The Jackson 5, but also revived with much success in 1992 by Mariah Carey.

By August 1993, the second Take That album was almost finished, except for one track. For 'Relight My Fire', a revival of the Dan Hartman disco classic of the late 1970s, Nigel suggested they could collaborate with a veteran pop idol who was about to celebrate 30 years in the business. Lulu had first hit the charts in 1964 (aged only 15) with a searing version of The Isley Brothers' 'Shout', but had many hits thereafter including 'Boom Bang-a-Bang' (the UK entry in the 1969 Eurovision Song Contest) and a cover of David Bowie's 'The Man Who Sold the World'. Early in 1993, the pop-dance song 'Independence' had returned the singer to the British Top 20, exposing her to a whole new generation of fans. In October, 'Relight My Fire' became her first-ever number one in Britain – and Take That's second.

Hot on its heels came the *Everything Changes* album, most of which had been made in only two months. In general, it was a big improvement on *Take That & Party*; the performances were confident, the production more ambitious and, for the most part, the songs were frankly much, much better. 'Multi-vitamin enjoyable,' declared *Q* magazine. 'A masterpiece of pop,' cheered *Smash Hits*, 'and *the* must have album of the year.'

Though some of the songs on *Everything Changes* had been in Gary's repertoire of compositions for several years ('Another Crack in My Heart' was almost as old as 'A Million Love Songs'), others had been completed in a hectic blizzard of energy the previous Christmas: 'I realised it might be the only bit of free time I could get, so I just got on with it. People told me to rest, but I couldn't. I didn't like the thought of unfinished work hanging over me.'

Hard-working Gary's talent was much ballyhooed, but there were some humiliating moments for him when it came to image and looks. By his own admission not the best-looking one in Take That, he found that his love for food was already being scrutinised by their management and record label. 'The photograph for the sleeve of *Everything Changes* had to be airbrushed so a roll of fat could be removed from my stomach,' he told *The Sunday Times* in 1997. 'How demoralising is that? Not only to be told in front of the rest of the band, but also knowing that everyone at the record company was probably having a good laugh about it.' There was further embarrassment after one group photo-shoot: 'Pictures of me with double chins were circled and sent to my manager with a note that said, "This is a waste of a shoot, Gary's too fat."'

As the years went by, columnists and headline writers seldom passed up the opportunity to write TAKE FAT or CAKE THAT or CAKE FAT, or some other strained, tiresome pun.

Take That's fan club membership now numbered more than 160,000. Though it appeared that the vast majority of the fanbase was female and under 18, there were signs that the band's appeal was broadening. Style magazines for adults such as *Arena* and *The Face* were starting to cover the group, and famous fans were stepping forward: Bono, Neil Tennant from Pet Shop Boys and the outspoken newspaper columnist Julie

Burchill, who proclaimed: 'Their dancing and their prettiness gives them a head start, of course, but there is a freshness there that Wham!, even at the start, never had.'

An autumn tour found them supported by D:Ream, about to hit number one themselves with 'Things Can Only Get Better', and featuring Manchester University physics student Brian Cox on keyboards, before he turned his back on music to become a professor. By December, the *Everything Changes* album had been certified double platinum, meaning over 600,000 copies had been sold. 'Babe', with a lead vocal by Mark, made it a hat-trick of number ones, but the group were denied a number one placing in Christmas week due to the dreaded Mr Blobby, the irritant sidekick of Noel Edmonds from BBC1's *Noel's House Party*.

Even so, Take That finished 1993 as the best-selling singles act of the year. The only albums to outsell *Everything Changes* were, in descending order, titles by Meat Loaf, R.E.M. and Dina Carroll. They won eight awards at the *Smash Hits* Poll Winners' Party at Wembley Arena, and a recording of The Party Tour raced to the top of the video charts. If anything, Take That had had a better 1993 than 1992.

It wasn't all one big party, though. Being in Take That could be exhausting. In December 1993, the *Daily Mirror* documented a typical day in the life of the group while on tour. They would usually rise at eight in the morning. After discussions of the previous night's gig, a coach would transport them to the city of their next live venue and their hotel. By 4.30, they'd be soundchecking at the concert hall, before conducting interviews for local media regarding the live show and new record. After meeting and greeting some of their many fans backstage, they would prepare for showtime at half past eight. By 10.45, the exhausting, exhilarating set would be over, and it was back to the hotel for a bite to eat and a winding-down drink. Bedtime (at least officially) was cited as midnight. It was roughly the same again the following day, and so on for the rest of the tour.

Yet, as pop columnist Kate Thornton revealed, the group was mostly not yet wealthy. It was claimed they were each surviving on just £150 per week, a management decision that the bandmates insisted they were satisfied with. 'We won't be making the same mistakes Bros did,' said Robbie, referring to the financial problems the late-1980s teen idols suffered from. 'Our £150-a-week keeps us under control.'

But Gary was quite a bit better off. While Robbie, Mark and Howard continued to live at home with their parents and Jason moved in with one of his siblings, the wealthier song-writer had indulged in a home of his own: a house worth around £60,000 in the Cheshire town of Knutsford.

Gary seemed to have found what he always wanted: acceptance as a musician and songwriter. It was a driving force that had been an integral part of him since his teenage years: 'Something has bitten me. It's an addiction. All my life I knew I was going to be somebody. I wanted to be recognised.' But he, like the others, also knew only too well that there was a darker side to fame. The constant attention from fans and the media was starting to chip away at his confidence: 'I used to be very outgoing. Now I'm withdrawn.' For the likes of Mark, still living at home, his family had had to change their telephone number three times: 'We were getting calls every 60 seconds. It drives you mad.'

Gary's priority remained work. If others in the group revealed a few dalliances with soft drugs in *The Face* magazine, he admitted he couldn't even risk smoking tobacco, for fear it might affect his singing voice. For all five members of Take That, but especially Gary, the group was a job, and they could not afford to take their success for granted.

'I never dreamed we'd be where we are now,' gasped Jason Orange. 'It's incredible. But we'll never forget where we came from. Remembering the bad times puts the good times into perspective.'

CHAPTER 9

THE FAB
FIVE

There would be no new Take That album in 1994. It was a year of consolidation, and a world tour for *Everything Changes*. They began the year with another European tour, facing 100,000 fans at venues in the Netherlands, Scandinavia and Germany. 'The international work is hard and can be very tiring,' admitted Gary, 'but once you're on stage and you hear the cheers of the fans it makes it all worth it.' During rare moments away from the limelight, he found time to indulge in his latest hobby – buying antiques.

Take That-mania was spreading across the globe, although there were still territories left to conquer. Australia remained relatively immune to their appeal. In fact, London rivals East 17 had quipped that one of the best things about visiting Oz was that no one asked them about Take That as they weren't well known enough. 'Pray' had reached number 10 in the charts there, but subsequent singles struggled. Compare and contrast with East 17 – five Top 10 hits there and a number one with 'It's Alright'. Only in 1995 would Take That break through Down Under.

Cracking North America remained something of a challenge too, despite occasional visits. For a time, it looked as if Take That might achieve success via television, as well as music. In the spring of 1994, despite the poor reception in the USA to several Take That singles, Nigel Martin-Smith was in talks with the NBC television network for a series mixing drama and songs, which could then be syndicated throughout the world. The plans, however, came to nothing, and even whispers of something similar happening on home turf (BBC1 controller Alan Yentob thought of a wacky sitcom along the lines of *The Monkees*) became nothing more than talk. Ultimately, Gary argued, branching out into television and acting could dilute, not strengthen Take That's appeal. 'It is all very flattering,' he said, 'but first and foremost, we are a music act, not TV presenters or comedy stars.'

At the end of March 1994, the title track of the *Everything Changes* album was issued as a single, backed by a Beatles' medley the group had premiered at the BRIT Awards only weeks earlier. Gary tried to calm Beatles' purists by stressing that the decision to perform the Fab Four's greatest hits was born out of affection. 'It was a tribute,' he said, but was trumped by an astute observation from Robbie: 'It's very good for marketing.'

Later on, Gary elaborated on the decision to cover the lovable moptops. 'People thought we were comparing ourselves to The Beatles, but we weren't. We do think we have something in common, though. They were a band who had fun, and that's what we've always tried to do.' Something else Take That had in common with The Beatles, though: they were also a manufactured and carefully managed outfit with built-in original songwriting talent. And, for many teenagers in 1990s Britain, Take That had a scream factor every bit as powerful as John, Paul, George and Ringo had had some 30 years earlier.

For the whole group, including Gary, it was getting trickier to preserve their anonymity. 'It always happens to me in Marks & Sparks,' he told the *Sunday Mirror*'s Kate Thornton in May 1994. 'I'm stood there in holey tracksuit bottoms, I've got a basket on one arm and a shopping list in the other, and a group of women want me to sing for them in the middle of the shop.' It was a surreal and puzzling way to live, even if he had spent most of his young life dreaming of being a star singer and songwriter. But Gary generally professed to be unfazed by the attention except for when he had work to do, creating future songs, at his Knutsford bungalow. 'It's the best place for me to write but it's not always easy when you've got flashes going off outside your front-room window.'

By the summer of 1994, while Robbie was still living with his mum in Stoke-on-Trent, and the others were renting, Gary was preparing to move again. By then, such were his riches from the catalogue of original songs that he could afford to buy a 1920s country mansion by the name of Moorside (said to be worth £300,000), located slightly away from Knutsford in the village of Plumley. He set about filling it with antiques, one of his newfound passions, and even bought a house for both his mum and dad, and one for brother Ian.

Despite his burgeoning wealth, Gary remained frugal. Writing in *The Sunday Times*, Alex Kadis – who knew the group well in the 1990s – reported an example of the songwriter continuing to save money wherever possible: 'On returning from a gruelling European tour, he took himself off to Harvey Nichols with the intention of buying himself a bed. Upon spotting the bed of his dreams, he attempted to barter for the price. "You're in another world here, sir, this is Harvey Nichols," the snooty assistant informed him. "We don't make deals here." Whereupon Gary promptly hailed himself a taxi to the bed manufacturers, where he bought one for cost price.'

He allowed himself the occasional extravagance, though. At one point, Elton John (with whom he had become friends) advised him to hire a butler, which, for a time, he did. Maurice did all the cooking and the cleaning and took care of things in general. 'I was totally into that "What are pop stars supposed to act like?" frame of mind,' commented Gary.

Gary and his peers in pop were much more financially savvy than the pop stars of 20 years earlier. Jeremy Marsh, an executive at the group's label RCA, commented in 1995: 'There is more presence from lawyers and accountants and general advisers and managers. The artists are much more aware of their income streams and are just more financially adept and aware.'

Jonathan Morrish, a record industry boss at Sony Music, observed that young successful pop stars could now look back at the chequered fortunes of their predecessors: 'Twenty years ago, the industry was fairly new and there really wasn't a rule book, so people made the most appalling mistakes. Today, pop stars can learn from history.'

Gary explained his cautious nature with money: 'I keep a close eye on my money. You've got to. All this could be gone tomorrow.'

Meanwhile, Take That had surpassed all expectations. They were respected and admired by the British music industry, and had millions of fans to boot. Gary continued to win prizes for his songwriting. 'Pray' had won Best British Single at the BRIT Awards in February 1994, and then, at the end of May, he was honoured at the Ivor Novello Awards in London. Hiring a £4,000 Versace suit for the occasion, Gary scooped two gongs: one for the Best Contemporary Song prize, and another for the Best Songwriter, presented to him by his friend and hero Elton John (also a Take That fan). Gary had now recorded with Elton, having contributed backing vocals to a new song, 'Can You Feel the Love Tonight', soon to be featured on the soundtrack to the Disney animation *The Lion King*, due to open later that year.

That summer, critical acclaim also came from the panel of the prestigious Mercury Music Prize, an award for the Best British Album of the Year. Inaugurated in 1992, the Mercury was less concerned with sales figures than the BRIT Awards, instead choosing to honour musical innovation and excellence. Primal Scream and Suede were previous victors. For 1994, *Everything Changes* featured in a list that also included the likes of Blur's *Parklife*, Paul Weller's *Wild Wood*, Pulp and The Prodigy. Some rock purists frowned at their inclusion, but the judging panel's statement considered that Take That's music was 'too good to be the exclusive property of their fans'. On this occasion they failed to win, but the winning album was almost as surprising a selection for a prize that seemed to favour indie-rock, not pop or dance: M People's *Elegant Slumming*.

By the summer of 1994, Take That had sold four million albums worldwide (*Take That & Party* topped a million, and its follow-up, *Everything Changes*, three times that figure), and 850,000 videos. By now, the group were so used to topping the charts that anything less was a flop. 'Love Ain't Here Anymore' was their only single to miss number one in nearly three years. It had still reached number three in July, but failed to overtake the summer's monster hits of All-4-One's 'I Swear' (number two for seven weeks) and Wet Wet Wet's 'Love Is All Around' (which parked itself at number one for 15 weeks until even the group members themselves begged for the single to be deleted).

At the end of the summer and into the autumn, Take That embarked on another arena tour, taking in Glasgow, Manchester, Dublin, Sheffield, Cardiff, London's Wembley, Birmingham and Belfast. Among the delights of the new show, along with a cameo for Lulu on 'Relight My Fire' and that Beatles' medley, was the preview of a previously unheard song (and inevitable future number one): 'Sure'.

The *Independent on Sunday* was effusive at 'a show that overflows with effort, energy, imagination, and above all respect for the audience. The eight backing musicians are polished, the dancing superlative, and Gary Barlow's songs – especially the ballads – nearly worthy of the attention they have been given.' It stopped short of favourable Beatles' comparisons in light of the medley, though, preferring to cite Stock Aitken Waterman. As for reports on the singing, there were encouraging signs of 'a good'n'throaty soul voice' in

Robbie Williams. Take That were not only big business – the tour was being sponsored by Kellogg's Corn Pops – but now had a considerable critical following, too.

Interspersing the songs was a sort of jokey, knowing, end-of-the-pier level of badinage between the members of the group. Take That were not just a band, they were purveyors of variety and light entertainment, too – though, admittedly, the banter wasn't exactly at the level of the Marx Brothers:

> Robbie: I tell you what, Gaz, I wouldn't mind having a rest. Do you know 'Why Can't I Wake Up With You?'
> Gary: Do I know it, Rob? I *wrote* it!

Alex Kadis knew the members of Take That better than most. As the group's fan club magazine editor for a few years, and a frequent companion on their world tours, she felt comfortable around Gary. Even in the centre of attention, she believed, 'He's never lost the ability to laugh at himself. He's learned to enjoy his success and achievements. He used to sit in the corner at parties nursing a Diet Cola. Now he drinks cocktails and is always first on the dancefloor.' She also emphasised that he was forever looking ahead: 'Gary's always been a planner, and likes to know what tomorrow holds. I'd say he's even more ambitious than he used to be.'

But how much longer could Take That last? Already there were whispers that the group's days were numbered. It was highly unusual for a teen idol act to have more than two or three years at the top, and Take That had already been by far the biggest pop group in Britain for nearly two years. Asked about the future, Gary was vague but acknowledged it would have to end at some point. 'It really depresses me when I think of it all coming to an end. We all know it will finish. It might be next year or in 10 years but it will go on as long as we want it to.'

The comparisons between Gary and George Michael were starting to become commonplace, although within the group itself it was the source of much irreverence. When Jason proudly called Gary 'the next George Michael' and pronounced himself 'taken aback at how brilliant he is', Robbie Williams quickly declared, 'Yeah, and I'm the next Andrew Ridgeley!', as a reference to George's partner in Wham!, who had been a pop star but not much of a musician. After Wham! split in 1986, Ridgeley attempted an album (1990's *Son of Albert*) which did tend to show that George had been the overpowering talent in the duo.

Just as George Michael had disbanded Wham! to enjoy even greater global success (most notably in the USA), so it began to be suggested at the end of the summer of 1994 that Gary might split Take That if they were unable to progress Stateside. Tilly Rutherford, then an executive at Pete Waterman's record company PWL, which had guided the careers of Kylie Minogue and Jason Donovan, felt a solo career was inevitable: 'I would have thought it was certain Gary would go solo, despite his saying that he will never do it. The boy has got so much talent and he's the only one who can sing.' On the subject of Take That needing to crack America to survive, Rutherford said: 'It is important to conquer America and as a solo artist Gary could launch himself on the rock radio stations, like Elton John and Rod Stewart have. Take That are too gimmicky for America.'

For now, however, the only way Gary was going solo was in latex form. In November 1994, a puppet of him made its debut on the satirical ITV series *Spitting Image*. Inclusion on that show was as double-edged as fame itself – you could expect jokes at your expense, but being included at all was a sure sign that you had made it into the pantheon of stardom. One item poked fun at the fact that Gary never seemed to get the girls, but he himself claimed to have found the sketch amusing. 'I had a real giggle at it,' he told one paper, while backstage at the MTV Awards in Berlin (where Take That had won the Best Group gong). And he went on to explain that, like all the best comedy, the sketch was unwittingly based on truth. 'Just last week there were about 50 girls outside my house. I thought, this is great, and went out to see them. But when I went down to the gate, it turned out they thought Robbie was here.'

Gary later confessed the sight of the chubby puppet had triggered him to lose weight. He hit the gym, and tried to emulate the diet regime practised by Jason: no fat, no sugar and a daily diet of seeds. But, for such a passionate lover of food, dieting would always be a constant battle.

The *Spitting Image* puppet workshop didn't bother to craft models for Jason, Robbie, Mark or Howard, instead spending its time making grotesque versions of other famous names such as the incoming Labour Party leader Tony Blair and the actor and star of the movie *Four Weddings and a Funeral* Hugh Grant.

There was more competition between the Take That boys in the run-up to Christmas when it was announced that 12-inch-high models of each member of the band were being made by a toy firm called Vivid Imaginations, to be sold in Argos. Sales for the doll of Gary (RRP £11.50) trailed those of Mark and even Robbie, but he still fared better than Howard and Jason. 'We didn't stock the other two,' explained an Argos spokesman, 'because there wasn't room for them.'

All this demonstrated that, while there was equality onstage between the five members of Take That, there was ferocious competition between the boys as to who was the most popular among fans – not especially a problem while the group remained together, but a worrying sign for when the band would inevitably take its final bow and go their separate ways.

CHAPTER 10

BACK FOR NOW

After 'Sure' hit number one in October 1994, there would be nearly six months before any new Take That product. The prospect of another single before Christmas was ruled out, leaving the field clear for East 17 to reign supreme with what turned out to be their only chart-topper, 'Stay Another Day' – a deceptively dark song, which turned out to be about the suicide of songwriter Tony Mortimer's brother. It was number one for a month, but the ubiquity of the song was not easy for his family. 'If I get to open my soul to the public, it's an honour,' said Mortimer, 'but my family had no say. When they hear the song it's hard – it takes them right back.'

Take That introduced 'Stay Another Day' when they guest hosted and linked the Christmas Day edition of *Top of the Pops*.

At the same time, a new five-piece boyband from Dublin called Boyzone – managed by one Louis Walsh – was scampering up the charts with a cover of The Osmonds' 'Love Me For a Reason'. 'Take That have already reached the pinnacle of their success,' was the verdict of Boyzone's 17-year-old frontman Ronan Keating. 'There is not much further they can go. They've been around for five years and I think they now want out of the teeny-bopper scene.' Keating felt that Take That might be outgrowing their audience. 'We are younger and hungry for success, and we are appealing to the new breed of 12- and 13-year-olds.'

Also in December, Take That had topped the bill at the Concert of Hope, a charity event at Wembley Arena before Diana, Princess of Wales. Staged on 1 December – World AIDS Day – others appearing included Lulu, and other favourites from the year's singles charts (EYC, China Black), plus brilliant Scottish singer Eddi Reader. Meeting the Princess was very exciting, as Gary explained. 'We went round the day before for drinks and Diana was fantastic. Jason turned up in a denim shirt and trousers. The next night [at the gig], we met her officially and Diana turned to him and said, "Oh, I see you've still got the same clothes on." What a woman to remember something like that.'

The third Take That album could have been recorded at a top recording studio in the Caribbean. Instead, it was made in about two months at Gary Barlow's own home studio for the bargain price of around £150,000. 'It was like going to school,' recalled Mark Owen of the low-key sessions. 'It was really relaxing because we would just sit in Gary's garden and wait to be called into the studio.' Tracks included 'The Day

After Tomorrow', another ballad for Mark to sing, and 'Never Forget', which seemed to take stock of where Take That were, and where they had come from. The latter would inspire *Smash Hits* to write, 'If the boys ever needed a parting record, this would be it.'

Gary would later claim he regretted giving away the lead vocal of 'Never Forget' to Howard. 'The only thing wrong with "Never Forget",' he told Robbie over 15 years later, 'is that I'm not singing it. We used to divvy up stuff per record and when we first recorded the song, it wasn't the stand-out hit it became, so I said, "Here you are, Howard." Then it had a big mix and it was just a different record when it came back.'

The song 'Nobody Else', which would double as the album's title, was dedicated to the rock-solid relationship of Marge and Colin, Gary's parents. During one of his visits to their home, he had found them in the loft sifting through old photographs of themselves. 'I began to think about the hopes they must have had when they were young,' he explained, 'and how their lives have turned out pretty good. They're still in love and still happy. So I wrote the song for them.'

Nobody Else was the boldest attempt yet to break the group in North America. 'America is a very big market,' observed Gary, 'and if you are going to crack it there, you've got to do it properly.' Dance and pop producers helped out with the new album (Brothers in Rhythm, Chris Porter, Dave James and David Morales), but it marked the first time on a Take That album where Gary had co-produced every track. 'It's the most I've ever been involved with the making of the music,' he told *Music Week*. Though still a group project, it was acknowledged by certain members just how vital to Take

That's success Gary's creative power was. 'We'd be finished without him,' Mark said succinctly.

Perhaps the best song on the album, and certainly the most celebrated, was 'Back for Good' – a catchy, tuneful ballad in the vein of 'Love is All Around' and the Chi-Lites' soul hit of the 1970s 'Have You Seen Her?' According to song factory Gary, 'Back for Good' was written in just 15 minutes. 'The songs that I write the quickest seem to come out the best,' he said. He seemed to revel in the spontaneity of songwriting, the process of creating something from scratch against the clock. 'I just like sitting down at a piano,' he said in 2005, 'and there being no song and half an hour later, you've got something. The possibilities are so exciting – is this song only going to mean something to me or will it connect with thousands of people?'

But he also emphasised that just because songs of the calibre of 'Back for Good' had come quickly did not render them throwaway. 'I know some people think that if we put out a record of us burping it would be a huge hit, but that doesn't mean we're going to go down the easy road for easy hits. We want to make quality records. We want to better ourselves.' The truth is, though, even when songwriters create a song 'in 15 minutes', it's a swift gathering together of technical know-how and life experience, as well as a burst of energy.

'Back for Good' was first aired in public at the BRIT Awards in February 1995, traditionally an occasion where live guests revisit a familiar hit from the previous 12 months. But such was Take That's confidence in the new song that they broke with tradition, and such was the reaction to 'Back for Good' that its release date was brought forward. There were a few disappointed reactions – rock weekly the *New Musical Express* (*NME*) felt a tiny bit betrayed: 'Proper song alert! What I want from Take That is rippling pants, jumping around and Lulu at the end. "Back for Good" is just too classy.'

Take That were growing up, but most were happy at the prospect if it meant more songs like this.

When 'Back for Good' came out, on 27 March 1995, it became the fastest-selling single of the decade thus far, shifting 350,000 copies in its first week. This outranked the total sales for the other nine records in the Top 10, and even dwarfed sales of a previously unreleased Beatles single, 'Baby It's You', which had been issued the same week. Not since December 1984, when Band Aid sold 600,000 copies of 'Do They Know It's Christmas?' in seven days, had a new single received this sort of response. Number one in the UK for a month, by which time its sales would be approaching one million, 'Back for Good' was Take That's best-selling single to date. The song's appeal stretched far beyond the teenage demographic who had lapped up many of their previous smash hits. It would also bring them their strongest international acclaim yet, topping the charts in much of Europe, Australia and Canada. Finally, they would break in the United States, partly thanks to a deal with new record label Arista, and an appearance on the US television series *Baywatch*. They would appear in an episode, filming a video on the beach.

By the spring of 1995, Take That appeared invincible; it seemed as if every new single was destined to outsell all competition, at least among their pop rivals. East 17 had perhaps posed the greatest threat to their dominance, but a bigger threat was the emerging Britpop movement, a poppier take on alternative guitar rock. Born out of the indie boom, groups such as Pulp, The Boo Radleys and Supergrass were scoring huge hits by 1995. After an uncertain period, commercially Blur had firmly established themselves as inventive and imaginative chroniclers of British suburban life. And then there was the Mancunian guitar band Oasis, whose 'Some Might Say' was the record that (at the end of April) dislodged 'Back for Good' from the top of the charts.

Meanwhile, the ban on steady girlfriends for Take That members had effectively been lifted. Nigel Martin-Smith always insisted that the group would be hottest with teen audiences if they were perceived to be available and single. A *Smash Hits* magazine poll conducted in May of that year appeared to back this up. Readers were asked which of the five they liked the best. Mark topped the list with 32 per cent, with Gary on 27 per cent, trailing Robbie by just one percentage point. A long way behind were Jason (7 per cent) and Howard (6 per cent), but, as the magazine's editor Mark Frith pointed out, both of them had already talked openly about the fact they had girlfriends.

The *Nobody Else* album was released on 8 May 1995, and sold 600,000 copies in three days. The cover shot was from a fashion shoot held by the style guru Gianni Versace, and the group had helped him display his latest collection in Italy (all long coats and tight trousers) at the end of the previous year. Much of the shoot had appeared in the Italian edition of *Vogue*, though the fivesome had also worn the Versace suits at the MTV Awards in Berlin. Gary confessed to feeling flattered at Versace's invitation to model the outfits. 'I must admit we had never considered doing any modelling but when the offer came up we thought, "Why not?"' He had even felt a little intimidated by the grandeur of the occasion (there was also a lavish feast). 'It was good to see how the other half live. But I wouldn't know what to do with that kind of lifestyle – I'm more your three-bedroom detached kind of bloke.' Even when drowning in wealth, Gary couldn't help but be the boy next door.

The album had been given an international press launch in March in the German city of Munich. 'Clearly a new George Michael in the making,' said *The Times* of Gary Barlow's latest songs. There was evidently a newfound maturity, even solemnity, on some of the ballads on the album like 'Holding Back the Tears' and 'The Day After Tomorrow'. But there was also a nod to the swingbeat and R&B arrangements of American 90s pop on up-tempo offerings such as 'Hate It', 'Sunday to Saturday', and the familiar 'Sure'. 'Lady Tonight' even opened with a rap, and proceeded with a light hip hop backing. *Q* magazine did wonder aloud if the most time and trouble had been taken over 'Back for Good' and the next single, 'Never Forget': 'There is still an air of production-line haste in the tracks unlikely to become singles.' But Gary laughed off suggestions that the record was a conscious effort to seduce the USA, the last major territory Take That had not yet conquered. 'If it sounds American, it certainly wasn't intentional,' he told *Music Week* a few weeks before the album's release. 'I'm not a fan of US music and I don't think it really influenced what we did.'

Take That, though, were back for good – or were they? A few hints that all might not be well had started to sneak into the gossip columns. 'I can see us taking a break from each other to do various projects,' warned Robbie, but he quickly reassured, 'that is way down the line.' It was also reported that, in April 1995, when Nigel Martin-Smith (now running a management company called NMS) renegotiated his contract as the group's manager, it was renewed for only one more year. *The Sunday Times* wondered if the arrangement between group and manager would continue for much longer once the new 12-month contract was up. 'Can he and Take That go much further together? Will he want to? Take That's audience is growing up, and the last thing tomorrow's screaming teens want is yesterday's teen idols.'

Besides, Nigel seemed a lot less bothered about international acclaim than the group itself, perhaps because he had always envisioned them as a homegrown act, a 'British New Kids On The Block'. When Take That had taken off globally, he tended to stay in Manchester. 'He got jet lag flying to London,' one band member would later tell *The Sunday Times*. Other difficulties had started to appear in his relationship with the boys. He had branded himself their mother and, according to Jason, called them his 'surrogate children'.

Just as Nigel signed his 12-month contract, Take That signed a new recording deal with the RCA label, estimated to be worth £20 million, and announced another British tour for the late summer of 1995. 'It's hard to believe that all this is happening to us,' said Gary, 'especially as so many people have said we wouldn't last. They said we were going to split up but that couldn't be further from the truth. Things are just getting better and better.'

It seemed nothing could go wrong. Funnily enough, though, things were about to – in quite spectacular fashion.

CHAPTER 11

JOVIAL BOB
SIGNS OFF

The summer of 1995 was a season of departures and settlements in pop. Just as Oasis topped the charts for the first time, at the end of April, they fired their drummer, Tony McCarroll. In June, Louise Nurding (one of the female vocal quartet Eternal) left for a solo career, resulting in several hits, and eventually marriage to the footballer Jamie Redknapp. In the first week of July, it was announced that George Michael had settled his three-year dispute with Sony Music, and was now free to sign with a different record label. But overshadowing all three of these events was one that had been on the cards for some time.

On 23 June, Robbie Williams had attended the Glastonbury music festival without telling the other members of Take That or their management. With bleached white hair, he hung around backstage with Oasis, and couldn't resist joining them onstage during their song 'Shakermaker'. Hungover and listless, he returned to Take That rehearsals. He was drinking too much, taking drugs and seemed bloated and directionless. Later, he admitted, 'I couldn't bear to be by myself. I was always the last to bed. I'd look around the bar and think, "Ah, a German double-glazing salesman! I'll go and talk to him."'

Years later, Mark Owen would recall of Robbie: 'Sometimes we'd joke and say we wanted to be in Oasis but he actually *did* want to be in Oasis. I feel a bit guilty now that I wasn't mature enough to hear his cries.'

Matters came to a head on Thursday, 13 July. Take That were rehearsing at Staffordshire Territorial Army Centre, preparing for a series of arena dates in Manchester and London, due to begin only a few weeks later. Robbie told the others that he wanted to leave the band in October, when his five-year contract was up. Even then, he was given the weekend to reconsider. He disappeared to St Tropez, where he was seen on a yacht with George Michael and the TV presenter Paula Yates. 'When he came back,' Mark Owen said in a subsequent radio interview, 'he hadn't changed his mind. It was quite obvious to us he wasn't happy.'

The bubble had burst – the members of Take That had rarely been seen apart from each other, in the company of other celebrities. First Oasis, next George and Paula. Gary Barlow knew now that Robbie would go: 'Once the strangers were let in, having their say, we knew that was it.'

The story officially broke in the media on 17 July. It was reported as a shock departure, but for a while there had been hints that all was not well. Part of Robbie's need to break away came from the uncomfortable truth that he had grown up in public, as a professional entertainer, and defined by management contract clauses. Most teenagers have the luxury of living out their adolescence in relative privacy, with their friends and family, trying to establish their own identities. Robbie Williams, who described himself as 'Jovial Bob, the joker from Stoke', had formed his identity in the glare of the world's media. 'I've never had a chance to grow up and be an adolescent,' he told the *Daily Mirror*'s Kate Thornton in March 1995, four months before he quit. 'I came from school straight into this. The others have all had a couple of years to find their feet and do the things teenage blokes do.' While Howard was already 22 when the ink was drying on the Take That/Martin-Smith contract, Jason was 20 and Gary was 19 (with six years of regular performing experience). Even Mark had turned 18. Robbie had been only 16. 'I'm not the wild one of Take That,' he reasoned. 'I'm just the youngest.'

What hadn't helped Robbie's unhappiness in the group was that, as the lead singer on 'Could It Be Magic' and 'Everything Changes', he had made no major lead contribution to the *Nobody Else* album. In short, his voice had gone. 'I was going out too much, I abused my voice and I paid the price. I just wasn't good enough to carry a lead vocal.' Later, he reflected on his reasons for leaving, and wondered if he just never felt part of the group. Certainly, he found it hard to relate to the group's songwriter, or so he claimed: 'There were never any big arguments with Gary, but we never talked. We were just total opposites. I would hang around with Jason and he'd stick with Howard – it was always like that. But I had to get out in the end. I felt there was no choice.'

In hindsight, Gary would admit that he had never really

taken Robbie sufficiently seriously during the first half of the 1990s. 'Should have done because he was a valid band member, but he was never interested in any of the business that surrounded the band.' Then again, perhaps Robbie's lack of commitment in that department at the time was down to his age: indoctrinated into Take That at such a young age, he was only just 21 when he left. Growing up in the glare of the paparazzi, the rush of live gigs and most of all the idolatry from the fanbase can be a lot to deal with, no matter how strong one's character might be.

Later, Robbie gave a vivid insight into how the fan attention could spill over from inconvenient into intimidating and terrifying. He had expected to be able to keep fame and home life separate. 'In my head, what was going to happen was we'd play the NEC [in Birmingham], then I'd come home and go to the pub and get pissed with my friends.' Instead, the Williams' household seemed constantly under scrutiny: 'To my mother it was hell. She was miserable, which made me miserable. We were constantly under threat of being burgled. I slept with a starting pistol and a hammer under my pillow.'

In July 1995, it wasn't immediately clear whether Robbie had jumped from Take That or had been pushed. Regardless, he had left just three weeks before a 20-date sell-out British tour was due to begin on 5 August, to be followed by dates in Australia, Japan and the Far East, and then a promotional tour of North America. In his absence, the others would have to cover for any lead vocals he had contributed to recordings and shows in the past. All the merchandise for the tour (T-shirts, posters and so on) depicting him as part of the band would have to be discarded and revised, no doubt at considerable expense. 'The four of us are still 100 per cent committed,' declared Gary, 'and looking forward to a long future together.' But no replacement would be drafted in: 'There's no other Rob. If we searched the world, we'd struggle to find one.' Finally, Gary insisted: 'If he has a change of heart, the door's still open, and we'll be waiting.'

Robbie's departure made the flavour of the next Take That single all the more poignant. Titled 'Never Forget', it was about the group's own rise to stardom, reviewing where they had come from, and where they were now. The video was a montage of photographs and footage from their childhoods. It was a curiously self-aware evaluation of the Take That career thus far, an understanding that it could end at any time.

And wherever Robbie was now, he was out of Take That. He would be missing from the *Top of the Pops* appearances; when 'Never Forget' became their seventh number one, the others had to cover for the Robbie solo dance, which was now missing.

In the wake of Robbie leaving Take That, there was almost endless speculation about how it would affect the dynamics of the group, and that Gary's own departure could not be far away. 'I'd be surprised if Take That were still together in 1996,' an RCA executive warned the *Daily Mirror* that same month. 'Gary has a huge talent, and a solo career is the obvious move.'

Manager Nigel Martin-Smith remained undeterred in the wake of Robbie's leaving, and perhaps relieved too. 'I believe very much in fate,' he declared in *Music Week*, 'but I think this will be a shot in the arm for everybody. To me, it's given us another three or four years of Take That.'

In his first post-Take That interviews, Robbie explained how regimented life in the group had been, with a constant feeling of constraint. 'It can be like being in the Army. You have to get up at a certain time, go out at a certain time, eat certain things and every single second of your day is accounted for.' Of course, he had enjoyed some of it, but, as he conceded to MTV, 'I'm bored with it now. I want to do something else, something more outrageous.' He didn't want to be 'one of Gary Barlow's backing singers'.

Naturally, before Robbie could make any solo records, there were legal and contractual requirements. Leaving a group is not a simple case of quitting; there are clauses in contracts to heed and, in the case of Take That, there was an agreement that a member wanting to leave was obliged to give six months' notice. Robbie hoped to launch a solo career by the end of 1995, but was prevented from doing so by contractual ties. He looked forward to making his own records, but his pedigree was not good. So far, his only writing credit was a short section of Take That's 'Sure'. He might be fine writing lyrics, but what about melody, which was Gary Barlow's real gift?

Take That insider and journalist Alex Kadis prophetically said of Robbie Williams in 1995, only weeks before he left the group in dramatic fashion: 'Rob has yet to show the full extent of his talents. The hell-raiser the public knows is just a small part of a much bigger picture.'

The first Robbie-less Take That tour was to take place at just two venues – Manchester Arena and Earl's Court in London. A fleet of special Take That coaches would transport many of the 350,000 fans expected to attend.

Behind the scenes, over 100 key people were helping to co-ordinate the logistics of the shows and ensure that all would run smoothly: caterers and technicians, designers and musicians. Accompanying Take That at all the shows was a new mini-Take That: Stuart Morris, Calum Gallaghan, Gavin Wood, Bryan Mitchell and Simon Bright. All were boys aged between 10 and 13 years of age, and this junior quintet would join them on stage for three songs.

If Gary, Mark, Jason and Howard were missing Robbie, they didn't show it too much in the live summer shows. At the first Manchester show, right from the off – 'Relight My Fire' (this time with soul singer Juliet Roberts in place of Lulu) – the four remaining bandmates burst forth in flamboyant costumes, which had been designed by budding fashion students in London. Gary emerged on to the stage on the back of a Take That logo. The energy of the show hardly dropped for almost two hours, in front of a 20,000-strong crowd. Later in the set, 'Back for Good' was sung from the top of a pair of American cars, while 'Pray' and 'Never Forget', performed with an orchestra and a 20-strong choir, were saved until the encore. At one point, an audience member was chosen from the crowd to be personally serenaded by the group.

The previous year, there had been a Beatles' medley on the tour. This time round, the lads tackled rock music, with Jason playing guitar, Mark on bass and Howard on drums. There was a cover of 'Another Brick in the Wall' by one of Jason's favourite groups, Pink Floyd. Then came an irreverent rendition of Nirvana's 'Smells Like Teen Spirit', a controversial choice for some, especially as the US grunge icons' frontman Kurt Cobain had only died the year before.

Originally, Robbie was to sing on both, but, with him now out of the group, there was a hasty change of plan.

'Smells Like Teen Spirit' turned out to be Mark's idea. 'It's something we started practising on the last tour. We thought it would be a laugh, but I can see the headlines now: "Kurt Cobain turns in his grave".' Though it was Gary who thought of 'Another Brick in the Wall': 'It's the only record I played at my ninth birthday party and it holds fond memories for me' – it was closer to Jason's taste. He later insisted he had liked most of Take That's singles, especially Gary's ballads. His favourite music was the Floyd, as well as Neil Young and hip-hop.

After ten performances in Manchester, the tour continued and concluded at Earl's Court in London. No one could have known that 31 August 1995 would be the last time they played a full-length concert in Britain. Then they were off to Australia, Japan, the Far East and, finally, to North America, where 'Back for Good' and *Nobody Else* were being belatedly released. Before the album came out in America, with a rejigged running order incorporating a few former hits like 'Pray' and 'Babe', its sleeve had been changed, with Robbie's image removed. On the single's flip side was a 'remix' of 'Love Ain't Here Anymore', meaning that Robbie's vocal contribution had also been withdrawn.

'Back for Good' did break through Stateside. It spent seven months on the Billboard Hot 100 singles chart and eventually climbed as high as number seven, at a time when few British groups were making much impression in America. But Take That would have no other major US hits, and the album failed to rise higher than number 69. Part of the problem was down to image – relatively few understood they were a pop group, and it transpired that most of the people who bought the single were over the age of 30. Take That wanted to be a grown-up band, but even this came as a bit of a shock. Gary began to realise the group's demographic was one more like Elton John and George Michael, who had outgrown a teen audience and carved out a long-term career for older listeners, than teenage favourites like Boyz II Men or a new group called the Backstreet Boys.

'We always wanted to go over there,' said Gary of America, 'and show 'em how it's done. Many groups feel the need to remix their music to make it sound more American. Why? We wanted to break America sounding British.'

Regardless, 'Back for Good' would be Take That's only Top 10 hit in the USA.

The overall global picture, on the face of it, looked brighter. *Nobody Else* had shifted more than six million copies worldwide, and Take That were officially reported to be planning a full world tour in 1996, as well as a new single and album. In private, things looked much less certain, though. Journalists would later tell of band members whispering backstage about how vulnerable Take That as a group now was. Take, for instance, Howard Donald backstage at the MTV Awards in Paris, in November 1995: 'I have to think about the future, but I don't know what it holds for me. I mean, this time next year I could be redundant.'

Gary Barlow was a little more ambiguous about the year ahead. After the *Smash Hits* Poll Winners' Party on 3 December, he told one reporter: 'All I want is to have a new album out. I've finished it, the only thing left is recording it.'

But was this a solo album or a Take That album? When asked a question about the future of the group, he politely changed the subject.

Earlier that day, for the fourth year in succession, Take That had been voted Best Group in the World at the *Smash Hits* Awards, despite the competition of Britpop giants like Blur, Pulp and Oasis. Meanwhile, the departed Robbie Williams had been dubbed Saddest Loser of 1995. All the while, during the show, Gary had intently watched several rival boybands take to the stage to perform, including Ireland's Boyzone and the USA's Backstreet Boys. Though he was careful not to name names, he felt Take That's days were numbered: 'They all looked like us, and they all danced like us, and they didn't sound any different. I thought, "We can't be here next year."'

CHAPTER 12

THE RUMOURS ARE TRUE

Nigel Martin-Smith later said one of the biggest mistakes he made in managing Take That was to give them a whole month's holiday at Christmas 1995. It was enough thinking time for Gary Barlow. There were no public sightings of the group, only as individuals, and the only official news was that Gary was back in the studio with producer Chris Porter, who had worked on *Nobody Else*, and before that various George Michael records.

At the end of January 1996, just as George himself was releasing 'Jesus to a Child', his first single in almost three years, news came of fresh Take That product. Their next single, their seventeenth, was rather curiously not an original number, and so was somewhat at odds with the image of Gary as star songwriter of the group. Instead, it was a cover version, their first on record since 1993. 'How Deep Is Your Love', like

'It Only Takes a Minute', 'Could It Be Magic' and 'Relight My Fire', dated from the 1970s, but this was their first cover of a ballad. It was originally written and recorded by the Bee Gees as part of their soundtrack to the 1977 John Travolta film *Saturday Night Fever*. Gary regarded it as one of his favourite songs, but it still seemed a relatively safe choice for a single, given his prolific nature as a songwriter. Why were Take That releasing *another* cover version?

On Monday, 5 February, the telephone rang in the *Smash Hits* office. The Take That interview arranged for that Friday in Paris had been shelved. Eyebrows were raised; the group had never before cancelled an interview or a photo shoot. By way of explanation, they were told that the upcoming Take That record would be 'a greatest hits album, and the lads feel they've got nothing to talk about at the moment'.

A week later, the truth was out: Take That were no more, and 'How Deep is Your Love' would be their swansong release. After six years, enough was enough, and the remaining four members were going their separate ways, with Gary tipped for even greater solo stardom. Plans for any more albums as a group were torn up, and there was to be no farewell tour. Instead, there would indeed be a greatest hits compilation.

In the industry, it was known that Take That had admired the way that George Michael orchestrated the split of Wham! in 1986, preparing the ground with solo George singles, then rounding off the duo's four-year career with a farewell single, greatest hits compilation and sell-out concert at Wembley Stadium. Now Take That intended to do the same. 'In Take That, we always talked about the end,' Gary later said. 'We talked about bands like Wham! and The Jam, the ones who cut it when they were right at the top. That's what we had to do: keep it all positive until we could just feel it drifting away a little bit and then – bang!'

As it was announced the group were splitting, Gary revealed that the writing had been on the wall for six months – ever since their British tour the previous summer. 'I stared out into the crowd,' he told the *Sun*'s showbiz reporter Andy Coulson, 'and realised that the flat-chested 13-year-old girls who had helped make us stars were now 18-year-olds with boobs. I knew then that just as the fans had grown, so must we. And that would mean only one thing – splitting up.'

Gary, Mark, Jason and Howard held a press conference at Manchester's Hilton Hotel at 1pm on Tuesday, 13 February 1996. When reminded that it was Robbie Williams' birthday, Gary simply deadpanned, 'Is it?' Tight-lipped on Robbie matters for legal reasons, he went on to admit that the split was necessary to enable him to launch his solo career. Any frustration that the record company felt about the split was tempered by the knowledge that at least they still had Gary. And he still had 'lots of material' held back to go it alone, rather than covers from the 1970s. A solo single would be out by the summer, he promised. Hot on its heels would be an album, then a tour. Career prospects for Mark, Jason and Howard seemed less certain, though all looked set to make some money from record sales and business shares. Inevitably, though, Gary as principal songwriter would see healthier profits.

Louis Walsh, manager of rival boyband Boyzone, was generous in his summing-up of Take That: 'It's the end of the biggest pop band of the Nineties.'

For Simon Cowell, who had turned them down at IQ

Records, back in 1991, there were mixed feelings, but it was a kind of relief. 'With every Number One hit they had – and there were eight of them – I felt physically ill, but you have to hold your hands up and say, "I screwed up".'

As for Robbie Williams's response, it was one of indifference, tinged with affection. 'I'm more concerned about how Port Vale do in the cup tonight,' he told reporters, but then added, 'I did my grieving when I was kicked out. However, Take That was six years of my life and I know how the guys are feeling.'

The reaction to the Take That split from fans bordered on hysteria. Their record company received many tearful phone calls from fans, and set up a helpline to try to comfort the distressed and upset. ChildLine, the national children's charity, were also besieged by callers wracked with grief and alarm. Gary tried to console them: 'All I can say to the fans is, when you're feeling sad, think back to all those excellent times we had.'

Splitting up Take That wasn't just about going solo for Gary. The previous summer, he had established a relationship with a 23-year-old dancer called Dawn Andrews. She had been one of the dancers on the spectacular *Nobody Else* tour in Manchester and London. 'We ordered 15 dancers and let Jason audition them,' Gary later recalled. 'We were putting our orders in: "Get me a dark one, get me a blonde one" or whatever. Jason said he'd sorted us all out, but when I turned up I saw Dawn. She wasn't the one he'd ordered for me but we just got to know each other – that's when we became inseparable.' He would describe his ultimate turn-on as 'a girl who can dance and really knows how to use her body'.

For Gary, it had come as a relief to declare that he was in a relationship, and not have to stay on-message as a perpetually single person, as all of Take That were expected to do. 'The official Take That line was always, "We don't have relationships". Of course everybody did, and it was tremendously hard to keep under wraps. All the English newspapers were on our backs, day and night. Sneaking people into hotel rooms was horrible, it really was.'

He had always been determined to observe the 'no steady girlfriends' rule for Take That members, and getting together with Dawn probably hastened his decision to split the group. For him, it marked a maturity regarding relationships. 'I don't think I ever communicated with any of my girlfriends before Dawn,' he told the magazine *Arena*. 'I don't remember having a decent chat with any of them.'

The couple had, of course, met several years earlier – at the Kurtis Rush video shoot in Nottingham in the summer of 1989, and briefly again in 1992, at the Children's Royal Variety Performance. In the meantime, Dawn had even beaten Gary to the number one spot. A year after the 'Love is in the Air' video, in 1990, she appeared in the promo for 'Itsy Bitsy Teeny Weeny Yellow Polka Dot Bikini', Timmy Mallett's bid for chart glory under the name Bombalurina.

There would be no farewell Take That live concert, but there were still contractual duties to be carried out before the start of April 1996, when Nigel Martin-Smith's managerial contract ended. On 19 February, they made a final appearance at the BRIT Awards, where they had originally planned to announce the split before snowballing rumours had made it impossible to delay the revelations any longer. Their nomination in the Best British Single category – 'Back for Good' – could not help but seem sourly titled in light of the split. They won the award anyway, but, as it turned out, Take That's performance at the BRITs was outflanked on the night by the disruption of Michael Jackson's stage act by an offended Jarvis Cocker from Pulp. Cocker felt that Jackson's act, which appeared to paint him as a biblical figure, was in highly dubious taste.

'How Deep is Your Love' came out on 26 February 1996, and would soon become Take That's eighth UK number one, the most by any group so far in the 1990s. If the track itself was polite and anodyne, the video was darker and more provocative. Five different endings were shot for it. The one that was chosen depicted the foursome being dominated and tied up by model Paula Hamilton, before their clothes were seen floating on a murky river. There was, however, no sign of their bodies, which meant that the door was always open for Gary, Mark, Howard and Jason to regroup. Maybe one day...

The *Greatest Hits* package was unusually sequenced for a 'best of'. Many hit compilations arrange the singles chronologically, from the debut single to the most recent. This is fine if a group makes it big straight away, but, as none of Take That's first three singles charted highly, it would have meant a scrappy start to a greatest hits album. Instead, the roll call of hits ran in reverse order, starting with 'How Deep is Your Love' and ending back in the summer of 1991 with 'Do What U Like'. The effect was like rewinding a videotape back to the beginning. A bonus track was the Robbie-free US remix of 'Love Ain't Here Anymore'.

Traditionally, when a group splits up and releases a compilation, it lures the fanbase into snapping up the back catalogue. This didn't really happen with Take That – quite the opposite, in fact. When *Greatest Hits* was released, their existing albums tumbled out of the charts, partly because the mainly juvenile fanbase could only afford one piece of Take That product at a time. Over the previous five years, their records and videos had been carefully scheduled to ensure the market wasn't flooded. Many of their fans did not have limitless pocket money.

A tie-in book, *Take That: Our Greatest Hits*, revealed the stories behind their many hits. Gary revealed his three favourite Take That songs. Of 'Back for Good', he said, 'I can never have enough of that track. I could listen to it over and over again.' 'Why Can't I Wake Up With You?', his second choice, was an early Barlow composition, penned in 1988 when he was just 17, and before Take That came into being. His reason for selecting 'Never Forget' was very simple: 'Because it's just about us.' Of his favourites to perform live on stage, Gary confessed to preferring the ballads over the up-tempo fare 'because I don't have to move around the stage much. I never was the greatest dancer.'

At the end of February 1996, Robbie Williams settled his legal battle with RCA, hours before the case was due to reach the High Court. He could extricate himself from his recording contract to become a solo artist, but only in return for 'substantial' compensation. His departure from Take That was becoming expensive. Virgin Records and EMI were both interested in signing him as a solo artist. So now, Gary and Robbie would be competing against each other as solo recording stars.

There is always a great deal of pressure to being in a boyband. As Mark Ellen, former editor of *Q* and *Smash Hits*, commented, consistent behaviour was essential when it came to preserving the 'brand' of Take That: 'The impression I get with some boybands, and even The Beatles in their early days, is that when they go out they are, 24 hours a day, representing the corporate image of that group. I have never seen a picture of one Take That member in the wrong place or with the wrong person on his arm.'

Being in a boyband is, then, undeniably hard work. For all the acclaim and attention, there's the regime of keeping in trim, eating the right foods the whole time, travelling, answering the same questions a lot, and all that smiling. Admittedly, it's hardly putting out fires or working down mines, but it's a job nonetheless, and suddenly realising that you're having to play a role during every waking hour must be a bit of a shock, especially if you're still a young person and haven't worked out who you really are yet.

Though Take That had floundered prior to their break-through single, 'It Only Takes a Minute', they could fail in relative obscurity, as they weren't really founded as part of a trend; they were simply a British equivalent of a US act, the first of a wave of boybands in the 1990s. In some ways, they and East 17 laid down the rules to be followed by imitations like Let Loose, Boyzone, 911, 5ive and, later still, Westlife. All of these groups had to score a massive hit single first time out, and have members with personalities that gelled. As Alex Kadis, Take That's fan club magazine editor for several years, candidly put it: 'The less successful Bad Boys Inc and Worlds Apart were beset with rows because certain members within the groups simply didn't like one another. To spend all your time with people you wouldn't have independently chosen as your friends is trying, to say the least.'

Even after Take That's split, fans haunted by the shock continued to organise pilgrimages to the sites of their idols. Having reacted to the break-up as a death, and the final appearances and press conferences as wakes and funerals, certain fans mourned the group for months after. The *Independent* followed the progress of one fan's itinerary, from one club in Runcorn where Gary had performed as a teenager, to the Indian restaurant in Rusholme where the links for the *Everything Changes* video compilation had been filmed. Restaurant staff estimated something like 2,000 fans of the group had visited the premises since that video had come out in 1994. 'They come from all over – Germany, Italy, France, Japan, even Australia. They all want to sit where Jason sat. They always want to have what he had. The funny thing is, he never really came here before he made that film.' Even for the fans who were self-aware enough to know that their obsession with Take That was pure fantasy, that obsession could still not be extinguished. The solo careers of the group's members would just not be the same.

Gary wouldn't miss the idolatry. He had seen a particularly dark side to it all. Many of Take That's fans had been under 16, some under 14, and, while it could be stressful having fans loitering outside his house late at night, it was much more alarming still to discover that the young fans in turn may have been attracting paedophiles. 'There are girls under 14 outside my house until one in the morning,' he explained. 'And wherever our fans go, this network of perverts goes, too.'

Take That's last engagement was on a TV variety show in the Netherlands. They performed 'How Deep is Your Love' on Ivo Niehe's show in an Amsterdam studio in front of a mere 250 fans. When there was a fault with the backing track on the song, Gary sang the song acapella, augmented by the harmonies of the others. Once it was all over, they flew back to Britain; they looked glum. While the others returned to Manchester, Gary headed for London and his girlfriend Dawn. He confessed to feeling bored with his lot in the group. 'I was becoming complacent,' he told the *Daily Mirror*. 'That's what triggered the end of the band for me.'

They could have survived another two years just by touring, but Gary was ready to take a few risks. He had enjoyed being a songwriter for the group: 'I liked being under pressure like that – it's what keeps me going.' The last days had been tedious ones, treading water and waiting for freedom. 'We were generating millions of record sales, but it was past being good for business. We just wanted to be free of it all – and then we were more trapped than ever. We were absolutely bored shitless, on that last day. Flying back that morning [from Amsterdam] was like breathing new air.'

There were encouraging hints to the Take That fanbase that their heroes may yet return; they would just have to have some patience. 'We do care very much about our fans,' said Mark. 'Hopefully, if they hold themselves together for long enough, they will all see us back.'

Jason also tried to reassure the millions of fans: 'When we say it's the end, it's the end of Take That as it is now.'

But Gary Barlow – ironically, the one with the greatest promise as a solo performer – was the most explicit about the possibility of a Take That Mark II: 'Our dream is, after five or ten years, to do it all again.'

Few in 1996 could have imagined that Gary and co. would live that dream.

CHAPTER 13

BARLOW
AT LARGE

It was June 1996. Gary Barlow was a wealthy singer, songwriter and pop star. Still only 25 years old, he had just been honoured at the Ivor Novello music awards with a Lifetime Achievement Award. He had, in fact, been shortlisted in a total of four categories, and was victorious in the Most Performed Work, as well as the Best Selling Song Title, recognised in both cases for 'Back for Good'. This time he was accompanied by his parents and his new love, Dawn. Other winners on the night included Blur and Oasis (who shared the Best Songwriter award), while Seal won the International Hit of the Year prize for 'Kiss from a Rose'.

Gary had become tired of the fact that everything he was doing was headline news, in the tabloids or on TV. He grew nervous about his safety and security in London, especially with the press attention being at fever pitch. On the whole, though, he felt lucky to have survived his first phase of celebrity relatively unscathed. 'We've had the first-class hotels, the limos, the girls at the bar waiting, people offering us free drugs. And not one of us has a drink problem; none of us has a drug problem. And because we've stopped at the top, we've all got a chance to do our own things now.'

He was about to launch his solo career, but already he was expressing doubts about his level of fame and establishing more of a low profile; he had not yet released any solo records. 'I think I can honestly say, I'd crave not being able to play a keyboard but not a screaming audience. I really have had enough of the hysteria. I'm looking forward to having a family, and living in the houses I've bought and driving the cars I've bought.' For Gary Barlow, the end of his old group was the end of an era, and the beginning of a quite different, grown-up one: 'The last six months in Take That were a brain-dead scenario for me because we weren't getting anywhere. We weren't breaking new ground.'

Gary already had songs stockpiled for his solo years, partly because some of them would have formed the backbone for a Take That record. 'We were just about to start recording a new album this year,' he explained in the spring of 1996, 'I already had 17 songs written.' He claimed to have written another 20 over the next several weeks, and hoped to choose the best dozen for the first of four albums for RCA Records. His co-producer would be Chris Porter, a collaborator from the *Nobody Else* album, but before that a producer for George Michael since his Wham! days. Gary had bought every record Wham! had ever put out, and was a huge fan of George's, but believed the new material he was putting out had more in common with the work of Elton John. 'George's songs aren't as musical as Elton's,' he controversially told *Music Week* in June 1996. 'You can tell with his songs that a musician has written them, whereas George's are far more like a four-chord groove which he sings over. With Elton, I know someone very musical has written the songs, and that's more the way I tend to do things.'

The journey from teen idol to mature artist could be a rocky path. Wherever you stood on that route, you were looking up to someone more established. The manager of rising boyband Boyzone (fronted by Ronan Keating) noticed this in 1996 while watching a George Michael video. 'S'funny,' said Louis Walsh. 'George [Michael] wants to be Elton. Gary Barlow wants to be George. And Ronan wants to be Gary Barlow.'

According to a list in *Smash Hits* magazine in June 1996, Gary was estimated to be earning £5 million during that year alone, trailing only Seal, Noel Gallagher and the wealthiest of all, George Michael, whose *Older* album (his first in six years) was expected to rake in a cool £10 million.

Gary felt comfortable working with his new co-producer. Chris Porter was a far cry from some who had tried to advise him in Take That days. 'He's one of the few producers to take notice of the demos I've made,' he said. 'I hate working with producers usually because, in the past, they've all had a strong opinion about the record and, usually, it's been the wrong one.' From here on, Gary was insistent that he would have the final say in how his songs took hold in the studio. 'I'm not taking advice off anyone with this record,' he vowed. 'I've taken charge of everything.' He found the new recording process to be liberating, an open road, and he wanted to get a solo record into the marketplace as soon as possible. 'I'm not the sort of songwriter who takes three years to do an album. Its success will not be in the sales, but in the fact I've made it on my own.'

Gary had been careful when talking about Robbie Williams, but, in the months after the official split of the group, the gloves were off, or at least half-off. 'I'm disappointed in Robbie,' he declared. 'He said he was a prisoner, that we've never been friends. It's complete rubbish – we're all close and always have been.' But he accepted that Robbie was moving in different circles, and was belatedly revelling in being a teenager – in his early 20s: 'He'd missed out on his teenage years and wanted to live them now. He had a following of real trendies – not the sort of people we'd ever been friends with, really.' None of this sat well with Take That's image, nor did the way that 'every other week he'd be in the paper, coming out of a club with a girl on his arm'.

Even in a quintet where he was the only real pop fan, Gary felt Robbie took a particularly dim view of the sort of records Take That had made. 'I don't think he ever liked our music,' he told *Arena* magazine, 'and he hated tours because it meant he couldn't stay up until six in the morning. It was all coming to a head round about the time of Glastonbury Festival, when we heard he'd been on the stage with Oasis. That felt shocking at the time.' Nevertheless, he felt sure Robbie's career, after a break, would flourish: 'If he waited two years, it wouldn't be too late because he's just so good that, no matter what he's done, his talent will outshine all of it.'

Gary had mixed feelings about Take That. After all, he could hardly be critical of the financial riches his six years in the group had brought him. He was one of the richest young stars of the music industry. But he had felt uncomfortable about certain elements of the job: the aesthetic and the promotional aspect. He believed that his talent had been somewhat underestimated in Take That, at least on the aesthetic side: 'I was an afterthought. I was the last one the stylist bought clothes for because I never looked that good. The only thing I could shout about was the music.' Now, with his solo work about to be made public, he relished the challenge to balance a stabilising personal life with Dawn against his professional career: 'In my career, I love change because professionally I've got nothing to lose.'

One interview with the journalist Kate Thornton, published in *Smash Hits* in the summer of 1996, anticipates Gary's wilderness years. It found him demystifying his life, stripping it of glamour and intrigue. It was as if he wanted to drain the colour out of pop stardom and reduce it to the bare bones: 'I play piano and I sing a few songs – and that's about as exciting as it gets, and as exciting as I want it to get.'

Professionally, he wished to appeal to all age groups, citing the example of Sting and the solo career he had carved out after the demise of his group The Police in 1983. But set against his ambitious streak was a suggestion that he was turning his back on celebrity. Whether conscious or accidental, he displayed the attitude of someone who no longer had any interest in being famous, other than having enough clout to carry on making music and recording albums. The way he spoke about recording and chart positions sounded as if he was withdrawing from the competitive world of pop. In a statement that must have concerned his record label, he shrugged when asked how he would feel if an album flopped: 'I've got nothing to lose. If my albums go in at 35, then that'll do me, as long as I can still keep writing and recording.' His views on concert performance were even more *laissez-faire*: 'I'm not a performer like Robbie, who can blow a crowd away – the people who come to my shows will have to bring a good book!' Self-deprecating as all this was, it was perhaps not a great advertisement for any concert dates he might have lined up.

And what of his yearning to be an anonymous songwriter, creating works for others to sing? 'My ultimate dream is to not really be anybody, just to write songs in my bedroom for other people to perform. They can go out there and be mithered all day!' Seemingly, his ideal was to be ensconced in domesticity. He spoke contentedly of being at home with Dawn, recording in his studio between 11 in the morning and 7 in the evening, watching videos and eating, and indulging in new interests like photography, reading, fashion, and the same aerobics regime practised by his dad Colin.

Gary had met Dawn at just the right time, in the midst of the shock of Robbie leaving Take That. 'It made me fall in love with her even more. I thought I had been in love before, but I know now that I haven't.' This was in stark contrast to his time in the boyband, where a relationship was impossible: 'It was all just too frantic and fast. By the time you met someone, you'd be off on a plane the next day. There was never time, it was all too studied.'

When asked if they were planning a wedding, Gary said it was probably only a matter of time, and paid tribute to his parents' 30-year marriage. 'At the moment I can't give anybody the time they need in marriage. It won't happen in the next two years because of commitments to my career, but I'm really, really sure now that I want to be a dad. I won't have children until I have really bought into the marriage thing – only because my upbringing was perfect.' He also felt that he could hardly be there for his children if he was a full-time pop star: 'I don't want their dad to be flying around the world never seeing them.'

Said to be dedicated to Dawn, 'Forever Love' was Gary's first solo single release. A ballad written in November 1995, it was released on 8 July 1996 and emulated Take That's form by entering the charts at number one. But hot on its heels was a debut single from Robbie Williams. Signed to a five-album deal with the Chrysalis record label, who had paid RCA a million pounds to buy out his contract, Robbie announced news of his first single, which was a cheeky choice of cover version. Given that Gary was forever being dubbed 'the new George Michael', it was ironic that his rival was covering a George song, namely his 1990 single 'Freedom'. Robbie's choice of song doubled as a riposte to Gary and his image, and as a defiant cry of liberation. Even so, recording someone else's song as a debut single seemed a precarious way to start a solo career. When Chrysalis vowed that 'Robbie will be a huge solo star', it was hard not to dismiss the statement as sheer hubris. Where would the songs come from?

For now, maybe hubris would suffice. Gary's self-belief and confidence had been a key part of Take That's success, but Robbie had developed his own outspoken brand of confidence. From here on, it would become customary for him to snipe at Gary. 'When you walk into an audition,' he told *Attitude* magazine in 1996 of how Take That formed, 'you sit down and see a guy with spiky hair, looking really dated in these horrible tracksuit bottoms and shitty trainers, with a briefcase and music score sheets. And this bloke is a clueless wanker who says, "I write the songs because I'm Gary Barlow".'

Robbie's other tactic in interviews would be to slyly belittle Gary. For instance: 'I'd like to get to number one before him. If there was a big battle I would be glad to win it. But I'm not after him – I'm after Noel Gallagher, George Michael. The big shots, not Gary.' This kind of straight-talking was commonplace in rock journalism, the sort practised by Oasis's Noel and Liam Gallagher. It was a major departure from the good-humoured quips of Take That days, where the chat was cheeky but likeable. There was a darker edge to this banter, which would grow more extreme as time went on.

To begin with, Gary reacted to Robbie's jibes, a tactic which worked for as long as the two of them were on an equal footing. He found some of his former bandmate's pronouncements to be utterly ridiculous. After Robbie compared membership of Take That to being 'a prisoner', Gary retorted, 'Ring someone at Strangeways and ask them if being in a pop band is like being in prison.' He also divulged a few home truths of his own: 'We invested a lot in Rob. When he joined the group he was overweight and he couldn't learn the dance routines, but we stood by him.' Yet for a time both parties in the Gary and Robbie rivalries would routinely switch from sniping to issuing supportive missives of the 'I wish him well' variety. It was becoming increasingly difficult for those following the saga to separate teasing from genuine anger. The press didn't exactly help either by reporting every slight from each side as if it were a front-page story.

Gary eventually explained why Take That had to split up when Robbie wanted out. After he quit, the group would have had to tour for two years to pay him as he had a share in the name. 'For us to continue with the name Take That, of which Robbie was a shareholder, he wanted paying,' Gary told the *Daily Record*, 'but he wanted an extortionate sum. We were a big money-making machine but we'd be working for two years to make that up. We'd tour and he'd get paid – what band in their right mind would carry on?' So Robbie had felt trapped in Take That, but, when he quit, Gary was trapped, too.

The last major chart battle between rival acts had been in August 1995 when Britpop's two biggest figureheads, Blur and Oasis, released singles on the same day. Nearly a year later, Gary and Robbie's debut singles were issued three weeks apart, but, all the same, the record industry believed that only one of them could truly succeed as a solo star. Already there were signs that the media were siding with Robbie, simply because he gave sparky, lively interviews. Give or take the occasional obnoxious comment, he gave reporters what they wanted: plenty of soundbites and a bit of controversy. There was always something going on in Robbie's world.

For Chris Poole, who had worked as Robbie's publicist, the pair could always learn from each other. 'If Robbie adopted Gary's self-discipline and Gary had more of Robbie's personality, they could *both* have long, successful careers,' he said. But the odds on this happening were slender. As of 1996, no teen group of note had spawned more than one substantial solo career. In fact, there weren't many that had even led to one, apart from a few notable exceptions (Michael Jackson, Donny Osmond, George Michael and the New Edition's Bobby Brown).

Three weeks after Gary topped the charts with 'Forever Love', Robbie's 'Freedom' reached number two in August 1996, but neither record even approached the kind of sales Take That had enjoyed. There were some who observed that, while both of them had their strengths, they were best utilised when in the same group. Caitlin Moran, writing in *The Times*, yawned at Gary's single ('The sound of approximately nothing happening for four minutes') and suggested he opt for song-writing, not performing. Robbie had his place too as a consummate performer, Moran felt, but 'can do very little else. If the world was a perfect place, Gary would be writing songs for Robbie to perform. But then, they tried that before.'

In the event, that summer both artists' songs were completely overshadowed by the sensational arrival of the debut single from five lively and cheeky young women. 'Wannabe' by the Spice Girls had knocked 'Forever Love' off the number one spot, and stayed there for nearly two months. Like Take That, the Spice Girls had been carefully manufactured with five distinct personalities. One of its number, Geri Halliwell said, 'We've been likened to the new girlie version of Take That, but we're not as clean-cut. We're more like a girlie movement – 60s feminism spiced up for the Nineties.'

The Spice Girls would reach the British number one spot nine times between 1996 and 2000, and sell millions of records around the world, including the USA. Though other pop acts filled the gap left by Take That's split, they were the only ones to have the same sort of impact. They insisted they were not puppets and wrote their own songs, but theirs was no self-contained Barlowesque song factory; they contributed to the songs, certainly, though successful but anonymous songwriters toiled away in the background. One of them was Eliot Kennedy, who had written 'Everything Changes' with Gary Barlow.

The successes of the Spice Girls, and Take That before them, made manufactured pop look easy, but the market was saturated, often with also-ran pop bands. Who now remembers No Mercy, or Gemini, or Damage? The desperation about boybands seemed to be epitomised in a 1996 TV documentary for the *Inside Story* series about the ill-conceived formation of a manufactured group called Upside Down. One record industry observer commented: 'That documentary about their launch harmed the whole market, making it look as if you could cynically pick four nice-looking blokes, put them in the recording studio, then sit back to wait for the money to pour in. It doesn't work like that. The punters may be young, but they're not so gullible.'

In any case, scrabbling around to find the next Take That was rather missing the point. Part of the reason Take That had flourished in the first place was they had no competition and, frankly, didn't seem like successors. Before them, there hadn't been a durable British teen sensation since Wham! Gavin Reeve, the editor of *Smash Hits* magazine by the latter half of the 1990s, believed that, if there was a formula to cracking the teen market, it was a relatively simple one: 'You need a decent song, a good tune, before people will pay attention. And if you're good-looking and entertaining as well, you've got every chance in the world. The Spice Girls would never have got so far if the records weren't convincing.'

Gary Barlow knew that, without the launch pad of Take That, he would have found it harder to make it on his own. His six years in the group had made him a more generous and magnanimous figure, he felt: 'I wouldn't be here if it wasn't for Take That – definitely not. Had I had the sort of success we had, as a solo artist, I would have been the most unbearable person you've ever met.' He readily admitted to having been a snob at the start, wondering, 'What am I doing with these boys who can't do anything?' But if he had not enjoyed having to learn the dance routines, he soon came round to them. 'We'd bonded so much that I loved the dancing because I wanted to be doing the same things as the lads.' It had been a wild experience, but for someone who had disliked the promotional side of fame, preferring to hide in the background, he understood sharing the limelight with the others: 'It's good to have the compromise because wouldn't it be totally unbearable if you have everything you wanted all the time? You'd be a horrible person.'

That said, he now called the shots. He declared that the era had gone where his songs would be tailored and adapted by producers to fit the market and appeal to a demographic. Gone were the days of having songs tailored to a club audience, or for teenage listeners, or for more mature fans: 'There's none of that now. What you'll be hearing on this album is pure me.'

CHAPTER 14

AMERICAN DREAM, STATESIDE NIGHTMARE

Hindsight is a wonderful thing. The obvious follow-up to 'Forever Love' should have been the sprightly 'Open Road'. It would have been, and was even pencilled in for release in the UK in October 1996, but it was postponed while Gary's solo LP was being completely reworked to give it more of a chance in the US. He wanted to show that he could do more than slow ballads. That summer, he got a chance on TV when he appeared on Channel 4's live music show *The White Room*, covering the Roachford rock-soul hit of the late 1980s 'Cuddly Toy'.

The intention with Gary Barlow's first solo record was to aim as high as possible. He hoped it would spawn at least two or three worldwide hits, with the focus on the USA, the world's biggest record market: 'I'm hoping to sell 10 million albums and I know that, to do it, I need to crack it in

America.' Despite a Top 10 placing in the US with 'Back for Good' in late 1995, few of those who bought it had much of a concept of the group. As a result, Gary didn't have the same launch pad Stateside as he had in the UK, where everyone had a clear idea of how he slotted into Take That's line-up.

Roy Lott was an executive at Arista Records, Take That's American label. He had overseen Take That's campaign to crack the USA, and now faced the challenge of helping to establish Gary there. 'The challenge is that the general public don't know who Gary Barlow is,' he explained, 'and they don't really know the separate elements of the band, so Gary doesn't have a running start, like in the UK. Here, he is effectively a new artist.'

'Forever Love' had performed well in Australia, the Far East and across Europe, but it was decided that it was not a suitable launch single in America. His album was being reworked to make it more palatable to the international market. With this in mind, he was given three further tracks to record by the project's executive producer. Gary may have had a reputation as a perfectionist, but so did Clive Davis. A veteran record company executive since the 1960s, at CBS Records, Davis had nurtured promising artists like Simon & Garfunkel and Bruce Springsteen. Later, as Arista Records boss, he had guided the young Whitney Houston to massive worldwide fame in the mid-1980s, and had stepped in to help the likes of Aretha Franklin, Carly Simon and Dionne Warwick when their careers were stalling.

Davis's idea, for Gary to collaborate with other songwriters, and even record the work of other professional songwriters, was something he wasn't used to, and not necessarily why he had gone solo either. 'In Take That I was the one who spent all the time in the studio working on the songs. It wasn't until the very final stages of the recording that the rest of the boys would come in and do their parts.' On the other hand, as one record company boss said, giving a solo artist like Gary complete freedom had been a risk. Mavericks like Kate Bush and Prince had sung, played, written and produced their own adventurous and brilliant efforts, but, on the downside, executives still shuddered at Terence Trent D'Arby's excesses on his 1989 album, *Neither Fish Nor Flesh*, which had received good reviews but flopped disastrously. If he really wanted to crack America, Gary Barlow needed to collaborate with other writers.

One song he had been handed was the up-tempo 'Love Won't Wait' – very unlike the sort of song Gary would ordinarily write, which was in fact co-written by Madonna. 'As soon as I heard it,' said Gary, 'I thought, "This is a hit!" It was only later that I was told it was written by Madonna – I couldn't believe it.' It took a while to nail the song in the studio, though, as it hadn't been written with Gary in mind: 'She had written it from a female point of view.'

Gary's solo record would not appear until 1997. With no Robbie Williams album likely to be ready until the New Year either, it meant the first Take That member to issue a solo LP was Mark Owen.

Mark had cut ties from manager Nigel Martin-Smith, reasoning that he needed to sever himself from his Take That days, and teamed up with John Leckie, critically fêted producer of the Stone Roses and Radiohead. The result was a contemplative album, *Green Man*, which had far more in common with indie-rock than with Take That. Two of his singles, 'Child' and 'Clementine', both made the British top three, but Mark denied feeling disappointed that they hadn't topped the charts. 'Take That songs used to go straight in at number one all the time, and, although that was a nice position to be in, if this had done the same thing, people would've wanted the next one to do it as well, and I don't want that pressure. The most important thing to me is that my songs stand on their own.'

Mark was trying to shake off the teen-idol tag a little but it was a hard thing to control who would consume one's music: 'When I started playing live there were all these little girls down the front, screaming and throwing teddy bears. They just didn't understand where I was coming from.' But by the time the album came out, the audience was deserting him. *Green Man* peaked at 33, and then fell away sharply. Mark had to admit selling records mattered a lot after all. 'I made a point of saying I didn't care if people liked my solo stuff. I can pretend all day that I don't care but I do, very much.' By 1998, it seemed unlikely that RCA would fund a second album.

In November 1996, Gary broke away from manager Nigel Martin-Smith in what was said to be an amicable split. 'I created Take That around Gary and I have been heavily involved with his solo album,' Nigel explained to the *Daily Mirror*. 'But he wants to spend more time in America and I don't like it there. I'm more interested in discovering new acts than dealing with the problems of a star like Gary.'

The star's new manager was Simon Fuller, whose clients included the Spice Girls and Annie Lennox. 'It was the most horrible thing I've ever had to do,' Gary said of his ditching of

Nigel. 'It was all done through my lawyers. But there comes a time when you just have to be ruthless: breaking America is what I want now.' It meant that the only Take That member still on Nigel's books was Howard.

With Fuller behind him, Gary teamed up with Richard Stannard and Matt Rowe, who had written the Spice Girls' 'Wannabe', for another upbeat song, 'Lay Down for Love'. Gary admitted that he had problems coming up with suitable up-tempo material for his album, and had also needed help with lyrics.

In February 1997, Gary was backstage at the BRIT Awards, where he was presenting an award, when his mobile phone rang. It was Clive Davis in New York, who requested his presence the very next day at his traditional pre-Grammy Awards party. This was a bash for record industry figures and America's pop elite, and it was considered a great honour to be invited to sing at such an occasion. When Gary arrived in the US, he visited Davis at the Arista building in Manhattan. Once inside Davis's office, he was played a dance remix (by the producer Junior Vasquez) of 'Love Won't Wait', the song Madonna had co-written. It was a very different treatment of a song Gary was already uncertain about. 'On goes the stereo. And at once all these 50- to 60-year-old men in suits go into dance routines, like they're Marc Almond singing "Tainted Love". And I'm not only thinking, "What on earth are they doing?" but "What is this rubbish we are listening to?"' It transpired that the track that was inspiring middle-aged record company staff to bop around the offices was what he was expected to sing over that evening at Davis's pre-Grammys party. And he hardly knew the song in the first place.

At the Plaza Hotel that evening, Gary's performance at the star-studded party would be a complete fiasco. He later recounted the painful detail to *The Times* in what felt like real time: 'I don't remember the words. I come in at all the wrong places. I can see people drifting off to the toilets in droves. Talk about dying on your arse!' In just a few minutes, his American fortunes had crumbled to dust. He walked back to his hotel alone, sat in the bar, and woke up with a thumping hangover the morning after.

A poppier mix of 'Love Won't Wait' was finally released in the UK in April 1997. Gary's first single in ten months, it made him the first artist to achieve ten chart-topping singles in the 1990s – eight with Take That and two on his own. It outsold a new George Michael single ('Star People '97'), but it would be the last Barlow number one in any capacity for nearly a decade.

The *Open Road* album followed 'Love Won't Wait' a month later, in late May. It knocked Michael Jackson off the top of the album charts in Britain, but the critical response towards it was, at best, lukewarm. Those who accepted it was a polished, streamlined and highly smooth piece of product couldn't help finding it, as *The Times* did, 'depressingly workaday'. Awkwardly, the tracks that got the thumbs up often tended to be the songs Gary hadn't written himself, whether it was 'Love Won't Wait' or a cover of Johnny Bristol's 1974 proto-disco hit 'Hang On In There, Baby'. Guest vocals on the latter came from former Prince backing singer Rosie Gaines, who had recently charted high in her own right with the dance-floor hit 'Closer Than Close'.

Two of the Spice Girls' writers had helped out on the upbeat

'Lay Down for Love', but, all in all, it didn't sound like a record to set the world on fire. The dreaded words 'middle of the road' were never far away and, in the world of teen pop, 'middle of the road' equals mature equals a bit boring. Not even fare such as 'Everything I Ever Wanted', a leftover number from the *Nobody Else* sessions of Take That days, seemed to excite.

Gary wasn't convinced by some of the songs he had been recording. 'So Help Me Girl', lined up as his first solo single in the US, was a cover of a song by country artist Joe Diffie: 'It's bloody awful, but I think we've transformed it.' Of 'Hang On In There, Baby', included on producer Trevor Horn's recommendation, he commented, 'I wasn't chuffed, but it's now one of my favourites.' 'I Fall So Deep' was 'not one of my favourites, but everyone else likes it'. Definitely not the *Q* magazine reviewer, though, who lumped it in with 'So Help Me Girl' as 'such dogs that the Andrex puppy features on backing vocals'.

None of this sounded like a record where Gary had been able or permitted to be in control. It smacked of compromise, in an effort to get the album noticed in the American entertainment market. By far the best song on the LP was its title track, one the artist had written by himself in 1986: 'The lyrics are perfect for now. They describe my worries about the future, about being alone as a solo artist.' A self-aware song, it was catchy and accessible. Had it been released earlier than it was, it might have saved the album. As it was, it limped out in October 1997 as the fourth single in Britain. It would be Gary Barlow's last completely solo effort to reach the Top 10 for 16 years.

For all the writing talent hired for *Open Road* – including Diane Warren and David Foster, who had worked with everyone from Celine Dion to Toni Braxton – the end product seemed inconsequential. The record received some support from BBC Radio 2, which was slowly modernising itself from an easy listening station into a more mature version of Radio 1. Gary joined other groups like Wet Wet Wet, Prefab Sprout, Celine Dion and The Beautiful South on the station's playlists – a quieter station policy than the brash Britpop of Radio 1, but still a far cry from its MOR years.

In the summer of 1997, just as *Open Road* came out, Gary ditched Simon Fuller as his manager after less than a year, and instead hired Kristina Kyriacou, previously part of Take That's PR team. Fuller's hot new clients the Spice Girls had become world famous beyond anyone's expectations, and Gary knew that he was far from being his priority act. In particular, the Spice Girls had become far bigger in the USA than Take That ever were – '"Back for Good" may have reached the Top 10, but "Wannabe" had reached number one, and they were able to follow it up with several other major hits. I think they watched Take That for six years and took what we did one step further.' Asked why Take That hadn't had the same opportunity to break in America, he was blunt: 'It was partly because we didn't have the time to promote ourselves, but mostly it was down to our American record company being so crap.'

Gary also believed that the extent of the Spice Girls' global reach in a matter of months was partly down to lucrative sponsorship deals by international brands – far bigger than those who had courted Take That: 'Huge worldwide companies like Mercedes and Pepsi are paying a fortune to sponsor the girls. Take That had Kellogg's Corn Pops – I think that says it all.' Ironically, within six months, the Spice Girls would also fire Fuller, who went on to create a new manufactured group called S Club 7, which mixed talented singers with those who excelled at dancing.

Officially, Gary described his first solo album as the record Take That would have made, had they not imploded. 'I didn't want to change direction and start producing a style of music I know nothing about,' he told one reporter. 'I want the fans to enjoy it in the same way they'd enjoy a Take That record.' A total of eight producers were involved in its making, with Clive Davis as executive producer. It felt a long way away from the original plan, for Gary to simply make an album with Chris Porter in a studio and then release it.

CHAPTER 15

ROAD
BLOCK

By 1997, Gary owned 60 acres of land in Cheshire, known as Delamere Manor in Cuddington. The property was described by a local estate agent as 'one of the few private houses in England where you will not see another house at all. You have complete and utter privacy and look out a long, long way over your land to the horizon.' The privacy must have appealed to Gary – he, like the rest of Take That, had grown weary of the frenzied level of press and public attention.

Built by landowner George Wilbraham in the 1930s, just before the Second World War, Delamere Manor was at the time worth a million pounds. Gary shared the six-bedroom house with girlfriend Dawn, while the rest of his family also lived on the estate in separate properties. Brother Ian owned a golden eagle and an owl. His mum Marge kept a donkey in the garden, while his dad Colin was not only his gardener but also ran a farm on the estate. 'Nobody leaves our place without some eggs from Dad's farm,' Gary promised, who described the whole Barlow presence on the site as 'like the Beverly Hillbillies, us having moved into this place where none of us really belong'.

Already it seemed as if Gary was pulling up the drawbridge on being a celebrity. 'I'm quite happy with the quiet life. If nobody ever recognised me again, I wouldn't be bothered.' What's more, he had cut back on some of the excesses of old: 'You can only drive one car at a time, so why have two? I can't bear unnecessary spending.' Getting together with Dawn had grounded him, although, for now, there was no immediate talk of wedding bells due to career commitments. He had been spending two weeks every month in the US. 'If we can survive the mad period,' he said of his relationship, 'then I think we'll be together forever. If we keep it together, I'd want to have children and that's when we'd get married. Now is just the wrong time.'

After a spell in therapy and some legal wrangling, by 1997, Robbie Williams' first solo album was recorded and ready to go. It had been a messy two years, but he had discovered an effective writing collaborator. Guy Chambers was a former keyboard player with groups like World Party and The Lemon Trees, with a good ear for radio-friendly melodies. He was a perfect writing partner for lyricist Robbie, who would offer a confessional but self-aware running commentary on his own fame, together with cheeky and vulnerable musings about his time in Take That. 'I'm laying myself open like a nerve,' he said of his album, originally to be called 'The Show Off Must Go On', but finally retitled *Life Thru a Lens*. He also announced that he had bought a copy of Gary's *Open Road*, but denounced it as 'crap' and said he had taken it back to the shop.

Gary had lined up his first solo tour for the autumn of 1997, where he would showcase material from *Open Road*, plus plenty of highlights from the Take That back catalogue. Gary was just relieved that he didn't 'have to do those bloody dance routines again'. He admitted that the dancing aspect of Take That was one he had found a challenge: 'I believe there are two types of people – those who move naturally and those who don't. I am definitely in the second category. The other boys came out of Take That with badly damaged feet, because I spent five years treading on them.'

Perhaps bruised by his recent experiences in America, he admitted that he missed being in a group. Achieving success alone may carry with it a feeling that you are entirely responsible for that success, but there is no one to share the euphoria. 'When you get to number one as a solo artist,' he reflected, 'you just kind of go, "Hoorah!" But when you're in a band, you all go mad and hug each other and go out and celebrate. It's a team effort – you feel like you've achieved it together.' There was a fraternal feeling in Take That, an environment where all five were protective of each other, which was especially invaluable in the glare of stardom. 'We were all in the same boat and having the same experiences. We'd stick up for each other. I think I would have freaked out if I had gone through that on my own.'

So, how had the other three-fifths of Take That coped after the split? For Mark Owen, spiritualism had been a salvation. Even when the group was still together, he had been encouraged to meditate by Lulu. Subsequently, he consulted gurus in places as far apart as New York and Australia. 'If I hadn't found my spirituality I would still be insecure. I certainly never would have made an album.' But he still yearned for a satisfaction in life: 'I want to feel like a king. I knew in Take That we were top of the pile and I want to get back up there again.'

While Mark had managed to get an album out ahead of both Gary and Robbie, Howard Donald's musical plans remained in development. With Nigel Martin-Smith still managing him, he had written a song called 'Crazy Chance', for another of Nigel's clients, the singer Kavana, and the theme to a Channel 4 TV series called *Planet Pop*. He confessed to feeling bereft after Take That's break-up: '[It] was very traumatic for me. It was like a divorce and I was stuck in the middle of it.' And he still felt he had something to prove. 'People saw Gary as the songwriter, with me in the background. I want to prove I am more than the shy one with the body; I can prove I can write good songs.' He claimed to have a whole soul album in progress – one track, 'Speak Without Words', was sung in English and Spanish – but it would remain unreleased.

Jason Orange had taken some acting classes. He signed up with a theatrical agent and soon had a few TV parts: a soap opera for Sky about a football club called *Dream Team*, then as a DJ in Lynda La Plante's thriller *Killer Net* for Channel 4. Stage work included a stint at London's Royal Court in a play called *Let's All Go to the Fair*, and a role as a poet in a fringe production called *Gob*. He distanced himself from Take That's squeaky-clean image: 'You know how those things snowball.

One of the biggest misconceptions was that we weren't allowed girlfriends. We just had an agreement – an unwritten rule – that we would concentrate very hard on our careers and try not to get too romantically involved. But we were young. How could we not have relationships and sex?' But he had had fun, not based on the music or the fame, but on friendship: 'No one could come between us. The solidarity gave me so much pleasure. Compared to that, the adulation we got meant nothing. For me, the most memorable thing was the laughs we had away from the hysteria – a really good, boyish laugh. That's what I miss, more than anything.'

In September 1997, within two weeks of the death of Diana, Princess of Wales, Gary vowed to reunite Take That for one gig only, as part of a tribute concert in her memory. It would be held as part of World AIDS Day in December. He retained fond memories of the Princess from when the group had played the Concert of Hope in 1994. 'Usually the same old stars turn up at tribute concerts – it would be great to have something for younger people,' said Gary. 'Acts like Peter Andre, Boyzone, Spice Girls, the Backstreet Boys. Diana loved young people. She would have wanted them to be involved.'

But there wasn't much time, and some of Take That were unwilling to participate. Within a week, it was apparent the reunion could not take place. Gary had insisted that it would need to be all five of the group, not just four. 'Robbie would have to be there,' he said. But perhaps surprisingly, it wasn't Robbie Williams who refused the invitation. 'We're all busy doing our solo projects,' Mark told the *Daily Mirror*. 'But the main reason we don't want to re-form Take That is the time.

We would have a week to get ready and it would be wrong for us to perform at anything less than our best.'

The four-hour Concert of Hope was staged on Sunday, 7 December 1997 at Battersea Power Station in south London. As well as Robbie and Gary, the bill comprised new all-female quartet All Saints (whose second single 'Never Ever' would soon reach number one), Peter Andre, Boyzone and boybands 911 and Damage. Gary performed two original solo songs ('Love Won't Wait', 'Open Road') and two covers – 'Hang On In There, Baby' and a duet of the Isley Brothers' 'Harvest for the World' with Boyzone's Ronan Keating. The hotly predicted onstage truce failed to materialise, but Robbie did play a Take That song as part of his short set: 'Back for Good'.

The year ended with Gary and Robbie both recording Christmas covers exclusively for BBC Radio 1. While Robbie remade Run DMC and Aerosmith's 'Walk This Way' as 'Walk This Sleigh', Gary opted for a more sincere revival: John Lennon and Yoko Ono's 'Happy Xmas (War Is Over)'. The two former members of Take That seemed on an equal footing – just about – but Gary's momentum was starting to falter. The 'Open Road' single, surely a number one hit in theory, had only just scraped into the Top 10. Its parent album had sold reasonably well (250,000 in Britain), but not remarkably so – it ended 1997 with fewer sales than mid-table albums by Seahorses, Reef and Skunk Anansie, and was far behind the likes of the year's big sellers: Blur, The Verve, The Prodigy, the Spice Girls and, biggest of all, Oasis. The year's best-selling single had been Elton John's tribute to the late Diana, Princess of Wales. 'Candle in the Wind' sold over four million copies in the UK alone and remains to this day the nation's best-selling single of all time. Gary continued to look to Elton as his ultimate role model: 'He's still going strong. However much I've already achieved, I've really only just started.'

Yet there were ominous signs that Gary's career was on the skids. In the plot of the Spice Girls' *Spice World* film, released on Boxing Day 1997, a judge (Stephen Fry) consigns the group to the dustbin of pop history, uttering the dreaded words 'Gary Barlow' as a byword for how fleeting fame can be. Gary was becoming a synonym for 'uncool'. Meanwhile, his rival's star was rising. By the beginning of 1998, Robbie's single 'Angels', an emotive ballad, was heading for the top five, on its way to selling a million copies.

From here on, and for several years, the media as a whole began to favour Robbie over Gary. Robbie would win numerous awards, and enjoy a string of solo hits: 'Let Me Entertain You', 'Millennium', 'She's the One' among many others. A second album, *I've Been Expecting You*, released in the autumn of 1998, was another sensational seller. The well of stories about Robbie, an essential part of keeping any star in the public eye, refused to dry up, and he wanted to appeal to everyone. 'I'd like to be a cross between Tom Jones, John Lennon, Chuck D and Gene Kelly,' he declared, in a bid to cover all bases of popular culture, from musicals to pop for all ages to hip-hop.

'What Robbie has done well,' said *Smash Hits*' Gavin Reeve, 'is anticipate what the fans would be into at their older age. He is aware that a 13-year-old Take That fan could now be a 17-year-old Robbie fan. The fans grow up and have more mature tastes and Robbie has anticipated those tastes.'

In comparison, Gary was struggling. While Robbie would

sweep the board at the BRIT Awards, Gary had to be grateful for a mere nomination for Best British Male. He was surprised at his inclusion in the category, 'because when we were in Take That we were always overlooked. Awards dished out by the industry aren't a big deal – they don't buy my records or come to my concerts.' Take That had only ever won BRIT Awards in the public vote categories. Instead, Gary had to be content with winning the male category of Rear of the Year 1997.

The year 1998 began with a fresh attempt at breaking America, this time with a brand-new single called 'Superhero', a song that had not featured on *Open Road*. 'I hope that soon I'll see some results,' he told the *News of the World* that February. 'But if I don't, I'll leave America and concentrate on the rest of the world. It's not worth breaking your neck over.' He continued to be a prolific songwriter: 'I write a song a day but for every one I keep, I chuck ten away' – and busied himself with preparing himself for a solo tour.

The first Gary Barlow concert tour in March 1998 was a very different proposition to his dancing days in Take That. 'I won't be doing backflips,' he deadpanned, 'or spinning on my head in between six costume changes and firework displays.' His backing musicians had played on Take That tours, but the big hits – 'Pray', 'Never Forget', 'Back for Good' – were glued together in a medley at the piano. 'I want to concentrate on my new material,' explained Gary. On the other hand, he wasn't prepared to perform untried new stuff live. 'I want to keep the audience in the palm of my hand. As someone in an audience, when the band say, "We are going to play four new songs," I think, "Come on, let's go get a drink." I hate it.' He relied on a few covers, like 'Labour of Love' (a hit by Hue and Cry in 1987) and Otis Redding's 'Hard to Handle', both echoing a time when Gary was still working the clubs in the north-west in the late 1980s. From time to time, the dreaded phrase 'chicken-in-a-basket' was whispered. It may have been professional and slick, but it wasn't terribly rock'n'roll or thrilling.

'It's such a risk to take,' Gary told a journalist from the *Independent*. 'I was just so scared of putting all these dates on and nobody coming to see me.'

The screaming crowds of old at Take That concerts were a thing of the past now. Devoted fans tended to turn up to the solo gigs with their husbands in tow. 'His destiny, surely, is to be a Shane Richie or a Des O'Connor,' wrote one broadsheet rock critic, who attended a London show on the tour, 'still making albums but fronting his own ITV series too: some songs, maybe a duet with one of his celebrity guests, some saucy flirting with the biddies in the audience.'

More sympathetic reviewers, though, could not fault how Gary engaged with an audience. 'Never smug or remote,' argued *The Times*, 'generous to his band and hard-working almost to a fault, he put on a performance which commanded respect.'

This was showbiz, not rock'n'roll, but it had its place all the same and suggested Gary had the potential to be an all-round entertainer. He became a regular on TV talk shows and, with carefully honed anecdotes about embarrassing moments like vomiting in Lulu's guest bathroom, he demonstrated a penchant for deadpan humour. He would help comedy duo Hale and Pace become songwriters and wrote a Eurovision song with them for a documentary series called *Jobs for the Boys*, in which the pair tried out various occupations (The resulting song, 'More Than Enough for One Life', was longlisted but failed to be chosen as the United Kingdom's Song for Europe). Other television appearances in this period included a guest spot on a BBC2 series for the operatic soprano Lesley Garrett, where the two performed his own arrangement of Frédéric Chopin's 'So Deep is the Night'. Chopin, of course, had been the inspiration for Barry Manilow's 'Could It Be Magic', covered with great success by Take That in 1992.

In a way, being an all-round entertainer was Robbie Williams' aim as well. It's just that his itinerary was very different to Gary's. He would make a swing album, *Swing When You're Winning*, and crack jokes on stage, but he was just as likely to be interviewed by the *NME* as by Michael Parkinson. And he had mixed all the bits of the pop stars he had idolised over the years, from the Pet Shop Boys' Neil Tennant to Mick Jagger, Tom Jones, Elvis and Freddie Mercury. 'I'm not a real welder, I've just got the goggles,' he told one reporter, as if to suggest he was simply playing at being a star. A merchant of wisecracks with a decent voice, where he differed from Gary was that the irreverence often extended to the records. Whereas it seemed as if Gary was cautious and unwilling to frighten the horses, Robbie couldn't help himself, often saying the most shocking and outrageous thing.

Gary would try this tactic in 1999, in a brief bid to court minor controversy in this way, but the reaction was a mixture of indifference and contempt. In May of that year, he revealed that he had briefly experimented with cocaine, dope and Ecstasy. 'I've done drugs, but I've never had a problem. I'm glad I tried them, but I got it out of my system.' He insisted that he had stopped taking them so as not to ruin his work ethic and creative spark: 'The problem was, if I took E, I'd feel like shit for a week and just couldn't work. That's why I knocked it on the head.' At the same time, he confessed to speeding down the motorway at nearly 170mph without being stopped. And he claimed to have bedded girls all around the world in his Take That days. 'Wherever we went, there were girls. I took every opportunity to have one-night stands,' he said in 1999. All of which appeared to contradict the image Take That had worked so carefully to preserve. True or not, these were awkward, slightly desperate confessions, which didn't fit comfortably with the professional, polite persona Gary had become known for.

He now began to admit that he was losing ground as a star soloist, especially when up against Robbie's growing stardom: 'I am very competitive but it would now be a dream for me to sell as many records as him. In that way, I can't really compete with him anymore. If I compete with him, I'm competing with people like Oasis and bands who sell millions of records.' In some ways, he found his rival's recovery and resurgence quite baffling, especially when it came to songwriting, in which the Take That-era Robbie had rarely shown any interest. 'I never saw any writing talent. The Robbie I always knew was someone who wasn't really interested. In creative meetings, he'd be sitting in the corner and, when we recorded his vocals, we had to do it at my house because he felt nervous in front of producers.'

Even so, Gary was supportive of him, while aware that part of Robbie's appeal was a rebellious streak: 'I feel that one thing he learned from Oasis is how to have a good feud – and that's helped him sell records.'

Robbie had been an underdog, and the British love underdogs, perhaps because, if and when they recover, it seems all the sweeter. But, while Robbie got bigger and bigger, Gary increasingly struggled. Though he had still sold far more records than Mark Owen, and a lot more than the none shifted by Jason and Howard (neither of whom had recorded anything), Gary's relative failure seemed far more serious simply because it had been *assumed* he was bound to succeed. In just doing reasonably well, he had failed.

Now, Gary was the underdog, but at least it meant his own career might just recover again, as Robbie's had done. Like all the Take That fans who may have been expecting the group to reassemble, he would simply have to be patient.

CHAPTER 16

THE
OBLIVION
BOY

Gary Barlow was desperate to get back to basics with his records. He had plenty of material ready for a second album. 'I want to get back to my sound, not make albums for markets, or remix for markets, and not involve computers and fiddling with a drum sound for three days.' But the Barlow hit machine was running out of steam by 1999. He was used to being number one, but now he wasn't even in the Top 10 anymore. Added to that, he tried the patience of his fans by postponing a whole British tour not just once, but twice. First scheduled for autumn 1998, it was shifted to the following spring, and finally to the end of 1999, partly so that the artist could complete a second album.

Gary still had wealth – with an estimated £20 million in the bank, he was second only to the Spice Girls in an April 1999 list of British entertainment's richest aged 30 or under – but his credibility and profile was plummeting. He may have been primed to be the next George Michael, but the existing one wasn't so hot on the idea. 'I resent it when people make out my contribution to the early 80s was influencing future boybands. Just because he was fat and we both have inflatable cheeks,' George told Q magazine, 'does not mean we're working in the same area.'

In July 1999, Gary was back with a new single, 'Stronger', which caused some comment due to the title's uncanny similarity to a recent Robbie offering, 'Strong'. Pure coincidence, insisted Gary: 'When I heard about Robbie's song, I thought, Oh God. I was trying to distance myself so much from him, I just couldn't believe it.' Besides, he continued, it was only the song titles that had anything in common; the themes were completely different. 'His song is all about not being strong and my song is just about being strong, being re-born and feeling fresh. It's the total opposite, which is good.'

'Stronger' was co-written with a hitmaker of a different generation. In the 1970s, Graham Gouldman was one of the founder members of 10cc, a clever, witty and melodic pop quartet from Manchester, who knowingly plundered pop and rock history for inspiration, and came up with something new. Their many hits included 'Rubber Bullets', 'Dreadlock Holiday', 'Wall Street Shuffle' and, most famously, their 1975 number one 'I'm Not In Love'. Before 10cc, Gouldman had been a hit songwriter for 1960s groups such as Herman's Hermits and The Hollies.

Despite the pedigree of 'Stronger' – another of George Michael's producers, Jon Douglas, was involved in its making – its chart fortunes were disappointing. It entered the charts at a lowly 16, Gary's worst placing since Take That's 'I Found Heaven', seven years earlier. And it stood no chance of reaching number one – it was a long way behind 'Livin' La Vida Loca' from another ex-boyband member, Menudo's Ricky Martin. Others outselling Barlow that week included the Manic Street Preachers and soul siren Beverley Knight.

'Stronger' had been the likeliest single material on what would be Gary's second album, which was given the unwieldy title of *Twelve Months, Eleven Days*. It had been a long time in coming. 'I've been away recording for the best part of two years,' he told the *Sunday Mail*, 'so I'm not going to come straight back in at number one. I know it's going to take time, but I've got the confidence to make it happen. This isn't the end for me, it's just the beginning.'

The beginning of what, though? Obscurity? When 'Superhero' (which had sunk without trace in the US) was re-titled 'For All That You Want' for British release, it tanked in the lower reaches of the Top 30, peaking at 24. 'Could we have a moment's silence for the solo career of Gary Barlow?' groaned *The Times* rhetorically in October, on receiving its copy of *Twelve Months, Eleven Days*. 'He plummets to new depths of pop cliché,' it went on. 'If Barlow isn't being "torn apart", he is listening for the phone that "never rings", or finding answers "deep in his heart". None of which would matter if there were any decent tunes.' *Q* magazine called it 'a collection of George Michael outtakes'. *The Sunday Times* was sympathetic to Gary's plight – 'nobody deserves to crash so spectacularly' – but was nonetheless appalled: 'Programmed, gated, reverbed into a sweet blancmange of early-1980s lift music, without a doubt the worst album of the year.'

When Woolworths, at the time the most common record store chain, decided not to stock the album, its fate was effectively sealed. Released on 11 October 1999, *Twelve Months, Eleven Days* sold fewer than 3,000 copies in its first week on sale, and entered the charts at a wretchedly low number 35, lagging far behind new releases from other chart veterans such as James and Pet Shop Boys. In all, it sold around 30,000 copies, only a tenth of the number that even *Open Road* had shifted two years earlier. A third single, 'Lie to Me', was scheduled for release in December, but was cancelled. It was reported that Gary was no longer a priority for his record label, RCA.

As the 20th century drew to a close, there seemed to be no let-up in the humiliation being piled on to Gary Barlow. At that year's *Smash Hits* Poll Winners' Party, traditionally the ceremony where Take That had cleaned up, he appeared in only one category: Worst Male Singer. The *Sun*'s showbiz column *Bizarre* voted him 'Plonker of the Year', while the London Rock Circus museum of wax models announced that its Gary Barlow model was to be melted down to be remodelled as the new American teen sensation Britney Spears (It was later reported that models weren't melted down – they were simply taken out of public view – but that wasn't much better).

There were a few crumbs of comfort. Gary was asked to switch on the Blackpool Illuminations with *EastEnders* actress-turned-pop star Martine McCutcheon. He finally got to tour again, although the venues were only two-thirds full. Liberal helpings of the flop new album opened the shows, but there were inevitable sections dedicated to Take That hits of old (for many critics the only time the show really came alive), and a rendition of 'Happy Xmas (War is Over)' in the encore.

Gary had come to the realisation that the hardest part of being famous and successful in music is not at the start of one's career, but maintaining that success once it happens. 'When you start out and release a single that doesn't chart,' he said, 'you think you've failed, but at least no one knows. When you're already known like me and take a wrong turning, everyone's there laughing.'

About the only substantial work on the horizon lay in acting, of all things. It was for the long-established ITV Sunday-night drama series *Heartbeat*, a police period drama series set in the North of England in the 1960s, and which used a range of pop hits of the time as a soundtrack. Fourteen million people watched it every Sunday, and it had been a favourite of his grandmother's, who was sadly no longer alive to see him appear in it. So he agreed to an appearance in the series finale, which just so happened to be the 150th episode.

In fact, though, Gary's cameo in *Heartbeat* (as a hitch-hiker who becomes a suspect when a stash of precious stones goes missing) was almost an accident. He had been in talks with ITV about making some music shows, whereupon it had been suggested he should appear in the series. 'What tempted me,' he said, 'was that I could sing in it. I love the music in *Heartbeat*, and that's another reason why I changed my mind.' The song he sang – a 60s-style reworking of 'All That I've Given Away', from his unloved album *Twelve Months, Eleven Days* – would have been new to the vast majority of the programme's many viewers. 'To give the track a sound in keeping with the series, I remixed it in my studio at home. I was brought up listening to songs from that period – Motown and The Beatles – so it was easy. It was great to perform.'

Gary's scenes were filmed in early February 2000 on the North Yorkshire moors.

'To succeed in showbiz today you have to diversify,' commented cast member Bill Maynard, who played Claude Greengrass in the series. 'Gary, very wisely, is out to forge a new career as an actor. You've got to be multi-dimensional otherwise you soon become a forgotten face and name.'

The singer felt relieved to be once again working as part of a team, but had been apprehensive about branching out into acting: 'Put me on stage at Wembley Arena and I'm fine, but acting is something I've never done before. That has never been where my talents lie. When I was in the nativity play at school, the teacher cast me as a sheep!'

In the end, Gary knew his *Heartbeat* appearance had been a mistake. His life was music, which was never a problem so long as he was still able to write, record and perform. 'I'd be really struggling if I wasn't a musician,' he had told Q magazine in 1997. 'I can't do anything else – I can't even hang a picture on the wall.' That was probably an exaggeration, but, in terms of a career, it was hard to see where his future lay.

In March 2000, it was announced that Gary Barlow was being dropped by RCA Records. Eight and a half years after Take That had signed to the label, it was letting him go. Undoubtedly, the sales of his recent output had been calamitously low, but this had been aggravated further by the quite spectacular success of his rival, Robbie Williams. Gary wasn't the only one whose solo career was in the doldrums, though. Mark Owen had also just been dropped by RCA, and the label's priorities were two younger boybands: Westlife (protégés of Louis Walsh's) and 5ive. By the end of 2000, Gary's website was shut down. He had been a paid musician for 16 years, and he was still under 30 years old. And, though he had millions in the bank, he was essentially pop's forgotten man.

At least things were looking up in his personal life. On Valentine's Day 1999, he had proposed to Dawn in New York, and they were now engaged: 'The biggest thing I love about Dawn is that she's her own person. She's still working as a dancer. I am very aware that some people would want to be with me because of my fame or my money but she's not like that.' When it came down to it, Gary seemed satisfied to be taking a backseat from pop stardom: 'I have got my life back. I don't need to think about money and I've had time to get to know Dawn properly. It's been a beautiful time for me.'

In January 2000, Gary and Dawn tied the knot in secret. Family and close friends joined them on the Caribbean island of Nevis. The couple had intended to marry in Cheshire later that summer, but felt it was best to hold the occasion far away from Britain after what had been, career-wise, a terrible year for Gary. And then came the happy news that he and Dawn were to become parents, an announcement he posted on his own fan website: 'Well, everyone, for once, may I be the first to tell you some exciting and exclusive news... I AM GOING TO BE A DAD!!!!! As if getting married wasn't enough excitement for one year! I knew the year 2000 would bring great things and here's the proof.' On 17 August, their baby son Daniel was born.

For Gary, it was the start of a new chapter in his life. In many ways, he ended the 1990s as a near-forgotten figure in pop music: much-mocked, if mentioned at all. And yet, he had achieved far more than most performers and songwriters in the previous six or seven years. He professed not to care that he was no longer top of the pops: 'I am very content with my life, which is something people in music often fight against. They have a great public image but their private life suffers. This time my personal life is outweighing my musical one. It feels good. I haven't had that before.'

In his Take That days, he had held back from committing to a serious relationship, mindful of the long working hours and travel around the world. Now that he had little left to prove and plenty of money in the bank, he could relax and spend more time with Dawn, who had little interest in fame beyond her job as a dancer. 'She's very shy of all that [fame] and still does the job she did when I met her. She still goes away, and shares rooms and travels in Economy.'

In 10 years, Gary Barlow had gone from obscurity to stardom and crashed back into oblivion – but his story was by no means over. With millions in the bank, he was not necessarily under an obligation to work again, but his passion for music would win out. 'I'm not the type to retire to a Caribbean island or play golf all week,' he declared. 'I enjoy my work. I love my music, and it's not just for the money.'

In the next few years, without an outlet for performing, he would need those around him all the more.

Above: A young Gary steps into the limelight as one-fifth of hot new nineties boyband Take That.

Below: Gary and fellow band mates (from left, Robbie Williams, Jason Orange, Mark Owen, Howard Donald) send millions of girls' hearts racing.

Gary has always been keen to lend a hand to various charities.

Above: Meeting Princess Diana at a 'Concert of Hope' AIDS benefit at Wembley Arena, London in 1994.

Below: Gary joins the Duke and Duchess of Cambridge, the Prince of Wales and the Duchess of Cornwall at a concert in aid of the Prince's Trust in 2011.

Above left: Gary and ex-dancer Dawn Andrews became a couple in 1995 when on Take That's *Nobody Else* tour. They married in 2000.

Above right: Gary and Dawn attend a reception held at 10 Downing Street in aid of Children in Need.

Below: Gary debuting as the new head judge on *The X Factor*'s 2011 series alongside fellow judges (from left) Louis Walsh, Tulisa Contostavlos and Kelly Rowland.

Above: Gary takes centre stage at the Royal Albert Hall on his solo tour of 2013.

Below left: Gary receives an OBE for his services to music in 2012.

Below right: On stage at Odyssey Arena in Belfast on the opening night of his UK tour in March 2014.

All pictures © Getty Images

CHAPTER 17

HEY, MR SONGWRITER

After being dropped by RCA Records, Gary Barlow consulted concert promoters about a possible small-scale tour, but it came to nothing. 'I explored every possible avenue,' he explained in 2008, 'but within a couple of months it became clear that there was no way forward for me. No one wants any association with you at all. It's instant, brutal. You're unemployable.'

In the early years of the 21st century, if Gary's name was mentioned in public at all, it was rarely as a compliment. It was a synonym for the naff, the failed, the useless or the outdated. 'BT to stop making phone boxes,' announced one newspaper in February 2001, while wondering, 'Where will Gary Barlow's fan club meet now?' When it was reported that Dawn was expecting their second child, the *Sun* described it as 'a novel way of increasing his fan base'.

Television comedy shows were no different. Already there had been a sitcom called *Boyz Unlimited* about a boyband, starring a young James Corden as a singer called Gary. In 2001, two of its series creators, comedy performers Matt Lucas and David Walliams, mercilessly sent up Gary's friendship with Elton John on the droll series *Rock Profiles*. Lucas played Barlow, bossing around hapless housekeeper Howard Donald (Walliams) in front of Jamie Theakston (in a regular role in the series as interviewer). A follow-up episode satirised Gary attempting to assemble a group of top singers for a charity comeback single. 'I think our send-ups are affectionate,' insisted Lucas. 'They are just characters, not the real people. When we show Gary bossing Howard about at the Take That reunion it's just a characterisation, really.' Perhaps inevitably, Robbie Williams was a big fan of the show.

In the early Noughties, the real Gary was uncharacteristically in self-destruct mode. He had put on weight, almost as a form of rebellion. 'I wasn't in videos anymore. I wasn't doing photo-shoots anymore. I didn't have to look good; I could eat what I wanted. It was almost my little "fuck you" to the industry. But then, of course, it went too far – I was getting immobile.'

For five months or so, he barely left his house. There was always the prospect of walking down the street and someone asking him how Robbie Williams was, or putting on a Robbie album the moment he entered any shop or bar. 'That's what made me reclusive. There's a meanness, people relish your situation. You end up embarrassed to be who you are. It got to the point where I wouldn't even use my credit card over the phone.' Even when he did venture outside, he would tend to go in disguise, hiding under a hat.

Even so, Gary later denied his depression was associated with Robbie's unexpected and overwhelming success. It was more to do with being rejected by the industry as an artist: 'My life had been ripped away from me. I was just thinking, I've worked all these years and now it's all been taken away from me. That was the depressing thing.' Though he was still worth around £20 million, he found it hard to know what to do if he wasn't hard at work.

Gary was shocked by the way his career had crashed. It felt like a cruel rejection by the public and the industry. 'For years we had people around us and cars taking us everywhere,' he said of his time in the spotlight in the 1990s. 'With one phone call, it all stopped and you're on your own. It wasn't easy.'

With no record deal as a performer, he could at least continue as a songwriter. He invited various artists to visit him at his home studio in Cheshire. One early visitor was Ian Watkins, alias 'H' from the pop group Steps. Each member of Steps was co-writing a track for their next album (2000's album *Buzz*) with an established name, but, in the event, the Gary collaboration never even made it on to the running order.

For the next four or five years, Gary refused to be photographed or interviewed, and he hardly sang a note, 'not even on a demo. I locked the door on that side of me, told everyone around me I didn't want to do it anymore. I even convinced myself that it was true.' He grew to hate music itself, even the lucky white piano he owned, on which he had written most of his 1990s hits. 'Within six months of this not happening anymore, this piano drove me mad. I spent days going slowly insane, trying to work out why this thing wasn't delivering to me like it used to.'

'When you're not on a label anymore, lots of things disappear from your life,' he told Q magazine years later. 'The thing I noticed was how few phone calls I'd get in a day.' It was a bad time for Gary, no question. As he ballooned in weight, he lost confidence and even began to think that any kind of resurgence would be impossible. 'I'd completely given up hope. Never at any point did I feel like, "One day, I'll get back there."'

In 2001, Gary and Dawn decided to move to sunnier climes with their baby son, Daniel. They headed for Los Angeles in California, and rented an apartment there. For Gary, the move came as something of a relief. After his solo career tanked, his name meant little in the US, though at least neither did Robbie's. It was a world away from the press and the public who would remind him of his failure. 'We made friends with the neighbours, who knew nothing of who I was and had no fixed opinion of me. I loved that.' It made a pleasant change from having to read CAKE FAT puns in the tabloids.

In the States, Gary contributed backing vocals to an Elton John album, *Songs from the West Coast*, acclaimed by many as the star's best since his heyday of the 1970s. But, while he was proud to work with one of his all-time heroes again, Gary had had enough of singing, and instead concentrated on writing and producing. Thanks to an executive at Sony Music in America, he began to collaborate with American songwriters, working on material for Gloria Estefan and Christina Aguilera.

In August 2001, the Barlow family returned to Cheshire.

Gary stood on the bathroom scales, and discovered he'd gained 50 pounds in weight: he was now 16 stone 8lb. It was wife Dawn who rescued him from his plight. Concerned about his weight, she urged him to see a doctor. 'He said that, for my height, I was morbidly obese. They devised a plan – and it wasn't about going on a diet but getting to understand food.' Once Gary started working on that plan, he set about getting back to work. As he explained: 'Even though financially you don't need to do anything, there's this need to be a provider. I have to have a purpose.'

Soon, he was busy behind the scenes again. By the end of the year, he had set up a new production company called True North with a young writer called Tim Woodcock and Eliot Kennedy, an old friend. His connection with Eliot went back as far as 1993 when they co-wrote the song 'Everything Changes'. In the meantime, Sheffield-born Eliot had written for S Club 7, Boyzone and the Spice Girls. Now, they had teamed up to write and produce material for an album by the boyband Blue. True North Productions felt like a new beginning. 'I went back to where I started,' said Gary, 'sitting in a room writing songs for other people, and eventually I was getting other artists into the studio.'

He was just one 90s star who was writing for the 21st-century breed of popstars. Many of his contemporaries from that period had also opted for the anonymous but extremely lucrative world of songwriting. Cathy Dennis, OMD's Andy McCluskey, Karen Poole (formerly of Alisha's Attic) and Betty Boo (under her real name of Alison Clarkson) were all successful composers, wealthy without having to deal with fame.

In 2002, Gary and Eliot produced *Somewhere in Time*, a

new record of cover versions for former teen heartthrob Donny Osmond. By now 44 years old, Utah-born Donny was a fan of Gary's work, and Gary knew just how important the Osmonds had been to 1970s pop. While Gary had been in his early 20s before stardom occurred, Donny had become a chart-topping star at 14. 'I didn't know Gary but I was a huge fan of Take That. He's a brilliant songwriter. I've experienced teen hysteria, so I was able to relate to what he'd also gone through.' Two years later, Barlow and Kennedy wrote most of the songs for a follow-up Donny album. The opening track, 'Breeze On By', gave him his biggest hit in the UK for over 30 years.

The songwriting and producing commissions continued to trickle in: Atomic Kitten, Charlotte Church, English teenager Amy Studt and several pop stars in Australia, including a teenage singer called Delta Goodrem, who had acted in the TV soap *Neighbours*. He was even asked to provide a song for an album by the Lancashire tenor Russell Watson at a time when classical crossover had not really taken off. Sessions followed for *Tissues and Issues*, the first pop album by the classical singer Charlotte Church. It anticipated the work he would do for Katherine Jenkins and Camilla Kerslake later on in the decade.

In August 2003, Gary found a song of his in the Top 10 for the first time since 'Open Road' in 1997. Thanks to his victory on Channel 4's *Celebrity Big Brother*, Mark Owen had landed a recording contract with the Island record label. His comeback single, 'Four Minute Warning', written with Gary and Eliot Kennedy, reached number four. Two months later, the boyband Blue (for whom Gary had contributed songs intermittently for a couple of years) reached number two with another True North song, 'Guilty'.

Every now and again, there was some claim in the papers that Take That were getting back together, but it all came to nothing. Nigel Martin-Smith felt it was a waste of time for them to regroup. 'If you look at groups like Abba,' he said, 'the fact that people still like them has an awful lot to do with them quitting at the head of their game. Similarly, I think Take That are best remembered as they were. It will certainly be more lucrative for the boys to receive royalties from past work than it would be for them to perform together.'

Meanwhile, Gary refused to comment. He was still not giving interviews. 'Gary's phrase today is "I used to be famous",' said his spokesman, Martin Barter, in 2005. 'It was always his intention to become a great songwriter. Celebrity and the media are not part of his life anymore.'

Throughout his time in obscurity, there was always his family – his children Daniel and Emily (the latter born in 2002), and his wife Dawn. 'When you're famous, there are always the wrong people hanging round. I've been incredibly lucky to find someone genuine,' he said of Dawn. He was ecstatically happy with his children: 'It's the best thing ever, having kids. I like being woken up in the mornings, when they climb into bed and kiss you.' He would talk affectionately of the 'chaos' at Barlow Towers, saying, 'It's a very normal set up. It's kids not eating dinners, climbing all over me before I've even got my shoes off. That kind of normality is the key to everything.'

CHAPTER 18

REALITY
CHECK

While Robbie Williams became the biggest star in British pop, and Gary Barlow languished in obscurity, Take That's success of the 1990s became a template for the reality formats of 21st-century television entertainment. From 2001, talent shows like *Popstars*, *Pop Idol*, *Fame Academy* and eventually *The X Factor* all aimed to unearth fresh new pop talent, with the budding stars of tomorrow performing for the public and a judging panel of industry experts and established stars. From these formats would come, among many others, Girls Aloud, Will Young, Gareth Gates, Leona Lewis, Lemar, JLS, Olly Murs and One Direction.

Many of those involved in the new TV shows had a pedigree of working with the 90s' biggest acts. Louis Walsh had been the manager of Boyzone and Westlife; Nicki Chapman handled publicity for Take That and the Spice Girls. Then, of course, there was the outspoken Simon Cowell. He might have turned down Take That in 1991, but he went on to oversee many of the biggest-selling records of the late 1990s: Robson & Jerome, Teletubbies and, finally, Westlife again.

When the members of Take That had auditioned for Nigel Martin-Smith in Manchester, it was done in private, away from the cameras. The new talent shows on television laid bare the brutality of the audition process. Hopefuls would be invited to sing in front of a panel of professionals. They could be rejected for all sorts of reasons, often not for lack of talent but really a feeling that they might not be ready for the sudden rude awakening of fame: tabloid newspaper attention, national TV and constant attention from the public. A lot of people think they want to be famous, but the reality of fame is something very different and extremely difficult: it can be fun, but it is also hard work and stressful. At the end of the day, it's a job. 'You have a moral obligation,' said Nicki Chapman of her role as a judge on *Pop Idol* and *Popstars*. 'Are these people going to be happy; is it what they want to do, or is it going to ruin their lives? You have to go for strong people: they don't have to be the loudest or most extrovert person in the room, you're looking for inner confidence.'

Shows like these demonstrated to viewers how to create stars out of the boy or girl next door – exactly how Take That had been created in 1990. But what none of the new creations would have was a Gary Barlow: a single autonomous writer able to pen number one hits efficiently. Instead, like the Spice Girls, successful finds might be teamed up with established (if anonymous) songwriters. But how might Take That have fared, had they been discovered on such a show? It's hard to say. It took them four attempts to have a sizeable hit, and nine to top the charts. In the world of reality TV pop, an act *had* to be number one immediately.

In 1999, Gary had commented on the manufactured pop of the time: Steps, B*witched and S Club 7. In retrospect, his remarks seem curiously prophetic of the way he would assess new talent when he became a judge on *The X Factor* from 2011. 'I look at the new releases each year and despair over who will be the next Elton John, Sting or George Michael,' he declared. 'Who in these bands has the musical or writing creativity and singing skills? A lot of the groups don't sing on their records – it's just so obvious.' And he pointed out that, while many of the new groups technically received songwriting credits, they were minor contributors compared to the professional (but anonymous) songwriters in the shadows. 'They get a joint songwriting credit for changing a few words. For someone like me who sits here and creates a record from beginning to end, I just find it very amusing.' None of these groups was the whole self-contained package, they relied on too many collaborators. Unlike Take That, he sighed, 'There are no songwriters. I could write, we could sing and we could dance.'

By the early 21st century, reality television had become a big part of British TV. *Big Brother* had spun off a celebrity version in 2001, and, in November 2002, Mark Owen beat Les Dennis, Sue Perkins and Melinda Messenger to win *Celebrity Big Brother*. It rescued Mark from the wilderness, three years after being dropped by RCA Records. He had made solo recordings at his home in the Lake District but no one wanted to release them, and the torrents of fan mail he had previously received dwindled to a trickle. 'When you are on the rollercoaster that is the pop world,' he said in 2000, 'you lose your grasp on reality. You think that it will never end, and when it does it comes as a total surprise.'

The media publicity surrounding *Celebrity Big Brother* landed Mark a recording contract with Island Records to make a new album in 2003 called *In Your Own Time*. 'I never expected to get a break again. When you hear people shout your name again, it's a frightening thing.' He worked on three songs for the album with Gary, including the single 'Four Minute Warning', and admitted to feeling slightly nervous at the prospect: 'It was the first time I would be writing with him on the same level. When we were in Take That he was always the writer and as I was travelling up to his house I wondered whether I'd speak up if I didn't like something, or if I'd be like, "Yes, Gary, yes, Gary". But we got on great. When we were in the band, it was "King Gary".'

'Four Minute Warning' returned Mark Owen to the top five in August 2003, but the album only scraped into the charts, peaking at 59, and he soon found himself once more without a label. He issued a third album (*How the Mighty Fall*) himself in 2005, and reflected on his time with Take That, now a decade ago. 'We all had a great time,' he stressed, 'and travelled to places we'd never have had the chance to see. But at the same time, we were all just five normal guys. We weren't trained for what happened. It was a great experience, but it was crazy.'

Meanwhile, Howard Donald did not turn his back on music completely. He had always wanted to be a DJ long before Take That had taken off, and, by the 21st century, he was doing just that. Commitments took him everywhere from holiday camps at coastal resorts to club venues in Britain and Europe. He had no interest in the limelight anymore. 'I simply don't want to be wheeled out on television every now and then as this bloke who used to be famous.'

Jason Orange, meanwhile, had travelled around the United States, and had then gone back to college in the Cheshire town of Altrincham, where he studied psychology and sociology.

And then there was Robbie. The one voted the Saddest Loser by *Smash Hits* readers in 1995, and widely tipped to vanish after leaving Take That, was bigger than ever. He had songs loved by millions, but also an unpredictable personality meaning he was forever in the papers and on TV. What had not changed was his tendency to keep sniping at Gary Barlow. It was sometimes hard to tell whether a heavy rock cover version of 'Back for Good' (which he would often perform live) was meant affectionately or not. Probably not, on reflection, given some of his other comments about life in Take That. For instance, when asked a question about whether a biopic of the group could ever be made, Robbie rose to the bait: 'There's one in production – it'll be a bit like *Absolute Beginners*. We're thinking of calling it "Absolute Shit".' In a hidden track on his 2002 album *Escapology*, there was another disparaging reference to his former colleague. And then, as if to atone, he would occasionally issue apologies. This became habitual behaviour over several years – a sure way of keeping his name in the gossip columns. In contrast, Gary stayed silent and even stopped granting interviews. After all, songwriters don't often get interviewed by the tabloid press.

When two public figures snipe at each other, it can only be perceived as good-natured when their profiles are equal but, before long, Gary and Robbie were no longer equal. 'I wanted to crush him,' said Robbie of his opposite number. 'And I didn't let go. Even when he was down, I didn't let go and for that I'm deeply apologetic. But I needed him to listen to my truth, to validate it for me.' Williams' jibes, especially when taken up by the media, had a cruel edge. At least Williams had the excuse of experiencing fame at a very young age, callow in an unpredictable industry. The columnists giggling on the sidelines had no such defence, though.

While Gary Barlow's prospects as a soloist had been likened to the career of George Michael, Robbie was being portrayed as a cross between George and a rebel rock icon such as Liam Gallagher or Shaun Ryder. By teaming up with tunesmiths like Guy Chambers and later Stephen Duffy, he sold over two million copies of each of his first three albums. 'Rob has never claimed to be the most original artist on the planet,' said Chambers, 'but there's a strong argument to say he is the most entertaining.'

But, as with Take That and solo Gary, the United States was the one place he couldn't really crack, with only the *Escapology* album making any real headway. 'The only one from Take That who had a realistic chance of conquering the States was Gary Barlow,' insisted Louis Walsh in 2003. 'Robbie is so blatantly British. His records don't suit the American market, and they just don't get his humour.'

In February 2005, when BBC Radio 2 listeners voted for a special BRIT Award for the Best Song over the previous 25 years, the winner was not Gary Barlow's 'Back for Good' or Gary Barlow's 'Pray'. It was Robbie Williams' 'Angels'. At the ceremony, host Chris Evans announced that Gary and Howard Donald would present Robbie with his special gong but it turned out to be Matt Lucas and David Walliams in disguise.

The rivalry between Barlow and Williams showed no signs of abating.

CHAPTER 19

TAKE TWO

In September 2005, after ten years at Delamere Manor in Cuddington, Cheshire, Gary decided to sell up the woodland estate, now worth about £8 million. Comprising a manor house, a lodge (where his brother Ian and his family lived) and a cottage (where his parents lived), it also had three recording studios, where Gary had recorded so many of his songs. He had now been married to Dawn for five and half years and they had two children: five-year-old Daniel and three-year-old Emily.

The eagle-eyed would have spotted Gary's name in the writing credits on many albums and singles by other artists in the interim period, but to the casual music fan nothing had been heard of him since the disastrously received *Twelve Months, Eleven Days* album of 1999. The radio would still play Take That hits such as 'Back for Good' and 'Pray', and occasionally someone would cover them on *The X Factor* or

Pop Idol, but Gary himself was invisible to the media world. He had hidden away in Cheshire from the bubble of fame, a quiet family man with Dawn and the children.

The Take That fans with long memories would always remember a few Gary Barlow asides in the late 1990s about the possibility that their idols might re-form one day. In 1997, Gary had said: 'I'm sure that in 10 years' time we'll all be sitting around bored one day and suddenly think, "Let's have a Take That reunion". I hope it happens. Wouldn't that be great?' Then there was the farewell press conference itself in February 1996, where Gary had said, almost as an aside, 'Our dream is, after five or ten years, to do it all again.'

Give or take a few months, it was indeed 10 years on. On 16 November 2005, ITV1 broadcast a brand new 90-minute documentary called *Take That: For the Record*. Made with the full co-operation of the band and manager Nigel Martin-Smith, it mixed candid interviews with special archive footage, looking back at the group's extraordinary 1990s career. Perhaps, unexpectedly, Robbie Williams was also on board to reminisce. 'Maybe in doing this, I can say the right things and put a few ghosts to rest,' he explained.

The reunion of Take That was first mooted when their record company RCA announced plans to reissue the group's back catalogue with some bonus tracks, like B-sides, live versions and remixes. Next, it was revealed that Gary had been sifting and trawling through all his tapes, and had found plenty of footage that few would have seen before. It seemed an ideal opportunity to release a DVD crammed with such goodies. 'There's some good stuff,' Mark said, and then warned, 'though there's some nasty haircuts.'

Take That: For the Record acknowledged the band and its millions of fans had grown up, and that it was high time to set the record straight and talk frankly about what it had been like to be in the top pop group of the mid-1990s. The group had been hugely successful, but at an emotional cost to its members. 'I was so lonely,' revealed Robbie Williams in the documentary, 'I would drink myself to oblivion every night by myself.' His drug use escalated as the band grew bigger: 'For me, the drug intake obviously sped up a lot, until it was my life. For the other lads it wasn't really part of their life, other than we used to like to smoke weed and then giggle. Perhaps Take That saved my life. I'd have had a problem with drugs anyway.'

Robbie wasn't the only one who had suffered low points in the 1990s. Howard Donald had a bad patch, although, unlike Robbie, the nadir came after the split, not before it. Now a house music DJ working in the UK and Germany under the moniker of HD DJ, he revealed that he had felt very depressed about the break-up, and had considered throwing himself into the River Thames: 'I must have felt emotional, and tired with what was happening. It was a bit stupid but I was thinking of jumping in the river. It probably wouldn't have killed me, though. I would have thought: "Oh, Jesus, it's too cold! I'm getting out."'

Mark Owen admitted to feeling lost when the framework of Take That was taken away: 'When it finished, the weirdest thing was to go from having your day-by-day schedule, then just closing the gates and going, "OK, what do I do now?"' And Jason Orange admitted to missing the lack of adoration, 'the adulation, the kids coming along and me performing'.

But it was Gary Barlow, the one who had just spent five

years being mocked relentlessly by everyone checking the 'Where Are They Now?' file, who had the fondest memories of life in Take That. 'We lived the life,' he said. 'In some ways I'm still living that life – I have so much luxury around me, and that's because of the Take That experience.'

All five had plenty to say about their amazing journey through 90s pop. They recalled their beginnings, of going to audition for Nigel Martin-Smith in Manchester. Jason described their manager's Svengali image as being a bit like 'Willy Wonka, handing out five golden tickets, and we were like these five kids going to this huge factory'.

They remembered the divide in the group between the creative ones, the ones who could dance, and those who looked good. Mark, the biggest pin-up of the group, felt shut out of the creative process: 'I was near the bottom. We all did a bit of dancing, and I remember Jason and Howard being really good at it, me and Rob being not so good, and Gary being pretty bad – it was probably the opposite way round for the singing.' This, though, was probably part of Take That's unique appeal in the first place – five lads with differing strengths and weaknesses, and with distinctive characteristics, but who (for the most part) got on well. It was this sort of chemistry that would spur on subsequent manufactured pop acts such as the Spice Girls.

Then there were the reminiscences about girls. While the group were forbidden long-term relationships, casual sex was positively encouraged by their management. Some, like Jason Orange, revelled in this: 'I remember Nigel saying "No full-time girlfriends", which suited me, because I could have lots of sex with different girls. No commitment.'

'When you look at the papers now,' said Gary, 'and see a girl talking about sleeping with a footballer, you wonder why there weren't millions of stories about us.'

Obviously, the departure of Robbie and the subsequent relations between him and Gary needed to be addressed in the documentary. Unlike Robbie, who had not had time to grow up away from the spotlight, and for whom fame and personal contentment were poles apart, Gary had been fortunate to live his teens mostly away from the cameras, very gradually coming to prominence. Now in 2005, he was still regarded as the uncool one, while Robbie was many times more famous and more acclaimed, but he still said of Gary and his stable domestic background in Cheshire: 'I would swap everything I have for what he's got.'

For his part, Gary couldn't deny having a period of envying Robbie's career, but not the man himself: 'I can honestly say I've never laid in bed wishing I was Robbie Williams. But I guess that, years ago, I lay in bed wishing I had his career.'

After years of wisecracks about Gary (many of them malicious), Robbie was magnanimous about his estranged colleague's talent, but less so about his ex-manager Nigel Martin-Smith. Reputed to have engineered Robbie's sudden departure from Take That, Nigel then sued him for £200,000 (for what he claimed to be unpaid managerial commission). There was no love lost between the pair. Nigel said of Robbie: 'I haven't got a nice thing to say about him.' Robbie fired back that Nigel was 'the third most disturbed person I have ever met'.

But, ultimately, Robbie was proud of Take That. He believed that no boyband had been so entertaining since their break-up, 'and you would be hard pressed to find one before, too. I'm not talking about The Beatles – I'm talking about your archetypal four/five lads on stage, singing and dancing. Boybands are frigging lazy these days. Ballad, stand, ballad, stand – it annoys me because I know how hard we worked.'

It was a pride shared by all five of the former bandmates. 'We did a lot for 90s music, especially pop music,' said Howard, though he was modest about his own contribution. 'Why was it me? Why wasn't it somebody else with more talent?' he wondered aloud.

Meanwhile, a level-headed Gary summed up Take That's first phase quite simply: 'I think if you asked someone in the street, they'd say, "Nice songs, great bunch of lads, and we thoroughly enjoyed it when they were together."'

Though the interviews were recorded individually, the plan at the end of the making of the documentary was to reunite all five in the same room. All of them showed up – except for Robbie.

In all, around six million people had watched *Take That: For the Record*. Its director, David Notman-Watt, discovered it had been a great nostalgia trip for the youth of the 1990s. 'I heard that groups of women in their early 30s have been getting together with bottles of wine to watch the show. It's fantastic.'

In fact, many of those working in the 21st-century media had been fans of the group as teenagers. Some were by now journalists and wrote nostalgic columns for newspapers about their memories of waiting outside TV studios, at signings, at live gigs, and even near the group members' homes, hoping for a glimpse of them.

Anita Sethi was one such journalist to share her memories. Writing in the *Guardian*, she wondered why she had loved the group so much: 'It couldn't have been the music, there were only a handful of their songs I liked. Perhaps the way they professed to love their fans, their personalisation (Funny One, Cute One, Deep One, etc), the divesting of exhaustive details about them made you sure, so sure, in your 11-year-old soul, that you knew them.'

The same week that the documentary was broadcast, a new Take That singles compilation appeared in the shops. *Never Forget: The Ultimate Collection* quietly jettisoned the 'Do What U Like' debut single in favour of a previously unreleased track, 'Today I've Lost You'. The collection sold 90,000 copies in a week, and entered the album charts at number two, behind the Madonna comeback album, *Confessions on a Dance Floor*.

As the compilation flew out of the shops, there was a huge pressure on the group to re-form. It was a tricky moment. Did they really want to put themselves through the rigours of the 1990s *again*? 'It's easy to remember the good times,' said Gary, 'but the schedule was non-stop. I could never go back to that life. I'm too old now and I've got a family to think about. I haven't had someone telling me what to do for 10 years.'

Howard also ruled out anything new beyond plugging the hits collection. 'We're going to do promotion for it,' he promised, 'but people will ask us to do live stuff again and expect us to go up on stage. That's not going to be the case.'

Could a wodge of cash possibly sway them, though, into going back on the road one last time? 'Possibly,' said Gary, who reasoned it could only be an improvement on doing shows alone. 'On stage on one of my solo tours, I thought, "I don't like this, this is shit." Sharing the moment with the band was easily the best bit.'

There was a sticky moment in that Robbie didn't seem to want to do it, but then the others were offered £1 million each to get back together, whether or not Robbie was interested.

On Friday, 25 November 2005, Take That officially announced they were re-forming for what was described as a 'farewell tour'. Gary's words deliberately echoed those he had spoken when the group had declared their break-up: 'We'd like to say thank you to everyone for giving us the last 10 years off, but unfortunately the rumours are true – Take That are going back on tour.'

They had not performed a full concert in a decade but the group understood that, after a decade apart, they needed to gel again, not just personally but also professionally. It came as little surprise to find that Gary hadn't kept up his dance moves, but then again, nor had Jason. Watching back the videos of their heyday, they knew they had a lot of shaping up to do. In fact, Gary not only had to lose some weight but also had to re-learn some of the songs as he hadn't performed in public in so long. His last tour had been six years ago.

Nigel Martin-Smith would not be involved in the reunion. It was felt that it would not be an equal hierarchy under him, and they decided instead to join forces with Mark's manager, Jonathan Wild, and become a co-operative. Later, Jason would cite Mark as injecting a collective confidence into Take That as a single four-pronged entity: 'It's he who's held it together. He's developed into a brilliant pop songwriter, meaning we now have two. Howard and I help wherever we can and the result is that it feels like a band effort.'

Tickets for *The Ultimate Tour* went on sale on Friday, 2 December. Gary wondered who might come beyond 30-somethings, but urged people with children to bring them along. Maybe a new generation could find out what their parents had been listening to in the 1990s. 'Many of our original fans now have children of their own and we'd be happy to see them at the shows. The concerts will be family-friendly,' he promised. 'We won't be baring our bums!'

But Gary felt tense. What if it was like his 1999 tour and hardly anyone wanted to come? On the eve of the tickets going on sale, he went out with a friend to drink the bar dry. 'I woke up the following morning and I had 27 missed calls. All the tickets had sold out! I realised: "Shit, this is big; we're back."' Suddenly, he felt 'valid again' – there was no need to go out in disguise anymore.

The 275,000 arena tickets for Take That's 11-date *Ultimate Tour* of April and May 2006 sold out in hours. Further stadium dates in Manchester, Cardiff and Milton Keynes were added for the second half of June. Among the support acts would be female trio Sugababes and US group Pussycat Dolls. Gary expressed astonishment at the enthusiasm for Take That's reunion. 'People of our own age are looking for tickets,' he gasped. 'When we were in our prime, they would have been too embarrassed to do that.'

'We didn't know how people were going to react,' said Howard, 'and to see how much support is still there has been a big shock to me.'

The group promised all those attending plenty of energy and

entertainment, as well as value for money. It would not be a set where the group would be mostly perched on chairs, said Howard, which was widely assumed to be a dig at Westlife's ballad-heavy repertoire. Gary was more direct: 'Westlife are OK, but they don't match what we did on stage.'

Why did Take That reunite? Part of it was a financial need; aside from Gary, the others were all a little strapped for cash. Also, realistically, with the group now in their 30s (Howard, the most senior member, was nearly 38), the time was right. 'If we don't do it now,' reasoned Mark, 'we probably never could. It's now or never.'

But there was a deeper reason. They recognised their audience would have grown with them. 'It's not going to be as chaotic as it was,' argued Gary. He also recognised that their audience saw the five (now four) of them as distinctive characters in a good-natured gang. 'Going on tour will probably be spookily similar to how it used to be. I think we've noticed that we all slot into place when we're all together doing interviews. We just seem to fall back into those characters.'

To prepare, the group wanted to research some of the spectacular shows being staged in the USA; to gather together some new ideas. And so, in early 2006, although Mark was busy on a solo tour of Europe, the other three visited Las Vegas. They figured they could not just show up and sing the hits; they had to provide the audiences with something that bettered their 1990s heyday.

Robbie Williams had given the tour his blessing but would not be appearing – mainly because he had a tour of his own going on for most of 2006. The same month that Take That announced they were re-forming, tickets went on sale for his own *Close Encounters* tour. In just one day, over 1.6 million people snapped up Robbie tickets for the tour, due to start in April in Durban, South Africa. It would have been impossible for him to do a solo tour and a Take That tour at the same time. By way of a joke, Mark Owen said: 'We couldn't afford Robbie, anyway.'

Well, not the physical reality of Robbie at least. Instead, for the Take That shows, Robbie rejoined the group in the form of a 10-foot-high hologram, to be beamed on to a giant screen of water. It seemed an appropriate and irreverent way to include the absent bandmate in proceedings. For 'Relight My Fire', they would be joined onstage by Lulu at the stadium dates and Beverley Knight for the arena shows.

The first concert of *The Ultimate Tour* took place in Newcastle on 24 April 2006. They began with a song that on its original release in January 1992 had been almost completely ignored: the big number 47 sound of 'Once You've Tasted Love'. To start with a relatively minor Take That song demonstrated huge confidence, but the lavish set, performed at a breakneck pace, was underway. Their many real hits of the 1990s came thick and fast. 'Today I've Lost You' made its live debut, and even the trusty Beatles' medley made a comeback. There was a flamenco take on 'It Only Takes a Minute', a radical update of 'Sure' (featuring a sample of 'Dirty Harry' from Damon Albarn's Gorillaz), a self-deprecating routine called 'How to Build a Boy Band' (with the four dressed as white-suited robots) and, as promised, the huge Robbie hologram, which introduced 'Could It Be Magic'. One former teenage fan, by now a broadsheet journalist, commented: 'When we were 13 we may have known the lyrics off by heart, but we never really listened to them. Suddenly we are seeing Take That with new, adult eyes, and strangely, it makes us feel like giggly schoolgirls all over again.'

It seemed no one was disappointed, much to Mark Owen's relief: 'We wanted to put on a show that was a bit spectacular. That was our biggest worry. We didn't want the reviews to be like: "They shouldn't have bothered coming back." There would have been nothing worse than that.'

Meanwhile, Nigel Martin-Smith looked on in wonder: 'I thought they would do the tour and that would be it. But now they could tour every year and pack stadiums.'

It was as if to confirm that Take That's mix of qualities – singing, writing, dancing, attractiveness – operated best when they were all together rather than apart. In the two-hour *Ultimate Tour* shows, no single member of the group was bigger than the group itself... except for that giant hologram.

'The only reason we did *For the Record*,' said Mark, 'was to close the door on Take That. But we ended up kicking it open even wider.'

CHAPTER 20

LET IT SHINE

Just as *The Ultimate Tour* was due to start in April 2006, Gary and the rest of Take That announced that they were going to make a new album after all. They were so amazed by the support for their concerts that they figured there was an available audience who might be interested in a record of brand-new songs. This was going beyond a look back at the 1990s, instead it was a 21st-century Take That, a Phase 2 for the group.

Recording comebacks that succeed are relatively rare in pop music. The initial thirst to revisit something from one's past can pall very quickly, and, by going back into the studio, Take That risked finding that the fans had only wanted to hear the old songs one more time. But this time round, it wouldn't just be Gary writing the songs. Now, all four would receive equal credit as songwriters. 'We've enjoyed getting ready for the tour so much we've started writing together,' announced Gary. 'If it's any good, we might be back for good.'

Take That opted not to sign to Sony BMG, the corporation which owned their 1990s back catalogue. Instead, they accepted a £3 million record deal with Polydor, part of the giant Universal Records company, whose artist roster included the Scissor Sisters, the Kaiser Chiefs, Girls Aloud and Eminem. The group's connection with Polydor boss David Joseph stretched back to their first incarnation, though – he had worked as head of artist development at their old label, RCA.

As they signed the Polydor deal, Take That already had five songs completed. When their tour of the UK finished in June 2006, they spent the summer back in the studio completing what would be *Beautiful World*, the first new Take That album since *Nobody Else* in 1995.

Meanwhile, Mark and his girlfriend, actor Emma Ferguson, had their first child, and Gary announced that he had written his autobiography. *My Take* (published in October) was a frank, revealing read, taking readers from his childhood to stardom, as well as saying how he really felt about the other members of the group, his time of fame, his period of oblivion and his estranged relationship with Robbie Williams.

In September, the group announced that the *Beautiful World* album was ready to go. Could their comeback single be number one for the festive season? Gary laughed off the suggestion. He still remembered what happened to 'Babe' in Christmas week 1993. 'Mr Blobby beat us and you can never tell what's going to happen at that time of year. We're a bit jinxed. *The X Factor* lot will probably get there.' (His prediction would be correct.)

On 10 October 2006, BBC Radio 1's breakfast show host Chris Moyles premiered the new Take That single, their first since 'How Deep is Your Love' in early 1996. It was called 'Patience', as if to playfully bait the fan base hoping for a new Take That record for so long. But it was a poignant ballad about loss and recovery, co-written by Gary, Howard, Jason and Mark. A video for the song had been shot in Iceland, where disappointment over the lack of northern lights was short-lived. 'All of a sudden,' said an amazed Gary, 'the sky started to light up and we stood for ages watching the reds and greens.'

He described the *Beautiful World* album as 'back to basics'. In his view, the vocals were the most important aspect of the record as the foursome were to all intents and purposes a vocal group above all else. The 12-track album was produced with the help of American John Shanks, best known for his work with Bon Jovi and the Backstreet Boys. Future single 'Shine' was an infectious pop song with a killer chorus somewhere between the ELO and the Scissor Sisters. Howard sang on 'Mancunian Way' (a nostalgic look back to the 1990s); 'Reach Out' brought to mind the anthemic work of Coldplay or U2; and 'What You Believe In' was seen by some as a future number one. The folky acoustic 'Wooden Boat' marked Jason's debut as lead vocalist and brought to mind the work of New Zealanders Crowded House. All in all, it was a versatile and assured collection of tracks, grown-up without being staid. It was abundantly clear that, after an 11-year lay-off, the re-formed Take That had made their best album so far.

'It's a genuinely co-operative effort,' said Gary, who sang lead on half of the dozen tracks. Creatively, he felt that a burden had been lifted from his shoulders: 'We've got an honesty this time.'

That said, the foursome (credited on all tracks as 'Take That') had a little help from other writing collaborators, like Billy Mann (whose credits included songs for Celine Dion and Joss Stone), Steve Robson (material for Busted and Blue), Anders Bagge (work for Janet Jackson and Madonna) and Eg White (tracks for Natalie Imbruglia and Will Young). The album's co-producer, John Shanks, was another co-writer across six tracks, including 'Patience'.

Some reviews wondered if this was less a Take That album than something along the lines of a Gary Barlow solo album. 'The result is very much a middle-management company car of a record rather than the ludicrous hen-night limousine of their prime,' wrote one broadsheet critic. Were there perhaps just a few too many ballads? Most saw 'Shine' and 'Mancunian Way' – the more up-tempo material – as the most memorable, but 'Wooden Boat' impressed, too. The *Observer* critic was smitten: 'Its mild-mannered adult rock is slicker than a tub of Brylcreem, but not so cloying as to make you want to wash your hands after listening to it.'

On 19 November 2006, 'Patience' returned the group to number one in the charts. It was a song that had some unexpected fans. 'I've always liked Take That,' Nicky Wire from the Manic Street Preachers told the *Guardian* in 2009. 'But this is something else. It's got such a dark lyric. There's a maturity about it that suits the boys all grown-up. Gary is a genius. You get so many alternative bands banging on about how to make perfect pop and this kicks all their arses.' Tellingly, though, when any male artist says they like Take

That, they have to immediately qualify that they're not joking. 'This is not an ironic choice,' Wire emphasised. 'If Neil Young had written it, people would be calling it a masterpiece.'

Beautiful World had the same sort of anthemic, epic sweep as the best work of Coldplay or U2, especially on 'Reach Out', its opening track. Coldplay had been a major influence over Gary Barlow's decision to return to singing and performing. It was *Parachutes*, Coldplay's debut album from 2000, that had particularly inspired him. 'I realised that you could be in a rock band and not have a husky rasp – Chris Martin has the most beautiful voice. I didn't sing for six or seven years. For the first time in years, I could see myself doing that again.' In fact, 'Yellow', the first Coldplay hit of all, had been played to death at Gary's home and was the source of inspiration for when Take That were resurrected: 'When I came back, I imagined that sound and the guitars, and imagined the stadium sound of a Coldplay song. I thought that could work for us as well, especially as a vocal group.'

On 2 December 2006, the same weekend that *Beautiful World* would enter the album charts at number one, ITV broadcast *An Audience with Take That*, part of an irregular but long-running series in which a star act performed in front of an audience of celebrities. This was the first-ever edition of the show to be broadcast live and interactive, meaning that viewers could vote by text message or via the Internet for the hit they would most like to hear performed. Meanwhile, a selection of tracks old and new would be sung; they would be joined onstage by Lulu to sing 'Relight My Fire' and a celebrity audience would ask questions of the four bandmates. Among the stars invited were Holly Willoughby and comedian Peter Kay.

As Take That signed a US recording deal with the Interscope label (home to Eminem and 50 Cent), they reflected on the extraordinary year they had experienced in 2006. Gary especially seemed at peace after a turbulent period of being the Aunt Sally of the group, the one who would always be mocked, the one who would be asked by passers-by where Robbie Williams was, and, worst of all, having no outlet and no audience for him as a performer. But he refused to discount and forget those difficult years. 'It's important to talk about them,' he insisted. 'All that happened has helped. There's a sense now that it's a good story, with a nice end and a positive message.'

When Take That appeared on the live final of *The X Factor* to sing their forthcoming single 'Shine', Gary was struck by the potential of finalist Leona Lewis. He described her as '50 times better than any contestant you've had on this show'. Perhaps surprisingly, given his later involvement in the series, Gary claimed to have little time for reality TV at this point, but he made an exception for Leona. 'I took a tape of the backing track to "A Million Love Songs" to her dressing room,' he told *The Times*, 'and she began to sing. She was fantastic to the point that I thought, "What are you doing on this show?" I was worried she might not get taken seriously because of it.' (Ironically, Leona's debut album, *Spirit*, would be overseen in America by executive producer Clive Davis, who had supervised Gary's *Open Road* album a decade before.)

More Take That live dates were lined up for 2007, which would take them to Europe (supported by rising star Mika), Australia and the Far East. They were also set to rake in profits from a whole range of new band merchandise, from clothing to stationery. Intriguingly, when the trademark was registered, there were five names listed, not four. Not just Gary, Jason, Howard and Mark but Robbie, too. It was explained that the absent member would also have had to give his consent as, when ownership of the Take That logo had passed to them, Robbie was still in the group.

'Shine' sounded like a number one on first hearing, and so it proved to be. It was released as a single in February 2007, accompanied by a Busby Berkeley-style dance extravaganza of a video. Gary preferred to stay behind the piano, leaving all the breakdancing moves to Jason. On the eve of its release, they performed the song at the BRIT Awards, where yet again they triumphed in the Best British Single category for 'Patience'. As with their three Best Single victories during the 1990s, for 'Could It Be Magic', 'Pray' and 'Back for Good', they won through on a public vote. In comparison, Robbie was only shortlisted in one category – for Best Live Performance, which was ultimately won by Muse.

The release of 'Shine' coincided with the announcement that, though there would be no new album in 2007, there would be a pre-Christmas tour of a *Beautiful World* show: 22 British dates in November and December. As ever, said Gary, they were thinking big: 'As a band, we have never seemed to come up with ideas that are small in scale, they've always been big ideas. Our fans can expect more of the same. It's going to be an absolutely massive show.'

Inspired by another trip to Vegas for ideas on staging and presentation, the *Beautiful World* show would boast a fantasy-tinged backdrop evoking *2001: A Space Odyssey* and Harry Potter. The fans, old and new, seemed just as word-perfect on the new material as the old favourites. 'Relight My

Fire' at one point morphed into a cover of Gnarls Barkley's 'Crazy', while there was a lapdancing sequence for 'It Only Takes a Minute', which featured Dawn as one of the dancers (but who was dancing for Howard). Gary explained the routine: 'We wanted to put something in that the boys in the audience could enjoy, too.'

Elsewhere, a radical reworking of 'Could It Be Magic', performed by Gary at the piano, reverted from a floorfiller to the tearjerker first popularised by Barry Manilow in the 70s. For the group it was a rare quiet moment in a gruelling, tiring show (at one point Howard – now 39 – was challenged to perform a backflip), but which seemed to enthral everyone who attended. In contrast, Gary played his mediocre dancing skills for laughs; after the others competed for the most audacious dance stunt, they turned to see their bandmate sitting reading the paper, and saying, 'I should have been in Westlife.' Gary was perhaps right to be cautious – on the European leg of the tour, in Austria, Howard was hospitalised with a collapsed lung the day after doing the splits at a show in Milan. He had to miss the Vienna date as a consequence, but his German girlfriend Marie-Christine travelled from their Berlin home to be with him. While he made a full recovery, it sounded as a warning that the daring dance routines might be taking their toll.

All in all, though, the *Beautiful World* live shows were a huge success, and consolidated Take That as a group that had been right to make a comeback. The bandmates had not just run through the old hits, but had also reinvented themselves with strong and brand-new songs. They had proven themselves once again in 2007, with appearances at Comic

Relief in March and a charity concert in memory of Diana, Princess of Wales in July. A stand-alone single, 'Rule the World', which doubled as the theme to the fantasy adventure film *Stardust* (starring Sienna Miller and Robert De Niro), was recorded over the summer and released in October. It was only prevented from reaching the number one spot by the *X Factor* contestant Gary had singled out for praise: Leona Lewis with 'Bleeding Love'.

In the wake of Take That's reunion, many other 1990s groups – from East 17 to Boyzone – did much the same, mounting comeback records and tours, and repackaging their back catalogue, to varying degrees of success. Perhaps most attention was granted to the Spice Girls' reunion in 2007, but, although their world tour was a sell-out, a newly recorded single called 'Headlines' was their first to miss the Top 10. Even New Kids On The Block, who inspired the creation of Take That, tried again. In 2008, they had their first US Top 10 album in 18 years. In the meantime, Donnie Wahlberg had experienced the most solo success, acting in films like *Saw* and *The Sixth Sense*. But this was a rare exception.

With Take That's revival, there was even a stage musical based around the group's back catalogue of 1990s hits. This had become common practice in the world of musical theatre, with the likes of Abba, Queen, Rod Stewart and Madness all having their past work presented in this way. It was to be called *Never Forget*, but was not exactly about Take That themselves; instead, it was about a Take That tribute band, with a story written by *Shameless* writer Danny Brocklehurst, and was described by its producers as a 'feelgood comedy about love, friendship, ambition and betrayal'.

Officially, the group played no part whatsoever in the musical's promotion. It transpired that their songs had been licensed by EMI to *Never Forget*'s producers in 2005, *before* the announcement that they were re-forming. Indeed, a statement was published on the group's website: 'The band wish their fans and the general public to know this production is absolutely and 100 per cent nothing to do with Take That.' Some involved in the production felt that Take That's disassociation after licensing their work had something to do with the success of the real Thatters regrouping – a level of success no one could truly have predicted. 'We'd much rather have them on side,' one of *Never Forget*'s producers admitted, 'but we can't force them to be. That's showbusiness.'

So it was an unexpected turnaround when the show, after a regional tour, hit the West End in May 2008, and Gary gave it the thumbs-up. Or at least warmed to it a little. 'At first I thought it sounded horrible,' he admitted. 'But the reports I've seen have been really good so there must be something good in it. I've had some friends who went to see it in Manchester and they said the cast were amazing.' Was he planning on going to see it himself? 'I don't think we can sit in the audience somehow,' he argued, perhaps knowing that, if they did, all eyes would be focused on the stalls, not the stage.

Now in their late 30s, Gary and the rest of Take That were once more as famous as they had been in the 90s.

CHAPTER 21

THE MANBAND

At the BRIT Awards in February 2008, Take That's achievements on their *Beautiful World* arena tour were recognised. They won the Best Live Act gong, beating the likes of Arctic Monkeys, and won the Best Single category (for 'Shine') but nevertheless Gary felt that their contribution to music elsewhere had been played down by the industry. 'When the public get to vote we always do well,' he told the *Sun*. 'But it gets to me that whenever we have been nominated for other awards we always get overlooked. I think we were in with a shout this year, but it just goes to show we don't fit the mould.' At least the group's songwriting prowess was confirmed at the Ivor Novello Awards later that year, although even here it was in a category based on public demand rather than critical standing. 'Shine' would win the Most Performed Work category. 'The Ivor Novello is worth more to me than anything else on the mantelpiece,' declared a proud Gary.

By the early summer, the group had cut short a four-month break to go back into the studio with producer John Shanks. Gary was said to have overcome a spell of writers' block and now the quartet was raring to go. By September, they had finished their follow-up to *Beautiful World*. 'It's not over-polished,' said Mark Owen of the final results. 'It sounds great but it feels real. I feel we've kept that original spirit. It feels very British to me. It feels like a British album.'

The first single, 'Greatest Day', was first unveiled in October then issued in November, when it became Take That's eleventh number one single. It came about because the group wanted a song good enough to open their live shows. 'We always think we've got great songs for finishing our concerts,' Gary told BBC Radio 1, 'so we wanted something to start a concert.' A video was filmed in Los Angeles on top of a sky-scraper in gale-force winds.

There was a minor kerfuffle when they had named the latest album *The Circus*, exactly the same title as a new Britney Spears album. What's more, both albums were coming out at the start of December 2008, in exactly the same week. The timing was an accident. Take That had wanted to give their album that title ever since they had seen a performance in Las Vegas of the alternative circus troupe Cirque du Soleil.

The Circus had a lot to live up to. *Beautiful World* had sold two and a half million copies in the UK, more than any of their 1990s albums. 'Our story is so far-fetched,' gasped Gary. 'I think it's taken a while for us all to get our heads round it, but everyone's enjoying it this time. I really don't think any other group has got an audience like ours. It's like we'd won before we'd even sung a note.'

The democracy of their reincarnation meant that the group had all been able to actually enjoy it this time round. Gary acknowledged that he had been too headstrong and controlling in the previous decade. 'Lead vocals were a sensitive issue, basically 'cos I wanted to do them all. I was young, ambitious and selfish. Robbie was the first to challenge that, but hearing him would only make me want to try to do the same song better. My own security issues, totally. I don't have them anymore.'

Plus, it wasn't just Gary playing the piano anymore. It seemed that all three of his bandmates had instrumental input into the records these days. 'There were a couple of keyboards and a couple of guitars, and we were all on different parts,' explained Mark Owen, 'getting different chords, trying to be heard and get our ideas across.' It didn't make them virtuosos, but considering the stick they had got from some quarters for their Pink Floyd/Nirvana tribute on 1995's *Nobody Else* tour, it was quite a revelation.

'It was a pleasure to work this way, to let them take the reins,' Gary said of his three colleagues, now on an equal footing. 'It's been lovely to watch, and lovely to be a part of it.'

In general, *The Circus* was considered an improvement on its predecessor, *Beautiful World*, and was hailed as witty, epic, triumphant and lovable. Its opening song, 'The Garden', featured all four Take That members taking turns at lead vocals. Jason Orange's second full track as singer, 'How Did It Come to This', was reputed to be a reaction to the troubled life of the talented singer Amy Winehouse. Another dark song was the title track. Despite its title, 'The Circus' was a downbeat number inspired by a best man's speech at a wedding Gary had attended a few years earlier. 'He had just split up with his partner and got drunk,' Gary said. 'When he got up to make his speech, he basically talked about himself for five minutes and how he'd ruined his life. Everyone was dying.'

The album's penultimate song, 'Here', was co-written with Olly Knights and Gale Paridjanian of Turin Breaks. It was a collaboration that raised some eyebrows, but to those involved it was logical, even if how it came about was a chance meeting. 'Our drummer's girlfriend was the chef on Take That's tour,' explained Olly. 'She was wearing a Turin Breaks T-shirt and Howard told her he was a big fan of ours and would love to write with us. Some people think it's an odd alliance but the world of music is a lot more open than the way it's defined. Those guys might decide to make pop, but the basics are the same as what goes into a Turin Breaks record.'

The success of the album lay in combining Gary, Howard, Mark and Jason's self-confidence, concentration and thoroughness. 'These days we study every detail of every song,' said Gary. 'Sometimes that means 33 takes of a vocal, but it works. We were never like that before. We used to amble on stage not even knowing what we were singing!' And, as one review noted, the album was the clearest indication yet that working as a team helped everyone.

The Circus was released in the UK on 1 December 2008. On its first day, it sold 134,000 copies. After a week, this had risen to an astronomical 432,000. It was an easy number one album. To coincide with it, the group appeared in a new ITV special, *Take That Come to Town*. Such was the way that they had re-established themselves that even the constant questioning of 'Where's Robbie?' was starting to dry up. It seemed to matter less and less that Take That were a four-piece group, and not a quintet. To them, it came as a relief, and especially to Gary: 'It still crops up but not as much, which is good. We love Robbie, but people see us as a four-piece now.'

The stadium shows for the *Circus* tour had been announced at the end of October 2008 for the following June and July. In under an hour, 300,000 tickets had been snapped up, breaking all records for a British tour, even beating Michael Jackson's *Bad* shows of 1988. After Howard's accident on the *Beautiful World* tour, it was fortunate that the music for *The Circus* album and its subsequent live shows was less obviously danceable.

The tour, estimated to have cost £10 million to stage, began in June 2009, with support acts of the calibre of Lady Gaga, The Saturdays, The Script and James Morrison. Fittingly, given the name of the show, the staging was a gigantic circus tent. The lads emerged from a vast hot-air balloon placed in the centre of the stadium, whereupon they launched into 'Greatest Day', that perfect show opener they had written specially for the album. The foursome perched themselves on ladders in the middle of a stage waterfall to croon 'Back for Good'. They all took their turns at vocal solos on new songs, before reviving their early 90s act in a medley of some of their earliest material: 'Do What U Like', 'Promises', 'It Only Takes A Minute' and 'Take That & Party'. At the end of that, they dropped their trousers to display boxers emblazoned with the distinctive Take That logo. A ringmaster puppet introduced 'Relight My Fire' before the group concluded the high-octane two-hour show with 'Rule the World'. As ever, Take That had given audiences a cracking night out. From ringmaster garb to riding unicycles, to a seven-metre-high mechanical elephant, this was a lavish yet human spectacle, with a beating heart. End of the pier but state of the art with it.

It seemed as if Gary Barlow didn't stop for breath during this period. Just as he was becoming a father for the third time – daughter Daisy was born in early 2009 – he was roped in to organise a celebrity charity climb of Mount Kilimanjaro for Comic Relief in a party that also included Chris Moyles, Fearne Cotton, Alesha Dixon and Cheryl Cole. He just had time to shoot the video for 'The Garden' in the grounds of Greenwich's National Maritime Museum before setting off for Africa. It was only one of several charity stunts he would co-ordinate; a couple of years later, he would be instrumental in organising a celebrity trek to the North Pole as part of BBC Sport Relief.

Yet he denied that he appeared to be working harder than ever. 'It's definitely a hobby,' he said of Take That. 'I don't think you should ever take this business too seriously. If you see it as a hobby, then it's something you enjoy and indulge in, and that's what we do. The day it becomes a job, we'll give it up. When we're making records, that's a proper day's work. When it comes to TV work, it seems we are doing more than we actually are doing.'

As we'll see, he was not just involved in Take That duties: Gary Barlow had wider ambitions in the music world. But, in the bubble of Take That, there remained unfinished business.

CHAPTER 22

THE TRUCE

For years, it was like asking the impossible. Robbie Williams would never rejoin Take That. In 2004, he had dismissed the question with the words, 'I'm afraid there's more chance of Hell freezing over.' But was this down to arrogance, or insecurity? Two years later, when Take That were touring Britain as a manband quartet and Robbie was on his own world tour, Gary felt some relief that his old bandmate was not physically present, and was only represented by a hologram, but explained that Robbie felt discomfort about getting back together: 'He felt respectful enough to say, "Those people have come to see you – they're not gonna wanna see me", which is not true. They would've wanted to see him.' Yet this would have caused an imbalance in how he felt Take That should be seen: as a group comprising equal parts. 'When you're in a band, it's not about any individual, it's about Take That.'

In the light of his 2006 world tour, it came as a surprise that Robbie's seventh studio album, the admittedly outré *Rudebox*, sold relatively poorly, only half the sales of its predecessor, *Intensive Care*. Coincidentally, *Rudebox* had come out at the same time as Take That's *Beautiful World*, but was nowhere near as commercially successful. Some believed that Robbie missed the hit-making skills and melodies of his former co-writer Guy Chambers, a professional association which had ended in acrimony. More troubling, though, was that he had had to cancel some shows on the Asian leg of his tour and, by the start of 2007, he was back in a rehabilitation clinic in Arizona. He was quoted as saying: 'I feel like I have overstayed my welcome a bit. I enjoyed tremendous success for 10 years – and now it's the time for the Williams to go away in people's minds.'

Gary and the group publicly supported Robbie during this especially turbulent time: 'We should thank him because I honestly think if it wasn't for him and for his huge success, there wouldn't still be the interest there for us that has put us back on the map.'

Nevertheless, as they told a *Sunday Times* interviewer, it was hard not to wonder about the timing of Robbie's announcement, and indeed the fact there'd been an announcement in the first place. 'One side of me wants to send him best wishes,' said Gary. 'I blame everyone around him. If it was me going into rehab, you'd never know. I'd be so embarrassed. But this bloody big press release giving all the reasons why... It's a big coincidence, isn't it? So who knows?'

Mark Owen, on the other hand, was quoted as saying, 'Emotions and feelings aren't something you can play around with. You can't say it's my birthday and they are going to win a BRIT so I'll go into rehab. I don't think he'd do that.'

It was while mixing was taking place in Los Angeles on Take That's *The Circus* in September 2008 that a delicate attempt at a truce began between Gary Barlow and Robbie Williams. There was still tension between the pair, over 13 years after Robbie's abrupt departure in July 1995. Gary decided to contact Robbie, who was now resident in LA, and received a response the very next day, by phone: 'He went, "I want you all to come up to the house – there are things I want to say that'll help us all move forward."' The following night, they met, for what Gary archly described as 'the you-said-I-was-fat-in-1991 conversation'.

Gary himself carried plenty of guilt about how Take That Mark I had treated its most junior member: 'We had a lot of guilt, the four of us, because Rob was the youngest, the most impressionable of all of us. We always felt like we didn't look after him enough.'

'I spent the last 15 years thinking what I was going to say,' Robbie later told BBC Radio 1. 'We had that big chat and the most amazing thing happened at the end of it. We both said sorry to each other and we both meant it. That's all we needed.'

In one evening, any iciness between the two had thawed dramatically. 'I went from having a real problem with this person,' recalled Robbie later, 'to literally rolling on the floor laughing with them, 10 minutes later. We were genuinely sorry that we'd upset each other.'

Robbie was not familiar with the *Beautiful World* comeback record. The first time he heard its follow-up, *The Circus*, was at his house in LA when Gary, Howard, Jason and Mark showed up. This was the moment he knew he had to work with his old group once more: 'If I write a hit, I do it by mistake – all the big ones were accidents. But Gary Barlow writes them on purpose. All these verses, middle eights and bridges were glorious. I was gripped by the fundamental pop of it all.'

And so Gary and Robbie's differences, which seemed to be irreconcilable, had been cancelled out by two things that had kept alive their professional friendship in the 1990s: laughter and music. There were plans to make a record together again but not yet as Take That. To begin with, they had unofficially changed their name: 'We figured there's been Take That Part 1, and there's been Robbie solo, and then Take That Part 2, so let's just drop all that and call ourselves The English.' Under a different moniker, they felt more confident to experiment with their sound. This way, they might not be so cautious and discard a song or its treatment because it didn't sound like Take That.

By the spring of 2009, Robbie was recording a new album at producer Trevor Horn's Sarm Studios in west London. Gary also had a studio suite at Sarm. Horn had doubled as producer and artist as one-half of Buggles for his first major hit – 1979's 'Video Killed the Radio Star', which almost certainly inspired the title of Robbie's album *Reality Killed the Radio Star*. Robbie had also temporarily moved back to the UK, buying a mansion in Wiltshire with his girlfriend, the American actress Ayda Field. Gary loved Robbie's new record: 'Rob's music still has an 80s electronic feel but it sounds fresh. I can hear Trevor Horn's influence on it. I would buy anything that guy does.'

Before the album was even released, all five of Take That

were in the studio again, working on brand-new material. The key meeting took place on Saturday, 26 September 2009 at Electric Lady Studios in New York City. It marked the first time in 14 years that the complete line-up were together in the studio. These Electric Lady studio sessions were originally booked for the final stages of mixing a live double album of *The Circus* for a Christmas release, but it also marked the genesis of a completely new Take That album.

When promoting *Reality Killed the Radio Star*, Robbie showed signs that his fractious relationship with Gary was calming. In live outings, he changed some of the words of 'No Regrets', a 1998 hit and previously one of the frankest condemnations of his Take That days, to reflect that Gary was no longer his sworn enemy. Then, on 12 November 2009, he was reunited on stage with Gary, as part of a Children in Need fundraising concert at the Royal Albert Hall in London. As Gary announced Robbie's arrival on the stage with the words 'What a perfect time to introduce an old friend of ours', Robbie was moved to tears. 'I was tearing up before I came on,' he said afterwards, 'knowing what was just about to happen and what the reaction was going to be like.' However, Take That performed separately, with Gary dedicating 'Rule the World' to his late father Colin, who had died a few weeks before of a suspected heart attack at the age of 71.

The first public admission from Robbie that he was once again recording with his estranged group came in an interview for BBC Radio 2 with old journalist friend Kate Thornton. When asked about the possibility of working with the other four again, he said: 'We'd have to have written some incredibly great songs together for me to be very, very excited about the project. I might be "very, very excited" about a project that's currently happening. Gaz is an amazing, amazing songwriter. I'm honoured to be in the same studio as him... erm... when we do, in the future.' But his attempt to switch tenses did not fool Thornton and she told him so, whereupon he admitted: 'Oh sod it, we've been in and the songs are absolutely amazing!'

A reunited Take That had been complicated for a while because four of them were signed to one record label, and the other bandmate to a different one. But this arrangement was about to change.

In January 2010, Gary Barlow, Robbie Williams and Mark Owen were just three of the many lead vocalists on a charity cover version of R.E.M.'s 'Everybody Hurts', to raise money for the victims of a catastrophic earthquake in Haiti. Simon Cowell masterminded the project, with other contributing artists including Leona Lewis, Kylie Minogue, JLS, Rod Stewart, Susan Boyle, Mariah Carey and James Blunt.

Take That's contributions to the project, which would be called Helping Haiti, were laid down in Los Angeles as the group set about working on their first album together since 1995. Gary signed a new publishing deal with Sony Music, and then, in March, it was reported that Stuart Price would be producing the new album. Since putting Madonna's career back on track with *Confessions on a Dance Floor* in 2005, he had produced the Scissor Sisters, but it was his work with The Killers that had made Take That enlist his help. They were looking to toughen up their sound, and make the boldest record of their careers.

Eventually, on a family holiday to the US, Gary met up with

Robbie once again. This time, they worked on writing songs. Over two days, they created what would become 'Shame', released in autumn 2010, a one-off single that would kick off a Robbie greatest hits album called *In And Out Of Consciousness*. Like the Take That *Greatest Hits* album of 1996, the running order of the album was in reverse chronology, rewinding through Robbie's solo years, but fittingly ending with Take That's 'Everything Changes But You', his biggest hit for the group as lead vocalist. A second brand-new song written with Gary, 'Heart and I', also appeared on the compilation.

Robbie described the retrospective hits album as 'not only a celebration of my past but also a bridge to the future. The fact that part of the future includes a name from my past makes it all the more poignant for me.'

In And Out Of Consciousness would be Robbie's last record under his contract for the EMI label.

It felt very exciting to be songwriting again. Gary had had many collaborators in the studio, but this was perhaps the biggest name ever. And yet they had met in 1990. 'We never did anything creatively together in the 90s,' Gary said of their new project, 'but once we wrote that, Rob said, "We've done it – now I want to work with the lads again."' To be pedantic for an instant, Robbie had a writing credit for one section of Take That's 1994 number one hit 'Sure' (as did Mark), but otherwise the point stood: Gary and Robbie had never written a song *together* as such.

'Shame' was released in October 2010, and reached number two in the charts. A tongue-in-cheek video to accompany it, a pastiche of the *Brokeback Mountain* film, was made in Los

Angeles, with the pair in matching cowboy gear. To promote it, they appeared on everything from *Strictly Come Dancing* to the Paul O'Grady talk show.

Just as 'Shame' appeared, Take That prepared to release their first album with Robbie back in the fold. They had reconvened in the studio in September 2009, but only in July 2010 – symbolically exactly 15 years to the week since Robbie had walked out of the group – had they officially announced that they had been working together again. 'I get embarrassingly excited when the five of us are in a room,' Robbie said. 'It feels like coming home.'

'Getting us in a room together,' said Mark Owen of Robbie's return, 'although always a dream, never actually seemed like becoming a reality. Now the reality of the five of us making a record together feels like a dream.'

The release of the new album, Take That's sixth studio record, would mark exactly 20 years since the group had formed in Manchester. It would be called *Progress*.

It wasn't just Gary and Robbie who were excited at working together as a quintet again. Of the group's original incarnation in the 1990s, Howard Donald commented: 'We never got the chance as individuals to work with him [Robbie] in this way – because Gary did all the writing then. We're all involved now.'

Jason Orange regretted that Robbie had become the scapegoat back then: 'I had a couple of years of feeling regretful about us not sticking by Rob. We had a lot of tensions going on, and it's easy in a group for one person to become the scapegoat.'

On first hearing the material for *Progress* that Gary had brought along, Robbie was astonished. 'I was like, "What the fuck have you been listening to?!" Then he tells you about the history of electronic pop in England and you're like, "Oh you know that, too." Brilliant!'

It was as if Gary's love for Depeche Mode 30 years before (recognised by many as seminal, not just for synth-pop in the UK but also for the development of electro and house music in the USA) was finally bearing fruit on record in a way it had never really done before.

Gary agreed that making *Progress* was a challenge. 'Me, Mark and Rob – three fully formed songwriters – could sit on our own and come up with songs. So when you try to decide which idea is better, it's really difficult.' Diplomatically, he described that process thus: 'We approached it as adults.'

The making of the album had been filmed for a documentary *Look Back, Don't Stare*. Gary asked a TV film crew to capture its construction, warts and all – a decision that might have been catastrophic, given how filming the making of The Beatles' album *Let It Be* early in 1969 had all but hastened the Fab Four's demise. Indeed, some of Take That were reluctant; Jason in particular hated the experience. 'I wanted to enjoy Rob; I wanted to enjoy the reunion privately. Everybody acts a bit differently when there's cameras on – I didn't want it to be captured on camera but it was. Gutted.'

In fact, there had been initial tensions anyway during the *Progress* sessions. After two months, Robbie walked away temporarily, concerned he was unable to handle the dynamics of being in a group again after so long as a solo artist. Gary was especially incensed, as it put the whole record and indeed subsequent tour in jeopardy (management deals and plans were already in place). It was Mark who calmed things down.

'Forget about touring. Forget about promotion. Let's just do this record and take it from there. Give us 30 days in the studio, that's all.' The simple approach worked and Robbie was back in the fold.

Progress was hailed as a triumph, both commercially and critically. Gone were the ballads that traditionally cropped up on typical Take That albums. And there wasn't much in the way of disco either. Overall, belying the warmth that had surrounded its making, it was an ice-cold, shiny paean to electronic pop, with nods to La Roux, American R&B, global icons like the Swede Robyn and even the stadium rock giants Muse. A track like 'Wait' wrongfooted those who were anticipating a Barlow-esque ballad: a piano intro gave way to an electro epic which the Pet Shop Boys would have been proud to write. 'Happy Now' brought to mind the vocal harmonies of the Bee Gees.

The most talked-about track was the most confessional. 'What Do You Want From Me?' was a contribution from Mark Owen. It was commonly felt to be about an affair he had conducted, which became a rare slice of negative press coverage for the group and briefly put his marriage under threat. Yet Mark insisted the track had been prepared before the affair reached the front pages. 'You know, when you reach a certain point with anybody in a relationship? That same song could relate to the band.'

Trailed by a single, 'The Flood', *Progress* was released on 15 November 2010. Gary said of its arrival: 'There aren't enough events in music any more – and this is an event.'

Many agreed with him. The most adventurous record Take That had made so far, it also received probably the best reviews of their career. 'A commendable leap into the unknown,' said *The Times*. The *Observer* praised it as 'the kind of record critics often carp on at pop stars for not making – oblique, eccentric, even bold'. It was hardly an avant-garde piece of work – Take That weren't into alienating record buyers – but, nonetheless, it was unexpected, which made it all the sweeter when it became the fastest-selling album in Britain in the 21st century so far. On its first day, it shifted 235,000 copies, more than the combined sales of the rest of the Top 20 that week. Not since Oasis's *Be Here Now* in 1997 (424,000 on day one) had a record sold so many in a single day. Before long, *Progress* had sold nearly three million copies in the UK.

It was made clear that Robbie Williams would not be rejoining Take That permanently. After the album was released, he would play over 50 worldwide shows with the other four, but nothing was certain beyond that. The *Progress* tour, set for the summer of 2011, would be a family affair: the group's wives and children would be coming with them on the jaunt across the UK and Europe. Each venue would have a family dressing room and crèche. The wild years of booze and sex excess were over. It promised to be 'a feast for the imagination, charting the evolution and progress of Take That and Robbie Williams through their extraordinary 20-year history'. To coincide with the British leg of the tour, the album was reissued with a second disc of eight new songs called *Progressed*, which included 'Love Love', the theme to the Matthew Vaughn film *X Men: First Class*.

Progress Live opened at the Sunderland Stadium of Light on 30 May 2011, climaxing at Wembley Stadium at the start of July. It was followed by European dates. 'The idea of actually going on tour is really exciting,' a pragmatic Gary explained, 'but there's always so much to do, so there is a worry. I'm not really excited until we're done and ready. I might not get that feeling until the first or second night, as late as that.'

Rehearsals for the tour, said to have cost £50 million (twice the bill for the *Circus* tour), took place in Bedfordshire in the utmost secrecy. Everyone involved had to sign strict confidentiality agreements. About all anyone knew was that there would be a section in the middle of the show for Robbie's solo material. Support acts on the tour included Pet Shop Boys, who were themselves celebrating a milestone anniversary: 25 years since their breakthrough hit 'West End Girls'. They performed a 40-minute section from their own lavish and bold stage show *Pandemonium*. Take That were big fans of Pet Shop Boys, another act who kept updating their sound and thought hard about their profile in a constantly shifting pop world.

The headliners' set began with Gary, Howard, Jason and Mark bursting forth with 'Rule the World', then 'Greatest Day', 'Hold Up a Light', 'Patience' and 'Shine'. Songs that were all less than five years old, but already felt so timeless and familiar they could have been around for 20. After these five songs, they left the stage.

For Robbie's section, he abseiled 20 feet on to the stage for his opener, 'Let Me Entertain You', and performed a spoof of The Beatles' 'Sgt. Pepper's Lonely Hearts Club Band' but irreverently changed the title to 'Robbie Williams and the Take That Band'. Inevitably, 'Rock DJ', 'Feel' and 'Angels' were all present and correct.

For the third section of the show, the other members joined

Robbie to race through highlights of the new album, before Gary sat down at the grand piano to lead everyone through a medley of Take That's old-school hits. Finally, there was a rendition of 'Eight Letters', in which the group left the stage and walked through the audience.

The British shows climaxed with a full eight nights at the 90,000-capacity Wembley Stadium. After one show, they shot a video for 'When We Were Young' as they waded through the litter left by the crowds to consider the effect of so many plastic cups on the environment. There was deep regret later in July when, for the very first time in Take That's career, they had to cancel a Danish show due to Robbie suffering from food poisoning. There was no way of covering up the hole in the show that his absence would have left, especially the middle section of his solo hits. At the very last show in Munich, he dropped his trousers and bared his bum. But overall, Robbie enjoyed the tour so much that he was keen to play live again solo – quite a turnaround from the stage fright that had been affecting him so badly during the *Close Encounters* tour of 2006.

The power struggles and quarrels of the early Take That years had mostly dissipated. 'Now it feels a lot more real,' said Jason Orange. 'Sometimes I think we shouldn't have bothered the first time, and just done the comeback.'

A minority of fans were said to have been a little disgruntled that the two factions had made up. 'It's like being angry with Ian Beale off *EastEnders*,' Robbie told the *Guardian*, 'then seeing Adam Woodyatt in the street and going, "You fucking bastard." People have invested into a storyline that fits what they think is happening to me and the lads. It's a bit of a soap opera, innit?'

Did Take That need Robbie back in the end? Perhaps not,

but they – and most of all Gary – *wanted* him: 'I was probably the most desperate out of everyone. It just gives our story a nice end. It's funny that, when it did happen, Robbie was in his own little crisis world. We all kind of helped each other, and that's how it should be.'

Progress had been an aptly titled project. Those involved had reviewed their 20-year career as five men who were thrown together, learned to work and socialise together, then quarrelled a bit, imploded, matured and made up again. Each stage of their career had been a fresh new chapter rather than a tacked-on postscript or desperate sequel. Somehow, they did it with sufficient care and grace that the audience continued to be gripped. Having some songs people cared about helped, too. Also, it was honestly expressing that there had been turbulence along the way that helped the audience stick around. One reason why the Spice Girls and others failed to make the same sort of impact second time around was that they pretended to be in the same roles as in their 90s incarnation. One writer even suggested the Spice Girls on their 2007 tour had become a Spice Girls tribute band. They had hardly developed their sound or character at all.

For Gary, he was always a solid figure in the midst of more changeable forces. He had always been the sensible one, in some eyes the dull one perhaps (in Robbie's rebellious eyes, he represented the dad figure), but the organised one and the focused one. And he had a theory as to why that was: 'Music is all I can do. I can't ever work a till at Sainsbury's, so I've always been the "We have to understand how the music business works" one in the band, because there's nothing else out there for me.'

CHAPTER 23

X-PANDING

From 2000 until 2005 – when Take That made their high profile return – Gary Barlow's life had looked like a sabbatical. He hadn't been in the headlines or granted an interview but he was very much involved in the background of various artists, writing songs and sometimes producing them, too. And the return to the charts of his old band from the mid-noughties did not stop him from working with others.

At Christmas 2008, while *The Circus* album and the 'Greatest Day' single were selling hundreds of thousands of copies, there was the small matter of a novelty single that Gary worked on with comedian Peter Kay. It came about after Kay had made a comic spoof of reality TV shows for Channel 4 with the catchy title of *Britain's Got The Pop Factor And Possibly A New Celebrity Jesus Christ Soapstar Superstar Strictly On Ice*, in which Kay appeared in the guise of contestant Geraldine McQueen. 'Peter called me saying he wanted a song,' Gary told BBC Radio. 'He had all these lyrics – an amalgamation of all *The X Factor* songs – and we wrote it together.' Titled 'The Winner's Song', it was released the same week as a single from the previous year's series winner Leon Jackson. Simon Cowell was unimpressed, branding it 'a pathetic waste of time'.

Gary was songwriter for hire with artists of almost all genres, from classical crossover to R&B. It seemed that everyone from Katherine Jenkins to John Barrowman to N-Dubz was requesting his services. In 2009, he worked with two female popular music icons from different generations.

Alesha Dixon was formerly a member of the all-female R&B group Mis-Teeq. After a false start at a solo career, she won television's *Strictly Come Dancing* in 2007 (later returning to the show as a member of the judging panel). This enabled her to release a second record in her own right, plus hit singles like 'The Boy Does Nothing'. Gary was drafted in to contribute a song called 'To Love Again', the story of how she had recovered from the break-up of her marriage to MC Harvey of So Solid Crew. 'I guess this is Alesha's story in the present,' commented Gary. 'She wrote the lyrics really quickly and they seemed very real. She then went into the vocal booth and killed it. Take after take, she nailed it. She has a contagious personality, a natural musical talent to create and perform.'

Just as 'To Love Again' was unleashed as a single, another of Gary's songs ('This Time') became part of *The Performance*, Dame Shirley Bassey's first album of completely original material in many years. Bassey, by now 72 years old, had been a star for over 50 years. Her collaborators on the record included many of the finest rock and pop songwriters, including Pet Shop Boys, lyricist Don Black, the Kaiser Chiefs, the Manic Street Preachers, KT Tunstall and Richard Hawley, and all produced by David Arnold.

'She's got that massive voice,' Gary said admiringly, 'and I could hear that as I was writing the song. It's impossible not to.' He hadn't sent her a demo. Instead, he performed it in person, which on balance was a far more nerve-wracking option: 'I sat down at the piano and my hands were shaking. Playing in front of an audience is one thing but playing in front of an artist like her... I mean, she's a legend.'

In 2011, he would turn his attention to the BBC's Children in Need charity appeal with a remake of 'Teardrop', the old Massive Attack hit, thanks to the help of Tinie Tempah, producer Labrinth and a whole host of MCs, musicians and producers, from Ed Sheeran, Ms. Dynamite, Tulisa Contostavlos, Rizzle Kicks and Tinchy Stryder. Coincidentally, the track was being made in August of that year, around the time of the rioting that took place in several cities across Britain. 'After the riots, the urban scene didn't get the best respect out of it,' remarked Gary. 'I really believe this song is going to say a lot after what happened and even speak to some of the kids that were involved in the riots.'

'Children in Need is a serious charity doing a lot of hard work for serious causes,' Gary went on. 'It's time to do something with artists who young people actually listen to. Labrinth and his manager have been the key to the whole thing.'

To coincide with the record, there was a concert, 'Children in Need Rocks Manchester', in which David Tennant, Fearne

Cotton and Chris Moyles would introduce JLS, Michael Bublé, Elbow, Coldplay and Lady Gaga.

Gary was always keen to try to encourage new talent. In 2009, he had launched his own record label: Future Records, a subsidiary of Universal, the label that had signed Take That Mark II. He explained that he went out as a talent scout with the group's tour promoter, circulating around the venues in London and sometimes Manchester. Future would be involved in three areas: publishing, management and signing acts to the label. It was not like *The X Factor*, though, he argued. 'I don't want to be Simon Cowell. He goes for people he thinks he can make into something. I try to find people who are already something.' Gary could relate to those who were the latter. He was playing a Nigel Martin-Smith role, looking for the 21st-century equivalents of the clubland Gary Barlow at the end of the 1980s.

Future's clients were an eclectic group of musicians and singers, exactly how Gary wanted it. He didn't want his label to be pigeonholed as making only one kind of music. There was the Brazilian rap star Aggro Santos, who broke through with his 2010 single 'Candy', featuring ex-Pussycat Dolls member Kimberly Wyatt. There was also the Glaswegian busker Emma Gillespie, who under the name Emma's Imagination had won the Sky1 TV talent show *Must Be the Music*. In addition, there was a country blues singer from Merseyside called Delta Maid, a London-based rock trio called Lonsdale Boys Club, the rock soloist Gary Go (one of the support acts on Take That's *Circus* tour of 2009) and the teenage electro-pop singer A*M*E.

Then there was Camilla Kerslake, an operatic singer with a

four-octave range who had bombarded Gary with demo tapes, which included her version of 'Ave Maria'. Once signed to Future in 2009, her debut album included a cover of Take That's 'Rule the World'. 'I had a small amount of classical training as a child,' said Gary, 'and my mother was disappointed I didn't go down that route. Now I've come round to her way of thinking.' A coloratura soprano seemed an unlikely signing, but Gary was entranced by her voice. 'She didn't have that wobbly, operatic sound,' he said. Before long, her singing voice was heard on TV adverts for Waitrose, ironically just as Take That's 'Shine' was plastered all over commercials for another supermarket chain, Morrisons.

Even in the age of the Internet, television still had the power to break a new artist, and Gary was keen to be part of that process, facilitating relatively untapped talent and giving them some kind of platform in front of millions of viewers. Television had been instrumental in breaking Take That in the early 1990s and Gary wanted to do the same with a younger generation of musicians, singers and writers. From 2011, he would join the panel of *The X Factor* on ITV1, but, three years earlier, he was part of the creative team that developed a musical drama series for the station.

Britannia High was set in a performing arts school centred around six talented hopefuls, and was promoted as a cross between Disney's *High School Musical* and the 80s film and TV series *Fame*. Gary was just one of a team of songwriters who submitted material for the series, which would then be choreographed by co-creator Arlene Phillips. To Robbie Williams' reported chagrin, one of the other composers was his estranged writing partner Guy Chambers.

ITV had high hopes for *Britannia High*, especially regarding related merchandise and multimedia platforms. Some of the traditional ways of breaking pop acts – teen press titles such as *Smash Hits* and Saturday-morning children's TV – were now consigned to the past. The nine-part series debuted on Sunday, 26 October 2008, but, despite Barlow's behind-the-scenes involvement, plus scripts from Jonathan Harvey (*Gimme Gimme Gimme*, *Coronation Street*) and cameos from Girls Aloud and Boyzone alumni, it flopped. Critics were merciless. 'No amount of starry-eyed optimism can hide the elephant in this particular dance studio,' groaned the *Guardian*. '*Britannia High* sucks the big one.' Fewer than four million viewers bothered with the first episode, and the numbers tailed off still further. On BBC1 at the same time, the *Antiques Roadshow* was being watched by over 10 million.

Perhaps a year later, with the huge success of the US series *Glee*, it might have done better. As it was, *Britannia High* was closed after just one series. It was an expensive folly, especially with the economic downturn affecting TV budgets.

Television audiences at the weekend had come to regard Gary Barlow and Take That as inevitable special guests on *The X Factor*. Gary had been considered as a potential mentor on the show since 2005, just as Take That reunited but it was only in its ninth series when he joined as a regular. Creator and executive producer Simon Cowell was to leave the judging panel to concentrate on launching the series in the USA, where he would be on the panel. But this did not mean he would not be keeping an eye on the British version he had carefully preserved since its premiere in 2004.

Take That had clashed with Cowell on the 2010 series when

a dance routine for their song 'Kidz' – with the five surrounded by a troupe of dancers dressed as police in riot gear and carrying shields – had been rejected as 'inappropriate' in light of the recent clashes between students and police officers over the government cuts to tuition fees. (Instead, the routine reappeared at the BRIT Awards in early 2011 instead.)

Even so, Gary was a natural choice for *The X Factor*. After all, he had the Midas touch for hit songs, certainly, and he knew all about the struggle towards fame, the success itself, a period of failure and oblivion, and even the redemptive era of the comeback. He had spent years toiling away in northern clubs waiting for recognition, and trying to persuade indifferent clients to listen to his performances. In addition, he had become a talent scout for his own record label, Future Records. His was a logical name.

Gary saw *The X Factor* as a chance to give something back after spending his time with Take That: 'I've spent five years being selfish with the band, so I thought what a good thing it would be to put my time and effort into other people's careers for five months.' After he joined the show, his Grammy Award-winning True North Productions associate Eliot Kennedy also became involved as the show's talent development producer.

The programme's judging panel had always been careful to cast industry figures (Cowell, Louis Walsh) against stars such as Dannii Minogue and Cheryl Cole, names who themselves had been discovered on TV talent shows, and so understood the pressures the competitors might be under. They could relate to what these budding stars of tomorrow might be going through. Gary Barlow, as a highly creative man and someone who as a teenager had taken part in numerous talent competitions, similarly was aware of both sides of the music business. Although Minogue and Cole would both be absent for the first Gary series of *X Factor*, one of the other replacement judges, Kelly Rowland, knew all about talent shows, too. Her former group Destiny's Child had emerged via the American series *Star Search* in the 1990s. Completing the new panel would be Tulisa Contostavlos from N-Dubz.

The auditions for *The X Factor* 2011 began in Birmingham on 1 June. Gary, who was juggling his new commitments with a Take That tour, had one goal, which was 'to find a global superstar'. As with Take That, the programme's quartet of mentors was a mix of personalities, markedly different characters who would all have their own lively and clashing opinions. 'Each of them brings a different attitude,' announced Simon Cowell. 'They have had a ton of hits between them.'

'I think people's perception of me is about to change,' warned Gary Barlow at the start of the series. He sat in the chair Simon had vacated, a significance Louis Walsh hadn't failed to notice. Indeed, he called him 'the new Simon Cowell'. Gary more than played up to the comparison. Whether by accident or deliberately (and the series had always had its pantomimic element), Gary was the new Mr Nasty of *X Factor*. He was blunt, terse and often even rude. And he seemed to know exactly what he was talking about. Like Simon, he was the last of the four judges to speak. As in Take That in the 1990s, Gary was having the last word. He would be flattered to hear auditionees singing songs he had written, but he quickly tired of all the Adele covers, despite being a fan of hers. Everyone wanted to sing 'Someone Like You'. 'This year has been all Adele, we're sick of Adele,' he sighed to one reporter.

The tensions on *The X Factor* could be deliberately orchestrated, contrived to make 'good television' and create headlines. What exactly *was* Louis Walsh playing at, declaring in one interview that Gary should be head judge ('He deserves to be head of the panel. He knows music; he's a master craftsman. I based Boyzone on Take That, so, if it wasn't for Take That, I wouldn't be here today'), but railing against the idea in another: 'After eight years and being the only surviving original judge, on day one Gary stole my head judge mug and sat in Simon's old seat. There's always next year, I suppose.' But everyone understood implicitly that the dullest kind of television would be four judges agreeing with each other and only saying positive things about the acts.

For X *Factor* host Dermot O'Leary, Gary displayed absolute authority as a judge. 'He has got quite an ambassadorial, almost presidential way about him. He speaks so slowly that you do hang on his words. You have to be confident to do that.' But it would not take long for Gary's comments to cause offence and upset. 'It sounded like a drunk singing' was one response of his. Another was 'You're great to watch... with the sound turned down.' He simply told one contender to shut their mouth. In Birmingham, he mistakenly presumed one female contestant to be male. To a self-confident youth who claimed to have matured his voice, he retorted: 'Things "mature" nicely – like a red wine or a cheese. You've matured like a bad curry.'

His outspoken manner startled some of his fellow mentors,

and probably surprised many viewers, too. Was this really the mild-mannered one from Take That? 'I thought I was bad,' said Tulisa, 'but Gary is the shocker. He always speaks his mind. If they are shit, he will tell you.'

But Gary denied being cruel for the sake of it: 'I don't think it's about dashing people's hopes, it's about being real with them. If I've disliked a performance, I've told them I didn't really enjoy it.'

Sometimes he got into trouble with established chart-toppers, too. When finalist Amelia Lily tackled 'China In Your Hand' by 1980s group T'Pau, and he commented, 'It was great to finally hear that song sung in tune', the group's singer Carol Decker was watching the show. She erupted on Twitter: 'Gary Barlow – what's your fucking problem? I actually have perfect pitch... *And* I had to suffer a Take That concert for the sake of my kids this summer.'

On that occasion, Gary retracted his comments and apologised. 'The things we do for our kids!' he quipped back.

There was even a connection to someone from Gary's own past. At the Manchester auditions, the green light was given to a four-piece boyband called The Mend, who just happened to be the latest clients of Nigel Martin-Smith. They didn't get much further on the show, though, as acts were forbidden from having managers – a rule that would be relaxed for the next series.

As the auditions progressed, an unofficial challenge was underway. Whenever the other judges were ready to shed a tear at an emotive showstopper, Gary's eyes would stay resolutely dry. 'That's our mission,' vowed Caroline Flack, a presenter on the ITV2 series spin-off *The Xtra Factor*, 'to make Gary cry.' The man himself calmly hoped for an amazing voice and stage presence.

One critic couldn't help but notice the way Gary sat at a sideways angle, facing the other judges rather than the act itself. 'His strategic deployment of his chair makes contestants feel as if they've burst in on a meeting to which they were not invited.' Could this have been the sort of reception the teenage Gary Barlow got when trying to interest record company bosses and music publishers in his early demo tapes? *The X Factor* was about attracting the attention of the judging panel and holding them in the palm of one's hand. Pulp frontman and radio host Jarvis Cocker tried to avoid the show, but, if he happened to catch it from time to time, he couldn't help but notice one particular Barlow habit: 'I do like Gary Barlow's "It. Was. Absolutely. Fantastic. I am going to keep my head in this position because I have been told I look good on camera like this."'

Bad acts could make 'good television' but sometimes this could topple over into manipulative and cruel television. Take the case of Ceri Rees, a woman in her 50s, who had reputedly been encouraged to audition four times for the programme. In scenes apparently cut from the final edit of the show, she proceeded to be humiliated by the panel, and even after her audition. Gary rifled through her handbag; people in the audience were booing. 'Perhaps they instinctively recognised that a multi-millionaire musician mocking a weak and vulnerable woman is as unedifying a scene as it is possible to imagine,' wrote one *Independent on Sunday* journalist.

Gary was unrepentant about the show's role and denied it was exploitative, though he refused to comment specifically on the Rees case: 'I don't want to single out any one case, but it doesn't matter if you're 90... the show has been on long enough, people know what it is.'

Robbie Williams was quoted as saying he wouldn't want to be an *X Factor* judge full-time. 'I would find it difficult. Who wants to break a 16-year-old's heart?'

As it turned out, Gary agreed with that last point. Rejecting a vocally promising but vulnerable 16-year-old boy from the contest, he was uneasy about how inconsolable the youngster was: 'He is just not ready. I have a responsibility here.' Maybe he was also conscious this was the age Robbie himself had been when joining Take That. 'Sixteen is too young to be in a competition with this kind of pressure. No wonder he cracked.'

The first episode of *The X Factor* to feature Gary, Louis, Tulisa and Kelly aired on ITV1 on Saturday, 20 August 2011. Gary and Louis would consistently be at loggerheads during the run. Louis was always trying to big up the novelty acts – the Jedwards and the Wagners, who divided viewers most drastically. Gary was a purist. He really was trying to find talent above all else, but, as Louis tended to argue, that doesn't always make for gripping TV: 'Gary doesn't get the novelty value of some acts that I'd get, or Simon would get. Simon and I like these odd people, because that's what makes the show. This is a television show. It ends up being a talent show but at the start of it, to get people in, you need big personalities.'

It wasn't just the singers who were competing against each other: so too were the four judges. Louis Walsh would be taking care of the Over-25s, Tulisa was to oversee the Groups category, Kelly would encourage the Girls, and Gary the Boys. His biggest hope was an 18-year-old from Brighton, who had tons of personality but signs of recklessness, too. 'I'm mental. I want to be famous. I want to sleep with as many women as possible,' announced Frankie Cocozza. He seemed an unlikely fit for the sensible, thoughtful Barlow, but he put him through regardless – perhaps because this was a surprising decision in itself.

After the auditions, Gary took the successful eight finalists off to Los Angeles for the next stage of the competition, where they would perform for him and guest mentor Robbie Williams. Gary told the hopefuls that LA had been important to him during the bad times of his career, when RCA had dumped him as a solo artist: 'When I lost my record deal I didn't know what to do. So I came to LA to start again and to think about everything. Being here took me back to the music, which is what it has always been about. This town is full of music, and I hope you find yourselves in the same way that I did.'

Choosing Robbie to partner him on the show was an inspired move. They remained polar opposites in terms of personality, but they were now firm friends. Giving additional advice was Marjorie Barlow, Gary's mum, whom he knew represented the viewer at home: 'She is in my ear about who she wants. That's what this show is about. It is an opinion, it is all about people at home thinking they are the football manager and can do better.'

In November, Frankie Cocozza left the programme after his behaviour spiralled out of control and broke the rules of the competition. Despite having limited talent – Louis had branded his act 'bad karaoke' – he had remained in the competition due to sheer spectacle, but boasting backstage about a night of sex and drugs (and there was no evidence such a night even happened) was deemed too much. The show's producers knew that good television came from having unlikely, quirky and even shocking acts, not just able singers. Gary felt partly but not exclusively responsible for Frankie's fate and cited the lad's young age as a contributory factor: 'We all played our part. None of us is guilt-free. He's wasted an opportunity, but he's an 18-year-old boy. I'm the only judge with children. He's been stupid, he broke the rules, but he's got to live with this and that's where I feel slightly bad. In our own ways we've all encouraged Frankie not only to be good, but to be bad.'

Frankie was gone, but, regardless, Gary had a tip for the top: Marcus Collins, a 23-year-old hairdresser from Crosby, near Liverpool. In the final, the pair sang Billy Joel's 'She's Always A Woman', and though he was narrowly beaten in the grand final by Tulisa's discovery – an all-female vocal quartet called Rhythmix, who eventually became known as Little Mix – Marcus seemed likely to get a record deal anyway. 'Marcus has got an old-school vocal,' said Gary, who foresaw a possible album as being in the vein of an Alicia Keys or John Legend type of project. Indeed, he became executive producer of the album, which featured a poppy cover of The White Stripes' 'Seven Nation Army'.

Traditionally, *X Factor* finalists had to wait nearly a year for an album to come out, but Marcus Collins' debut was completed in ten weeks and was out only three months after the final, while people still had him on their minds. 'Because people do forget – even the winners, they forget them,' insisted Gary. In fact, when Gary signed up to become involved in the show, he insisted on having some say in what happened to his discoveries: 'Right from when I was first asked, I said, "I've got to have access to the acts afterwards."'

Despite the panel revamp of 2011, with three out of the four mentors being replaced, some felt that *The X Factor* was starting to run out of steam. That year's final had been watched by four million fewer viewers than the 17 million audience of 2010. Simon Cowell was said to be undecided about whether Gary Barlow would return to the show for a second series, but ITV were keen to keep him in the frame and indeed he received a pay increase of around £500,000. People had assumed Cowell would be irreplaceable on the judging panel, but Gary had well and truly proven himself. 'Gary quickly established himself as a key member of the panel,' said ITV's director of programmes Peter Fincham, 'drawing on his years of experience in the music industry.'

For his second year on *The X Factor* in 2012, Gary had perhaps the hardest category: the Over-25s, which had unearthed Olly Murs as a finalist in 2009, but otherwise had not spawned a winner since Steve Brookstein won the first series way back in 2004. It was in the Over-25s category that the novelty acts tended to appear (Wagner Carrilho and Johnny Robinson), the sort of acts Gary tended to dislike. Nicole Scherzinger from the Pussycat Dolls had joined from the US version of the show to replace panellist Kelly Rowland. Gary's main find was Christopher Maloney, a 30-something singer from Merseyside.

Why did Gary Barlow agree to commit to *The X Factor*? He would soon admit it was an intense experience, especially in the glare of social media, where absolutely every comment, response and gesture would be analysed on Facebook and Twitter. 'Everyone has got an opinion. You can never say the right thing. This show doesn't end on a Sunday night,' he told the *Daily Mirror*. 'It follows you around all week.' And he confessed to feeling uneasy at not being in control of a project.

But ultimately he took part because he wanted to entertain his children, who expressed no great enthusiasm for his day job as a pop star or songwriter: 'My son sits playing Nintendo all the way through my concerts. But being a judge on *The X Factor*, they loved it. It's so seldom your kids engage with what you're doing work-wise.' He also claimed to have jumped at the chance precisely because he didn't really need to do it. 'People go on these panels to improve their career, or they've got something coming out. I don't have to go. All the reasons someone would do this – the money, to become more famous – I've got them already. I've joined just because I wanted to.'

CHAPTER 24

BY
APPOINTMENT

Gary Barlow's involvement in a television vehicle like *The X Factor* had made him a recognisable face, but, while it was an entertainment show, he participated in it to help find new musical talent. It was his urge to spot and nurture the stars of the future, plus his skills for organisation in charity events such as Comic Relief that led to other important work from 2010 onwards. He was sought out by the Establishment, by the British Royal Family and by the world of politics.

Gary had rarely made any overt political statements in his 20 years as a famous singer, either when being interviewed or in his songs. As early as 1996, rumours that he was a Conservative Party supporter were circulating in the press. 'There has been talk that Gary Barlow has right leanings,' suggested *The Times* in December that year, just as some of the Spice Girls were quoted in *The Spectator* as backing the

Tories. 'Thatcher was the first Spice Girl, the pioneer of Girl Power,' declared Geri. 'The Spice Girls are profoundly suspicious of Europe,' warned Victoria. 'All those countries look the same. Only England looks different.'

The Spice Girls' pronouncements came less than six months before a hotly contested General Election. When Labour Party leader Tony Blair defeated the Conservative Party's John Major to become British Prime Minister on 2 May 1997, much was made of the fact that, while at university in the 1970s, Blair had briefly sung and played guitar in a rock band called Ugly Rumours. Many bands had offered vocal support to Labour during the 1980s and 90s, but rock'n'roll's relationship with the Conservative Party had been much more guarded. It was the party of light entertainment – its list of celebrity supporters traditionally included Jimmy Tarbuck and Cilla Black, though a few rock stars like Bill Wyman of the Rolling Stones and Phil Collins were there, too.

If quizzed about politics, Gary Barlow erred on the side of caution, at least in his 20s. 'It frightens me when people write about politics in their records,' he told the *Independent* newspaper in 1998. 'A lot of young people are smart, but a lot of them aren't. There's been a lot to answer for that sort of thing.' It was not clear here if he was referring to young people in bands or young voters.

Increasingly, it wouldn't do for politicians to be seen as out-of-touch with younger voters. After Margaret Thatcher and John Major, who had shown little or no interest in pop music, the Blair administration had tried to align itself much more closely with youth, a tactic that the Tories tried to replicate during 13 years in opposition from 1997. David

Cameron was only 39 years old when he was appointed Tory leader at the end of 2005. When asked what sort of music he liked, he cited guitar bands like Radiohead, The Smiths and R.E.M. – along with Benny Hill's 'Ernie' to show that he had a sense of humour.

In 2009, when the prospect of a General Election was a few months away and Cameron was trying to court pop's finest to align themselves with his party in the campaign, Gary Barlow's name was mentioned again as someone who might endorse the Tories. But one of his spokesmen was quoted in *The Times* as saying, 'He wouldn't be interested in doing it.' In fact, very few pop stars were prepared to declare their voting preference. Doing so risked losing some of their audience and record sales. It wasn't as if musicians needed to be associated with political figures.

But the world of politics needed musicians and singers to be seen to give its leaders some credibility. Cameron's director of communications at the time was Andy Coulson, a former gossip columnist who at the *Sun* in the 1990s had regularly covered Take That's exploits. Coulson told all Tory frontbench MPs to inform him of any celebrity who was likely to endorse the party in the 2010 election campaign. The reward was a dinner with Jeremy Hunt, at the time the Shadow Culture Secretary. One Conservative figure was quoted as saying: 'Mainstream trumps trendy. We'd rather a Gary Barlow or Jamie Cullum than Razorlight.'

Cameron had had dinner with Simon Cowell and had been trying to drum up a word or two of support from Lily Allen, but there was no official word from the Take That star. That changed just three weeks before the election. In April 2010,

Gary publicly endorsed the Tory leader. The two met in the Cheshire town of Nantwich, on Cameron's campaign trail, at the launch of an *X Factor*-esque inter-school singing contest called the 'School Stars' competition, which aimed to back musical achievement in young people. When asked if this meant he was backing the Tory leader, Gary responded: 'I wouldn't be here if I wasn't', though he was careful to stress that his reasons for attending concerned music, not politics.

After Gary sang 'Greatest Day' at the School Stars launch, accompanied by a crowd of schoolchildren, the Tory leader said he found the sentiment of the song uplifting: 'When you feel down and depressed, it's great.' It was clear, though, that most of the excitable reception from the children was aimed at the pop star, not the politician. School Stars was to be introduced if the Conservatives won the election, with the first prize being the chance to record with Gary. While the Tories didn't win on 6 May, they were able to form a coalition government with the help of the Liberal Democrats. At the time of writing, little more has been heard of the School Stars project, leading some to dismiss the idea as a political campaign gimmick.

London would be the setting for the 2012 Summer Olympic Games, and Take That would be involved, as one of the many acts to take part in the Closing Ceremony. The show would be directed by Kim Gavin, producer of many a Take That tour over the years. Before that, though, in May 2012, Gary would headline a special preview performance at the Royal Albert Hall to honour Team GB. 'It will play such a crucial role in providing our athletes with the best preparation,' he said.

'This is the moment for the entire nation to rise up and unite in its support for Our Greatest Team.'

But, as 2012 dawned, Gary had been given another responsibility. It was reported that he had been given the royal seal of approval. He had been chosen to organise the pop concert that summer for Queen Elizabeth II's Diamond Jubilee. Her Majesty's 60 years on the throne would make her, apart from Queen Victoria (who reigned for 64 years), the longest-serving British monarch in history. The event would be staged in early June on the Victoria Memorial in front of London's Buckingham Palace. Around 250,000 people were expected to cram into the Mall, but crowds would also be watching from nearby Green Park and St James's Park.

It was a great honour for Gary. He had always been delighted to perform at royal occasions. From 1992, when he turned up with the rest of Take That for the Children's Royal Variety Performance in front of Princess Margaret, to 2012 at the Queen's Diamond Jubilee celebration, he was an avid supporter of the monarchy. Along the way he had joined the great and the good of showbiz at Windsor Castle bashes and appeared in many Prince's Trust charity concerts.

In December 2011, he played two fund-raising shows for the Prince's Trust as a solo artist at the Royal Albert Hall. It was a mix of Take That favourites old and new, plus a medley of Rat Pack classics and even an effective reading of Van Morrison's 'Moondance'. Finally, he performed a series of duets with Lulu (the usual), Olly Murs ('Shine') and Jason Donovan on the Australian's 1989 hit 'Too Many Broken Hearts'. There was a mild ripple of booing when Robbie Williams' name was mentioned, but Gary shushed them.

'None of that, it's Christmas!' When he greeted Prince Charles and the Duchess of Cornwall with the words 'I hope you enjoy tonight and I hope it's not too loud', he was assured, 'The louder the better' from Prince William, who was present with Kate Middleton, his wife of seven months.

William and Kate's Royal Wedding in April 2011 had received much worldwide attention, and the same was likely to be true of the Diamond Jubilee celebration. Television stations around the globe would be broadcasting proceedings as they took place. In Britain, BBC1 and BBC Radio 2 would clear their usual Monday-night schedules to cover the entire concert live.

Gary approached many music legends. Big names quickly secured included the titled, such as Sir Paul McCartney, Sir Elton John, Sir Tom Jones, Dame Shirley Bassey and Sir Cliff Richard, along with Annie Lennox, plus the pop-ska giants Madness (who would perform on the roof of Buckingham Palace). Current chart stars like JLS, Jessie J, Adele and Ed Sheeran were booked, too. The aim was to feature all the greats from seven decades of popular music, from the 1950s to the 2010s, as 2012 also just happened to be the 60th anniversary of the first-ever singles chart. There would be something for everyone (Princes William and Harry were said to have requested P. Diddy and Kanye West), though maybe Her Majesty might not stay for everything. 'There's points of the gig where the Queen's watching the show, and points where she isn't,' Gary explained. 'So there's a point where something quite modern would happen, which I know the Queen wouldn't be in her seat for, so we'll get away with it. It's quite strategic!'

But it wouldn't just be a pop concert: classical stars like the English tenor Alfie Boe and Chinese piano virtuoso Lang Lang would also perform. Before long, Robbie Williams was added to the bill. Everyone was ordered to keep things cheerful, positive and short. 'They've said it needs to be happy and uplifting music,' reported Sir Cliff Richard, whose set would include his 1968 number one hit 'Congratulations'. 'We have six minutes each.'

Gary was six years old when HM the Queen had celebrated her Silver Jubilee in the summer of 1977. He wanted to try to make the Diamond Jubilee occasion as inclusive as possible: 'We're trying to make this concert all-encompassing for everyone involved. That's why I was so keen on moving it out of the back of the Palace, and out the front.' While he had enjoyed the Golden Jubilee of 2002, he felt things could be improved upon. 'It did feel like the gates were closed and no one could get in without an invite. I wanted this to feel like the People's Concert – so that anyone could just get on a train to London, and turn up and watch the gig.' But it had taken time to get permission to use the space as a concert venue. 'It took five months because we had to go to the council and the police first. The Queen couldn't just approve it as the memorial is on a public road.'

When most pop fans now think of a record associated with the 1977 Jubilee, they tend to recall a song that, ironically, was banned at the time by all media outlets. Aside from one play on a BBC local radio station in London, the Sex Pistols' 'God Save the Queen' had been completely excluded from public broadcast. Though misunderstood as an attack on Her Majesty rather than a sardonic commentary on the royalty industry and the complacency of Britain, the single was the height of irreverence. Despite, or maybe even because of, the ban the song reached the number two position in the charts.

Thirty-five years later, Gary Barlow had a reverent, respectful anthem in mind, one that could hardly have been further from the minds and attitudes of Johnny Rotten & Co. He had been commissioned to compose a song in honour of the Jubilee, and so had teamed up with Andrew Lloyd Webber to dream up a song that could unite not just Britain but the whole of the Commonwealth.

Originally, the duo planned to record a song in the UK with the Royal Philharmonic Orchestra, only to be advised by the Prince of Wales that whatever they did should have as international a flavour as possible. According to Gary, Prince Charles had said, 'If you really want the Queen to like this, find people; go and travel and find people.' And so, Gary and collaborator Eliot Kennedy would travel the world in March and April 2012 on a journey that would be his biggest musical challenge to date. Gary, who had recorded so many songs in his home studio, would visit far-flung locations in the Caribbean, Africa, the islands of the Pacific Ocean and Australia. His trip would be recorded in a BBC television documentary called *On Her Majesty's Service*. This would be an entirely positive view of the monarch: it transpired that the visit to Australia would not feature an interview with its Prime Minister, Julia Gillard, as she was 'pro-republican'.

The concept of the new song was to combine international musical icons with members of the public, uniting both groups in the power of song. In Jamaica, they met reggae legend Bob Marley's widow Rita, who helped them to find suitable musicians. They were stranded in the Solomon Islands in the Pacific Ocean when tropical storms arrived. But the biggest problem was integrating the sound of bagpipes, a favourite instrument of the Queen. 'You either love or hate bagpipes,' said Gary, 'and the Queen loves them. In Australia, someone said they found me some pipers in Canberra. They had been trained by Scots and I thought it was fascinating that we were in the middle of Australia with a bagpipe orchestra, so we shoehorned them in at the end of the track.'

Gary and Eliot had travelled light, technology-wise. All they had brought with them for their global trip was a laptop and a hand-held recording device. The lyrics were written by Gary in Treetops, the location in Kenya where Princess Elizabeth had been staying in early 1952 when she learned of the death of her father King George VI, and discovered that, at the age of 25, she would succeed him as monarch.

On 21 April 2012, Gary joined Andrew Lloyd Webber at his mansion in Berkshire to perform 'Happy Birthday' to the Queen on her 86th birthday. Just over a fortnight later, on 8 May, the three met again – this time at Windsor Castle, where Barlow and Lloyd Webber presented her with the very first performance of their completed song. 'Sing' was a celebration of the Queen's commitment to the Commonwealth. With a simple six-note motif throughout, which almost anyone could emulate, the composers hoped that people would not just buy the track when it was released, but would also download the sheet music at no cost, to learn it in time for the June celebrations. Schools, colleges, choirs and all those attending street parties were encouraged to learn the new song. It had a very simple message – the power of song as a universal force of expression, no matter what language or culture. Yet it still sounded a bit like a Take That song.

Gary also explained the line-up, plans and logistics of the concert, but soon discovered that the Queen had a couple of awkward questions. 'She said, "So all that equipment, how long is it going to take to dismantle?" At this point I'm guessing, so I say "About six or seven hours", and she said, "So, the concert finishes at half-ten at night, which means you will be doing that all night at the front of the palace where my family lives."' Trying to change the subject, Gary showed the Queen the plans for where the Royal Box would be situated. 'She said, "How am I going to get there?" It was something else I didn't know the answer to!'

'Sing' was released on 28 May 2012. Over 200 people played on it, as well as featuring vocals from Gareth Malone's Military Wives choir, percussion courtesy of players from Kenya (called the Slum Drummers) and the Solomon Islands Police Force Band, and the indigenous Australian guitarist Gurrumul. Plus, it was the first ever hit single to feature a specially recorded member of the Royal Family. Prince Harry was first invited to sing on the track when he met Gary in Jamaica. He declined, but agreed to play tambourine instead. Even there, as Gary acknowledged, the Prince showed very little innate musical talent. 'Prince Harry was pretty sure that we weren't going to use it,' said Eliot Kennedy, 'but we have. It's in the track – I've actually put it in myself.'

For the Jubilee concert on 4 June, some of the contributors on 'Sing' were being flown in to help perform it live, like the Slum Drummers from Kenya, and the Kenyan Children's

Choir. Having performed a tepid duet with Cheryl Cole (a cover of Lady Antebellum's "Need You Now") earlier in the show, Gary redeemed himself; the collective's airing of 'Sing' was stirring and moving. The concert in general was regarded as a great success and, unlike the royal pageant along the River Thames the day before, was not washed out with torrential rain and gale-force winds. Unfortunately, the Queen's 91-year-old husband, Prince Philip, the Duke of Edinburgh, could not attend the concert. He was hospitalised with a bladder infection just hours before it began.

Gary felt honoured to have been entrusted with co-writing a song and organising a concert for HM the Queen, whom he had first met in 1995 for 'an arts do with about 100 people and I got my 30 seconds'. He was unquestionably a royalist and a patriot. 'It's easy to knock the royals,' he said, 'but I love 'em. I've so much respect for what the Queen's achieved. This country is my home. I bloody love it here and, in many ways, she's responsible for that. We won't see another king or queen like her. Not in my lifetime!'

Just days after the Diamond Jubilee concert, it was reported that Gary Barlow was one of the names in the Queen's Birthday Honours List for 2012. He was to receive the Order of the British Empire for services to the entertainment industry and to charity, in a list that also included OBEs for choirmaster Gareth Malone (who had assembled the Military Wives), the actor Jenny Agutter and the comic colossus Armando Iannucci. 'I'm absolutely thrilled,' said Gary. 'I enjoy every minute of the work I do, with a lot of it being a reward in itself, so for somebody to decide I should get recognised for that is just amazing.'

When he was awarded his honour in person at Buckingham Palace on 21 November 2012, it capped one of the most eventful years of his life so far.

CHAPTER 25

SINCE I SAW YOU LAST

When Gary Barlow went off to work on *The X Factor* in late 2011, Take That's future seemed uncertain. It marked the start of a hiatus for the group, one that would last at least 18 months, although relations remained positive between the five of them. While Mark set about making another solo record, Robbie (as had always been suggested) was also going solo again, although this time on infinitely better terms than in 1995. 'It ended perfectly,' Gary told the *Radio Times* of the one-off Take That record and live tour. 'And we can revisit it whenever we want. He's our brother, and if he's ever in trouble or he wants to have a year off being Robbie Williams, he's welcome any time he wants.'

Robbie was the biggest-selling homegrown male soloist in British music, with an estimated 60 million records sold, so, when he signed a new recording contract, it was big news. At the end of 2011, he signed with Universal Music, meaning he was now on the same label as Take That. Indeed, Gary would be collaborating with him on a new album. 'Gaz is great for me because he knows how I should sound,' Robbie told *Esquire* magazine. 'He wanted to make a Lennon and McCartney-type album. At the minute it's just me and him finishing the album and I love it.'

Two songs on what became the *Take the Crown* album were Barlow/Williams co-writes. One was 'Candy', released as a single in October 2012, just as Robbie became a dad for the first time. 'Some songs take an age to write,' he said, 'and some songs just fall out of your mouth completely formed, and you don't have to think about it.' 'Candy', with an almost infuriatingly catchy tune, was close to a novelty record. Robbie's self-deprecation, laced with insecurity, had never been too far away: 'I can do a number one, but you know, "Agadoo" [the Black Lace novelty hit of the 1980s] was a number one. Any piece of praise that comes along, I know how to shit on it.'

At least by 2012, he had made peace with Gary Barlow. Both of them had 14 number one singles. They were still in competition, but at least it was healthy competition.

Now in his 40s, Gary was still driven by work and activity but had realised that, while showbusiness could be hard graft, it was all relative. 'My brother's a builder,' he said of Ian, 'and he works much harder than I do. Here I am, still able to enjoy music, still able to be involved in it – that's a feat on its own in this industry.'

Gary had known what it was like to not have a professional purpose. Ten years before, he had no recording contract and, for a time, no one even seemed interested in his songwriting skills. He had enough money to provide for his family, but he still needed to contribute in some way; he needed a role of some kind. 'It wasn't not being famous any more, or even not being a recording artist: it was having nobody who needed me, no phones ringing, nothing to do. Now, I feel I've got more to give than I ever have.'

Those around him defended his commitment to hard work, essentially because he enjoyed it so much. For his 40th birthday in January 2011, he had celebrated by performing a special charity concert in London. 'It sounds very egotistical having a gig for my birthday, but my wife said, "What do you want to do? You should do what you really want to do on your birthday." I do love going on stage and singing.'

But his family remained his number one priority, especially when any crisis or tragedy occurred. On 15 October 2009, while preparing to launch the BBC's Children in Need charity appeal, he received the news that his father Colin had died, apparently of a heart attack, at the age of 71. Gary immediately cancelled his appearance and raced back to Cheshire, where his mother Marge and brother Ian still lived. 'Grief is more than the loss of a person,' Gary told the *Observer* two years after the tragedy. 'It's the realisation of who you now are: you're next. That crown is yours now.'

Similarly, in early August 2012, when Dawn went into labour with their fourth child, it was to everyone's great sadness when the baby girl they had named Poppy was delivered stillborn. Gary cancelled all engagements for the next month, except for the London Olympics Closing Ceremony on 12 August, at which Take That performed

'Greatest Day'. His *X Factor* duties were also put on hold. He had been scheduled to mentor acts on the Mediterranean island of Mallorca, but he stayed with Dawn, and an alternative venue in Northamptonshire was chosen, so that Gary wasn't too far away from her and the rest of their family.

In happier family news, daughter Emily had followed her parents' footsteps into the world of entertainment. From a young age, she had sat with Gary at the piano, where they would sing along to favourite tunes from the *Oliver!* or *Annie* songbooks. When she was nine, in 2011, she was cast as a munchkin called Jan in a West End stage production at the London Palladium of *The Wizard of Oz*, starring Michael Crawford. In Gary's 'wilderness' years, he had been able to shield his young children from the stresses and strains of pop stardom. Songwriters don't tend to be relentlessly pursued by the paparazzi but he knew that things were now changing with the re-emergence of Take That.

As his children were growing up, Gary was increasingly aware of how the entertainment world, more aggressively marketed than when he had been young, was targeting youngsters. He had rarely used his music to be provocative and was concerned about the content of some mainstream music videos. 'Music videos are so sexual these days,' he said. 'We had girls auditioning for *The X Factor* and you wouldn't believe the kind of moves they were doing.'

For a time after its 2012 series, it seemed unlikely that Gary would return for a third run of *The X Factor*. As mentor for the Over-25s category – which was always the toughest one to sell to the public – he had found it hard to have his acts taken seriously enough. His tips for the top in his second series on the panel had included the promising Glaswegian Melanie Masson, who had auditioned with a barnstorming version of Janis Joplin's 'Cry Baby', and 34-year-old Christopher Maloney, a former cruise-ship crooner from Liverpool – an act that divided the audience and the panel but made it to the final three of the series. After rows behind the scenes, Maloney abruptly left the show on the eve of the series final.

'I have enjoyed this series more than last year,' Gary said, 'but the show feels like it has been going on for a year this time.' He stressed he had enjoyed every minute of the experience, but a statement issued at the end of the 2012 series suggested he was ready to move on. 'He feels his integrity has been compromised,' it read, 'and the show has lost its credibility.' There had also been claims that Gary's putdowns had been scripted, along with reports that he had fallen out with Simon Cowell, said to have been furious that ITV had signed Gary up to a second series without consulting him. Yet in March 2013, Gary was confirmed for one more year on the show, after fellow judge Louis Walsh had reportedly said he would only sign again as a judge if Cowell agreed to take Gary back as well.

The Gary Barlow diary looked busier than ever but something had to give. It had been announced at the end of 2012 that his record label, Future Records, would be closing after three years in operation. Soprano Camilla Kerslake had done well with her first album, which reached number four in the classical album charts, but Future's pop acts had failed to take off. As the roster of artists was taken over by parent company Universal, it was said that Future had made a loss of £4 million. Maybe the label's fortunes would have recovered, had Barlow signed one particularly promising young singer. 'Emeli played for Gary Barlow when he had his label,' Sandé's collaborator Naughty Boy would claim in early 2013. 'I watched as she sang "Clown". He listened and said that he didn't think she was a star.' Former medical student Emeli Sandé would have the last laugh. She was snapped up by Virgin Records, and her debut album *Our Version of Events* became the UK's best seller of 2012. At least Gary had spotted chart-topping talent along the way, though: in April 2013, 18-year-old ex-Future signing Aminata Kabba would reach number one with Duke Dumont on 'Need U (100%)'.

Gary himself began 2013 with a live entertainment special for ITV called *Gary Barlow and Friends*, featuring special guests Peter Kay and James Corden, and made a cameo appearance in Miranda Hart's BBC TV sitcom *Miranda*. Then he set off on his first solo tour of the UK since his ill-fated undersold jaunt of 1999. At one point in the set, which contained material gathered from all phases of his 20-year career (everything from 'A Million Love Songs' and 'Pray' to 'Rule the World' and 'Sing'), he self-deprecatingly joked about a career low. 'Twelve Months, Eleven Days was very successful,' he deadpanned to his live audience. 'Listen, worldwide that album sold 15 copies! If anyone wants one, I have got a double garage full of those things.' An intimate affair, performing live as a solo act felt natural again. 'I know what the audience love now, what makes a great show,' he said. 'I can do this when I want to now, and I hope to always do it.'

The spring found him collaborating with former Abba singer Agnetha Fältskog, as part of an album called *A*, her first solo recordings in nearly a decade. Titled 'I Should've Followed You Home', the song had been written by Gary himself, but the pair had separately recorded their parts for the duet. 'It's a shame we weren't in the studio at the same time,' Agnetha commented. 'His vocals were so strong I did worry, "How am I going to match this?" But I love the end result. Our voices work so well together.' The two would finally meet during the filming of a TV profile of Agnetha called *Abba and After*, and in November 2013 Agnetha would make a live comeback at the 2013 Children in Need Rocks concert, once again curated by Barlow. It was her first appearance on stage in 25 years. At the same event, Gary and Robbie Williams would perform 'Could It Be Magic' with the song's original hitmaker, Barry Manilow.

*

By his own admission, Gary had tended to shy away from overtly confessional songs in the old days, partly because of how close he felt to them. 'I prefer to write about things rather than people,' he once said, 'because I get really hurt when people, like producers, start fiddling with them, or criticise them. I'm like, "How dare you say that?! Don't you realise that this is about my best friend?!' In Take That, the output became more personal in tone when Mark, Jason, Howard and Robbie came on board as fellow songwriters. Gary generally believed music was still primarily entertainment – 'My theory is that it's for people to enjoy. I don't really see how anyone can enjoy depressing music' – yet a return to solo recording would transmit his most intimate musical thoughts to date.

Since I Saw You Last, released in November 2013, was the first Gary Barlow album since 1999. Its title seemed less portentous than its predecessor, *Twelve Months, Eleven Days* – indeed, its friendly tone brought to mind a sort of round robin letter – and it was almost guaranteed to sell better (admittedly, not difficult). If he had detractors who had a strong dislike for what he now represented – whether that was to do with his role on *The X Factor*, or his political and royalist leanings, or simply the music itself – there were many others who were likely to buy his new record.

In terms of musical development, Take That's *Progress* album had been the most adventurous record so far with Barlow's name on it. In contrast, *Since I Saw You Last* seemed musically tamer. It was a record that seemed tailor-made for the mainstream of BBC Radio 2, and Gary conceded that it would be an unlikely fit for the more cutting-edge stations. 'I don't hope to make the Radio 1 playlist. It's not my demographic. Radio 1 is for young artists and I don't want to take their place.'

The new album superficially shared the streamlined, slick arrangements of his late 1990s solo output. But back then, he arguably had too many collaborators, and too many producers. This time round, he would be mostly writing alone, with a few exceptions here and there: the ever-reliable John Shanks, Robbie Williams again (for its opening track, 'Requiem') and Keane's Tim Rice-Oxley (for 'Jump', a paean to self-motivation).

Scaling back on collaborators mirrored the album's lyrical content, which was comfortably his most autobiographical to date. Often painfully honest about the trials and tribulations of Barlow's wilderness years in the early noughties (see 'Since I Saw You Last' itself for details), it was also a litany of thank yous. Wife Dawn and his family were serenaded via the closing track, 'More Than Life'. Meanwhile, 'Face to Face', featuring Sir Elton John, was a tribute to how Elton had continued to act as a supportive friend to Gary even in the dark days of 2000–5 when no one else in entertainment seemed interested. 'It's a respect song,' said Gary. 'I can count on the fingers of one hand the people who kept in touch with me when nobody else wanted to know me and he was one of them. I'll never forget that.' The pair had known each other for 20 years, but they only had limited time to put together the duet. 'I had him for three hours in Abbey Road studios before he went off for a Watford game,' said Gary, 'so we had to record the song and shoot the video at the same time.'

Elsewhere, there were some misfires – 'Small Town Girls' and 'This House' were a pair of twee sore thumbs – but the best results came via the darker stuff. 'Since I Saw You Last' was candid about the trials and tribulations of his wilderness years. The devastating 'Dying Inside' concerned itself with his anguished feelings about the loss of his daughter Poppy, a level of emotional honesty which came out of harrowing source material. He confessed to the *Daily Telegraph* it was a risk to include it. 'It comes with a government health warning. That's such a depressing song, it was on and off the album. But most people have at some point got to pick themselves up – you've got to turn up for work and get on with it.'

Overall, the directness of the lyrical content, coupled with the autobiographical dimension, gave the songs an emotional honesty that had been lacking in his earlier solo output. Here he dared to tackle some of his innermost feelings, and the record was without doubt an improvement on his previous two albums. Some critics, though, remained suspicious. 'A certain middle-England dowdiness stubbornly clings to him,' wrote Alexis Petridis in *The Guardian*. 'He has the air of a man who might well own a pair of driving gloves.'

Perhaps the most unusual song was the one that opened proceedings. 'Requiem', co-written – as we've established – with Robbie Williams, was a far cry from their daffy, silly creation,

'Candy'. Filtered through pastiches of The Beach Boys, Paul McCartney and ELO, it was a wry and irreverent song, Gary in the afterlife eavesdropping on eulogies from friends at his funeral: 'I'm in heaven, imagine my surprise!' (Gary had simultaneously helped out on a song for Robbie's new album *Swings Both Ways*, which took the form of a big-band pastiche called 'Wedding Bells'.)

If difficult life experience had fed a lot of the album's themes, Gary insisted actually making the record had been relatively easy. 'The one thing I was dreading was that the last album would be on my shoulder the whole time I made this one. But it wasn't. I'm not haunted by that time. My experience 14 years ago was completely different to now. Back then I had a lot of people trying to change me. This time, I don't know it all, but I know what I want to say.'

Since I Saw You Last was released in late November 2013. 'I had to do this record,' he said. 'I can't go all through my life and never do something by myself again.' And if it didn't match the huge sales of Take That, so be it. 'This is going to sound wrong,' he told the London *Evening Standard*, 'but I couldn't care less. I'm not looking to sell 10 million albums.'

Ahead of the album came a single, namely 'Let Me Go'. Many could not help but notice a new influence on Gary Barlow – the folk-rock of Mumford & Sons – but he insisted that the inspiration for it came from elsewhere. 'I was listening to Johnny Cash. I've always liked folky, acoustic music but I've never fully explored it. I love Mumford & Sons. It's good, English music, but let's be honest, they got it off Johnny Cash too.' Folk, country and their roots would colour the making of the entire album. 'The whole folk tempo felt right. It is a very good backdrop to write something quite negative over. I realised I could get away with some really dark lyrics and it unlocked the whole album for me.' Given a great deal of media exposure, 'Let Me Go' was confidently expected to be Gary's fifteenth number-one hit in the UK, but even though it climbed as high as number two in early December 2013, it could not surpass number one hits by Calvin Harris and Lily Allen.

The *Since I Saw You Last* album would also fail to top the charts, although it was competing head on with a new long-awaited One Direction album. Gary's effort would sell 116,000 copies in its first week on sale, and even though it only came out six weeks before the end of the year, only eight albums outsold it in the whole of 2013: 1D, Emeli Sandé, Michael Bublé, Robbie Williams, Olly Murs, Bruno Mars, Rod Stewart and The Arctic Monkeys. A two-week 'Since I Saw You Last' tour in spring 2014 would confirm Barlow as an artist with traditional values when it came to entertainment. Thirty years earlier, his teenage-self had been part of the last generation of social club entertainment. 'People would scowl at this young lad with blond spiky hair,' he reflected. 'But I loved winning them around. That was my apprenticeship. So when I go on tour and I have two hours to take an audience on a journey, where you have them going crazy at the beginning, you make them cry a bit in the middle and then you have them happy at the end. That to me is a lost art.'

The *Since I Saw You Last* album had been released just as Gary prepared to say farewell to *The X Factor* after three series. He said he had been persuaded to return for a third year on the grounds that his children were such big fans. 'My kids love the show and wanted me to do it again. It is addictive.' But it was undoubtedly hard work, long hours and relentless. 'It does get on your nerves. For three months, you cannot escape from it wherever you are.'

For Gary's final series, he and Louis Walsh were joined on the judging panel by Nicole Scherzinger of the Pussycat Dolls and – making a comeback – Sharon Osbourne. 'She has had a positive effect on everybody,' Gary said of Sharon. 'When you bring someone new in, it transforms the vibe of the whole show. For the first time ever I'm really looking forward to live shows because it's going to be a hoot.'

This time, Gary was mentor in the Groups category, but only a few weeks into the live show rounds, and while praising one of his favoured acts, Rough Copy, he casually let slip on live TV that he would be moving on. 'I'm so glad for my last year on the show I get to mentor you,' he said. He would later explain that his busy commitments for 2014 made further involvement in the show impossible. '*The X Factor* is a full time job,' he said, 'so it felt like the right time to hand over the baton.' Rough Copy were Gary's most successful competitors, but only finished in fourth place, just short of the December grand final, where Sam Bailey would be crowned series winner.

The announcement of Gary's impending departure coincided with news that series creator Simon Cowell would be returning to the UK version of the series, after plans were made to wind down the US remake. Despite huge effort to make *The X Factor USA* popular, it had struggled in the ratings in the States, and in December 2013, the third and last series ended. 'Simon is the show,' said Gary. Yet this would not quite mark the very end of Gary's association with the programme. Harry Hill and Steve Brown's 2014 stage musical about *The X Factor*, *I Can't Sing*, which was co-produced with Cowell himself, would find room for a singing dog character... called 'Barlow'.

At the end of October 2013, in between live *X Factor* shows,

Gary flew out to Afghanistan to spend time with British troops. It would be filmed for an ITV documentary, *Journey to Afghanistan*, shown that Christmas, and he would tell of the nerves he experienced during the escort in and out of the war zone at Camp Bastion. 'My heart was racing, palms sweating. You sit in full body armour, strapped in to the sides of this huge aircraft. Everyone has a rifle. Even when I was on stage, every single guy up there with me had a rifle strapped to his belt. It was probably the most emotional concert I've ever performed – despite the fact that every single person around me had a gun.'

As well as Barlow and Take That originals, he also performed covers of Michael Bublé ('Home') and The Hollies ('He Ain't Heavy, He's My Brother'), with the help of the Royal Artillery Band. But his 1,000-strong audience was far from reverent; instead, he received the kind of good-natured heckling he last truly encountered in his teenage days of the social clubs. 'It started within two minutes of going on stage. I'm not a comedian but there were plenty of them in the audience. They were shouting things and had banners up. It was great fun – the women were as bad as the men.'

It was hard to avoid Barlow in the last weeks of 2013. Aside from his Afghanistan documentary, shown at Christmas, and his swansong *X Factor* appearances, he hosted another Children in Need live music extravaganza for the BBC, an evening which notably tempted Abba's Agnetha Faltskog on to a stage again for the first time in 30 years. He performed at his fifth Royal Variety Performance, and even showed up in a TV advert for price comparison website comparethemarket.com, alongside the meerkat Alexsandr Orlov. Even on New Year's Eve, there he was on BBC1: he sandwiched the chimes of Big Ben at midnight with two instalments of a live concert at Westminster's Central Hall. At one point, he duetted with *himself*: footage of a younger Gary on a special version of 'A Million Love Songs'. Detractors begged for mercy. Was this too much Gary Barlow?

Most controversially, on 11 December 2013, BBC Radio 2 was to be designated 'Gary Barlow Day'. Listeners were promised that Barlow would 'take over' the airwaves for the day, with guest spots on various shows (Ken Bruce, Steve Wright), plus a live performance of 'Since I Saw You Last' from the BBC Radio Theatre in London, and even a video Q&A session on the BBC website. The plan was met with annoyance from some quarters, especially as Gary had already made several promotional appearances to promote the new record. Some even queried whether a non-commercial organisation should push a newly released album quite so strongly.

In the end, the plans were scaled back slightly, and the video Q&A was dropped, perhaps because of the slightly awkward Q&A Barlow had just experienced on Twitter. Many Twitter users had swamped the session with questions about the sticky issue of tax avoidance. According to a report in *The Times* newspaper in June 2012, Barlow (as well as fellow Take That members Howard and Mark, plus manager Jonathan Wild) was one of a group of almost 1,000 investors who between them had contributed nearly £500 million to Icebreaker partnerships, which Revenue and Customs claimed were artificial tax avoidance schemes. It was stressed that the schemes were perfectly legal, that all Take That parties were paying significant tax, and that (according to lawyers representing him) Gary had insisted that he had believed the investments to be legitimate. The story had first circulated at the time of a similar Jimmy Carr story, but outside *The Times* and

Private Eye, received far less exposure. In February 2014, *The Times* returned to the subject, claiming that the named Take That members had invested £40 million into a second Icebreaker partnership called Shirecroft.

Gary remained tight-lipped on the matter, but on 9 May 2014, a tax tribunal ruled that both Icebreaker partnerships in which Barlow, Donald, Owen, Wild and others had invested amounted to a tax avoidance scheme. They had been apparently set up as music industry investment schemes, but had made no profit. It was expected that the group would have to repay over £20 million to HM Revenue and Customs.

Reactions to the ruling were varied. *The Times* newspaper's leader column argued that while Gary's contribution to entertainment and charity work had been considerable, there were limits. 'Barlow was approaching the coveted status of a national treasure. He is that no longer.' Many, like the *Daily Mirror*, felt that he should be stripped of his OBE. Prime Minister David Cameron (whom Gary had publicly endorsed during the 2010 General Election campaign) disagreed; in his view Gary had done plenty for Britain and so didn't need to hand back his honour. Without naming Gary, Cameron simply said, 'I am opposed to all aggressive tax avoidance.' Some public figures did rally directly to Gary's defence – Sharon Osbourne, for instance, who tweeted the following: 'He needs everyone's support. Remember, there are two sides to every story. He is a decent human being.' Others blamed a complicated taxation system, and suggested that some wily accountants were at fault.

The tribunal had come just a few days after a celebratory hour-long BBC One documentary in which actor and Barlow fan James Corden spent time with the man himself and interviewed him about his life and career. While the *Since I Saw You Last* album had shot back to number two in the album charts in the wake of *When Corden Met Barlow*, sales would quickly fall away after the ruling. When its title track was released as a single, it fell well short of the top 100.

Another apparent casualty was Barlow's charity remake of Take That's 'Greatest Day', intended at one point to be the England anthem for the football World Cup in Brazil. In March 2014, Barlow had joined forces with the likes of Mel C, Emma Bunton and Kimberley Walsh from the pop world, as well as football icons like Gary Lineker, Michael Owen and Sir Geoff Hurst. The video was unveiled on Sport Relief day on 21 March, but by late May, the FA had quietly dropped plans to officially release the song. Conceived as an anthem for Take That live shows, 'Greatest Day' seemed a more awkward fit for stadiums, especially as the World Cup tends to last nearly a month. Football fan and comedian David Baddiel, whose 'Three Lions' record had topped the UK charts twice in the 1990s, branded the 'Greatest Day' cover as 'a bit rubbish'.

*

Gary Barlow has bounced back before, but the reaction to what he does next will be critical. As ever, he's a busy man. There's an upcoming musical version of the movie *Finding Neverland*, which he's writing with playwright James Graham, and which will star Matthew Morrison from TV's *Glee* as Peter Pan creator J.M. Barrie. But ultimately, no matter what Barlow does, Take That are never far away. In the 1990s, he had yearned for a solo life outside the group, but now older and wiser, he understood that

– at least in terms of pop – being a team player could be fun. His bandmates had helped to deliver his songs charismatically and colourfully to a loyal young audience of millions. Now, regrouped and older and wiser, Take That had a self-contained unity. They could do it all themselves. The truth was, they always could, but now it was all about the music. 'It was really hard for me,' reflected Gary, 'especially in the beginning of Take That, because it was really all about what I was writing. And I was really the only singer, to start off with. So I never felt I moved that far away from it.'

The group had reconvened in January 2014 to record a new album intended for release later in the year. 'I took Take That for granted,' Gary admitted. 'We all did, and now it's come back to us, we realise how precious it is. I include Rob in that, it's his band too. The band is for us all to take care of for the next 20 years. We can leave it and do other things and come back to it, but it's my number one priority. I see the solo album as a lovely little hobby for a year, but the main job is always going to be Take That.' He continued to regard Robbie as part of the group, but at the time of writing, it seems unlikely that Williams will be part of their next project, due to his own touring schedule and an impending second child.

Many teen acts flounder because their songs aren't good enough, or the chemistry between band members is unconvincing. Most often, though, they do not last because the only people whose music they touch are the most devoted fans. While every group or singer needs hardcore fans, the casual ones matter too, those who might not even consider themselves 'fans' but just like some of the music. The Beatles, Abba, David Bowie and Michael Jackson all succeeded in this way, and Take That have done the same. 'It started off with young girls,' explained Gary of his group's appeal, 'but the parents end up listening to what the kids listen to.'

Add to that the banter between the group's members, the way their story had peaks and troughs like all the best soap operas, and another breakout personality in Robbie Williams, and it's not surprising that they managed to engineer an even more spectacular comeback. 'Being a good pop band,' said Jason Orange in 2008, 'is not just about good pop songs. It's about a good story – our story is pretty good.'

Let's leave the last word to the man who was such a bitter opponent of Gary's for so long but, deep down, was ultimately one of his biggest supporters. 'Gary is one of the best songwriters of all-time,' declared Robbie Williams in 2010. 'The way he crafts songs, he writes hits on purpose. If I do it, it is a fluke. The guy just turns them out. I'm in awe of his talent.'

SOURCES

Arena, Attitude, BBC, *Birmingham Mail, Brighton Argus, Cosmopolitan, Daily Mirror, Daily Record, Esquire, Express, The Face, The Financial Times,* the *Guardian,* the *Independent, Independent on Sunday, The Irish Times,* ITV, *Manchester Evening News,* MTV, *Music Week, New Musical Express, News of the World,* the *Observer,* the *People, Q, Radio Times, Smash Hits, The Stage,* the *Sun, Sunday Mail, Sunday Mirror, Sunday Telegraph, The Sunday Times, The Times, Wales on Sunday,* WENN, *Western Mail.*

FURTHER
READING

Feel by Robbie Williams and Chris Heath (Ebury Press, 2004)
Let Me Entertain You by Robbie Williams and Jim Parton (Virgin Books, 1998)
My Take by Gary Barlow with Richard Havers (Bloomsbury, 2006)
Take That: Our Greatest Hits by Take That (Virgin Books, 1996)

DISCOGRAPHY

UK
PART 1:
TAKE THAT: 1991–96

SINGLES

DO WHAT U LIKE
Dance UK Records
UK Release: 22 July 1991
Peak Position: 82
7" Vinyl (DUK2):
Do What U Like // Waiting Around
12" Vinyl (12DUK2):
Do What U Like (Club Mix) / Here We Go! // Do What U Like
(Radio Mix) / Waiting Around

PROMISES
RCA Records
UK Release: 11 November 1991
Peak Position: 38
7" Vinyl (PB 45085):
Promises (Radio Mix) // Do What U Like
12" Vinyl (PT45086):
Promises (12" Mix) // Do What U Like (12" Mix)
CD Single (PD45086):
Promises / Do What U Like / Promises (12" Mix)

ONCE YOU'VE TASTED LOVE
RCA Records
UK Release: 27 January 1992
Peak Position: 47
7" Vinyl with Free Calendar (PB45257):
Once You've Tasted Love // Guess Who Tasted Love
12" Vinyl (PT45257):
Once You've Tasted Love (Aural Mix) // Guess Who Tasted Love
(Guess Who Mix) / Once You've Tasted Love (Radio Version)
CD Single (PD45257):
Once You've Tasted Love / Guess Who Tasted Love / Once
You've Tasted Love (Aural Mix)

IT ONLY TAKES A MINUTE
RCA Records
UK Release: 25 May 1992
Peak Position: 7
7" Vinyl (74321 10100 7):
It Only Takes A Minute // Satisfied

12" Remix (74321 10618 5):
It Only Takes A Minute (Deep Club Mix) / It Only Takes A
Minute (Blondapella) / It Only Takes A Minute (Dem Drums) //
It Only Takes A Minute (Wright Vocal Mix) / It Only Takes A
Minute (Love Dub Mix)
CD Single (74321 10100 2):
It Only Takes A Minute (7" Version) / I Can Make It / Never
Want to Let You Go / It Only Takes A Minute (Deep Club Mix)

I FOUND HEAVEN
RCA Records
UK Release: 10 August 1992
Peak Position: 15
7" Vinyl [Picture Disc] (74321 10813 7):
I Found Heaven // I'm Out
7" Vinyl with Poster (74321 10814 7):
I Found Heaven (Radio Mix) // I Found Heaven (Mr. F's
Garage Mix)
12" Vinyl (74321 11240 1):
I Found Heaven (Mr. F's Garage Mix) // I Found Heaven
(Original 12" Mix) / I Found Heaven (7" Radio Mix)
CD Single (74321 10813 2):
I Found Heaven (7" Radio Mix) / I'm Out / Promises (7" Radio
Mix) / I Found Heaven (Classic 12" Mix)

A MILLION LOVE SONGS
RCA Records
UK Release: 28 September 1992
Peak Position: 7
7" Vinyl [Limited Edition with Transfer Tattoos] (74321 11600 7):

A Million Love Songs (7" Edit) // A Million Love Songs
(Lovers Mix)
Cassette Single (74321 11600 4):
A Million Love Songs (7" Edit) // A Million Love Songs
(Lovers Mix)
*CD Single [titled A MILLION LOVE SONGS – THE LOVE
SONGS EP] (74321 11600 2):*
A Million Love Songs (7" Edit) / Still Can't Get Over You / How
Can It Be / Don't Take Your Love

COULD IT BE MAGIC
RCA Records
UK Release: 30 November 1992
Peak Position: 3
7" Vinyl (74321 12313 7):
Could It Be Magic (Rapino Radio Mix) // Take That Radio
Megamix [Do What U Like, Promises, I Found Heaven, Take
That & Party, Once You've Tasted Love, It Only Takes A
Minute]
12" Vinyl (74321 12313 1):
Could It Be Magic (Deep In Rapino's Club Mix) // Take That
Club Megamix / Could It Be Magic (Mr. F. Mix by Aron
Friedman)
CD Single (74321 12313 2):
Could It Be Magic (Rapino Radio Mix) / Could It Be Magic
(Deep in Rapino's Club Mix) / Could It Be Magic (Acapella) /
Could It Be Magic (Ciao Baby Mix) / Could It Be Magic
(Rapino Dub) / Could It Be Magic (Paparazzo Mix) / Could It
Be Magic (Deep In Rapino's Dub) / Could It Be Magic (Club
Rapino Mix)

WHY CAN'T I WAKE UP WITH YOU?

RCA Records
UK Release: 8 February 1993
Peak Position: 2
7" Single (74321 13310 7):
Why Can't I Wake Up With You? (Radio Edit) // Why Can't I
Wake Up With You? (Live Version – featuring Acapella) / A
Million Love Songs (Live Version)
7" Vinyl EP (74321 13311 7):
Why Can't I Wake Up With You? (Radio Edit) // Promises (Live
Version) / Clap Your Hands (Live Version)
Cassette Single (74321 13311 4):
Why Can't I Wake Up With You? (Radio Edit) / Why Can't I
Wake Up With You? (Live Version – Featuring Acapella) / A
Million Love Songs (Live Version)
CD Single (74321 13310 2):
Why Can't I Wake Up With You? (Radio Edit) / A Million Love
Songs (Live Version) / Satisfied (Live Version) / Take That
Medley (Live Version)

PRAY

RCA Records
UK Release: 5 July 1993
Peak Position: 1 (for four weeks)
7" Vinyl (74321 15450 7):
Pray // Pray (Acapella)
Cassette Single (74321 15450 4):
Pray / Pray (Acapella)
CD Single #1 (74321 15450 2):
Pray (Radio Edit) / Pray (Acapella) / Pray (Alternative Club Mix)

CD Single #2 (74321 15451 2) [released 19 July 1993]:
Pray (Club Swing Mix) / It Only Takes A Minute (Tommy
Musto Club Mix) / Once You've Tasted Love (Harding &
Curnow Remix) / It Only Takes A Minute (Tommy Musto
Underground Vocal)

RELIGHT MY FIRE
TAKE THAT FEATURING LULU
RCA Records
UK Release: 27 September 1993
Peak Position: 1 (for two weeks)
7" Vinyl (74321 16772 7):
Relight My Fire (Radio Version) // Why Can't I Wake Up With
You? (Live Version)
12" Vinyl (74321 16772 1):
Relight My Fire (Full-length Version) / Relight My Fire (All
Night Mix) // Relight My Fire (Late Night Mix) / Relight My
Fire (Percacapella) / Relight My Fire (Night Beats)
Cassette Single (74321 16772 4):
Relight My Fire (Radio Version) / Why Can't I Wake Up With
You? (Live Version)
CD Single #1 (74321 16772 2):
Relight My Fire (Full-length Version) / Relight My Fire (All
Night Mix) / Relight My Fire (Late Night Mix) / Relight My Fire
(Percacapella) / Relight My Fire (Night Beats)
CD Single #2 (74321 16861 2):
Relight My Fire (Radio Version) / Why Can't I Wake Up With
You? (Live Version) / Motown Medley (Live Version) / Take
That & Party (Live Version)

BABE
RCA Records
UK Release: 6 December 1993
Peak Position: 1 (for one week)
7" Vinyl (74321 18213 7):
Babe (Return Remix) // All I Want Is You
Cassette Single (74321 18213 4):
Babe (Return Remix) // All I Want Is You
CD Single #1 (74321 18212 2):
Babe (Return Remix) / All I Want Is You / Could It Be Magic?
(Live) / Pray (Live)
CD Single #2 [with free calendar] (74321 18213 2):
Babe (Return Remix) / It Only Takes A Minute (Live) / Give
Good Feeling (Live)

EVERYTHING CHANGES
RCA Records
UK Release: 28 March 1994
Peak Position: 1 (for two weeks)
7" Vinyl (74321 16773 7):
Everything Changes // Beatles Medley [I Wanna Hold Your
Hand, A Hard Day's Night, She Loves You]
Cassette Single (74321 16773 4):
Everything Changes // Beatles Medley [I Wanna Hold Your
Hand, A Hard Day's Night, She Loves You]
CD Single #1 (74321 16773 2):
Everything Changes / Beatles Medley [I Wanna Hold Your
Hand, A Hard Day's Night, She Loves You] / Everything
Changes (Nigel Lowis Remix) / Everything Changes (Extended
Version)

CD Single #2 (74321 19946 2):
Everything Changes / Interview [for BBC Radio 1] / Relight My
Fire (Live at Wembley Arena) [featuring Lulu]

LOVE AIN'T HERE ANYMORE
RCA Records
UK Release: 27 June 1994
Peak Position: 3
CD Single #1 (74321 21482 2):
Love Ain't Here Anymore (Live) / Rock 'n' Roll Medley (Live)
[Born to Hand Jive, Great Balls of Fire, Under the Moon of
Love, Teddy Bear] / Wasting My Time (Live) / Babe (Live)
CD Single #2 (74321 21483 2):
Love Ain't Here Anymore / The Party (Remix) [megamix of:
Relight My Fire, Could It Be Magic, It Only Takes A Minute
and Everything Changes remixes] / Another Crack in My Heart
(Live) / Everything Changes (Live *Top of the Pops* Satellite
Performance)

SURE
RCA Records
UK Release: 3 October 1994
Peak Position: 1 (for two weeks)
12" Vinyl with Tour Poster (74321 23662 1):
Sure (Thumpers Club Mix) // Sure (Brothers in Rhythm Mix) /
Sure (Full Pressure Mix)
CD Single #1 (74321 23662 2):
Sure (3.40) / Sure (Thumpers Club Mix) / Sure (Full Pressure
Mix) / Sure (Strictly Barking Dub)
CD Single #2 [with five free picture postcards] (74321 23663 2):

Sure / No Si Aqui No Hay Amor / Why Can't I Wake Up With You (Club Mix) / You Are The One (Tonic Mix)

BACK FOR GOOD
RCA Records
UK Release: 27 March 1995
Peak Position: 1 (for four weeks)
7" Vinyl (74321 27146 7):
Back for Good (Radio Mix) // Sure (Live) / Back for Good
(TV Mix)
CD Single #1 (74321 27146 2):
Back for Good (Radio Mix) / Sure (Live at Wembley Arena) /
Beatles Tribute (Live at Wembley Arena)
CD Single #2 (74321 27147 2):
Back for Good (Radio Mix) / Pray / Why Can't I Wake Up With
You? / A Million Love Songs

NEVER FORGET
RCA Records
UK Release: 24 July 1995
Peak Position: 1 (for three weeks)
CD Single #1 (74321 29956 2):
Never Forget / Back for Good (Live from MTV's Most Wanted) /
Babe (Live from MTV's Most Wanted)
CD Single #2 (74321 29957 2):
Never Forget / Interview

HOW DEEP IS YOUR LOVE
RCA Records
UK Release: 26 February 1996

Peak Position: 1 (for three weeks)
Cassette Single (74321 35559 4):
How Deep is Your Love / Never Forget
CD Single #1 (74321 35559 2):
How Deep Is Your Love / Every Guy (Live) / Lady Tonight (Live)
/ Sunday to Saturday (Live)
CD Single #2 (74321 35560 2):
How Deep Is Your Love / Back for Good (Live) / Babe / Never
Forget

ALBUMS

TAKE THAT & PARTY
RCA Records
UK Release: 24 August 1992
Peak Position: 2
Vinyl LP (74321 10923 1):
Cassette (74321 10923 4):
I Found Heaven / Once You've Tasted Love / It Only Takes A
Minute / A Million Love Songs / Satisfied / I Can Make It // Do
What You Like / Promises / Why Can't I Wake Up With You? /
Never Want To Let You Go (New Studio Mix) / Give Good
Feeling / Take That & Party
CD (74321 10923 2):
I Found Heaven / Once You've Tasted Love / It Only Takes A
Minute / A Million Love Songs / Satisfied / I Can Make It / Do
What U Like / Promises / Why Can't I Wake Up With You? /
Never Want To Let You Go (New Studio Mix) / Give Good
Feeling / Could It Be Magic (Rapino Radio Mix) / Take That
& Party

CD Reissue [released 2006] (RCA 88697044282):
I Found Heaven / Once You've Tasted Love / It Only Takes A
Minute / A Million Love Songs / Satisfied / I Can Make It / Do
What U Like / Promises / Why Can't I Wake Up With You? /
Never Want To Let You Go (New Studio Mix) / Give Good
Feeling / Could It Be Magic (Rapino Radio Mix) / Take That &
Party / *Bonus tracks:* Waiting Around / How Can It Be / Guess
Who Tasted Love (Edit)

EVERYTHING CHANGES
RCA Records
UK Release: 11 October 1993
Peak Position: 1 (for a total of two weeks)
Vinyl LP [Picture Disc] (74321 16926 1):
Cassette (74321 16926 4):
Everything Changes / Pray / Wasting My Time / Relight My Fire
/ Love Ain't Here Anymore / If This Is Love / Whatever You Do
To Me // Meaning of Love / Why Can't I Wake Up With You? /
You Are The One / Another Crack In My Heart / Broken Your
Heart / Babe
CD (74321 16926 2):
Everything Changes / Pray / Wasting My Time / Relight My Fire
/ Love Ain't Here Anymore / If This Is Love / Whatever You Do
To Me / Meaning of Love / Why Can't I Wake Up With You? /
You Are The One / Another Crack In My Heart / Broken Your
Heart / Babe
CD Reissue [released 2006] (RCA 88697044262):
Everything Changes / Pray / Wasting My Time / Relight My Fire
/ Love Ain't Here Anymore / If This Is Love / Whatever You Do
To Me / Meaning of Love / Why Can't I Wake Up With You? /

You Are The One / Another Crack In My Heart / Broken Your
Heart / Babe /
Bonus tracks: No Si Aqui No Hay Amor [*Spanish version of
Love Ain't Here Anymore*] / The Party Remix [Relight My Fire,
Could It Be Magic, It Only Takes A Minute, Everything
Changes] / All I Want Is You / Babe (Return Mix)

NOBODY ELSE
RCA Records
UK Release: 8 May 1995
Peak Position: 1 (for two weeks)
Vinyl LP (74321 27909 1):
Cassette (74321 27909 4):
Sure / Back for Good / Every Guy / Sunday To Saturday /
Nobody Else / Never Forget //
Hanging Onto Your Love / Holding Back The Tears / Hate It /
Lady Tonight / The Day After Tomorrow
CD (74321 27909 2):
Sure / Back for Good / Every Guy / Sunday To Saturday /
Nobody Else / Never Forget / Hanging Onto Your Love /
Holding Back The Tears / Hate It / Lady Tonight / The Day After
Tomorrow
CD Reissue [released 2006] (RCA 88697044272):
Sure / Back for Good / Every Guy / Sunday To Saturday /
Nobody Else / Never Forget /
Hanging Onto Your Love / Holding Back The Tears / Hate It /
Lady Tonight / The Day After Tomorrow / *Bonus tracks:* Sure
(Full Pressure Mix) / Back for Good (Urban Mix) / Every Guy
(Live)

NOBODY ELSE [NORTH AMERICA EDITION]

Arista Records
US Release Date: August 1995
Cassette (07822 18800-4):
CD (07822 18800-2):
Sure / Back for Good / Babe / Pray / Nobody Else // Never Forget
/ Holding Back The Tears / Every Guy / Love Ain't Here
Anymore / The Day After Tomorrow

GREATEST HITS

RCA Records
UK Release: 25 March 1996
Peak Position: 1 (for four weeks)
Cassette (74321 355584):
CD (74321 355582):
How Deep Is Your Love / Never Forget / Back for Good / Sure /
Love Ain't Here Anymore / Everything Changes / Babe / Relight
My Fire / Pray / Why Can't I Wake Up With You? / Could It Be
Magic (Radio Rapino Version) / A Million Love Songs / I Found
Heaven / It Only Takes A Minute / Once You've Tasted Love /
Promises / Do What U Like / Love Ain't Here Anymore (US Version)

VIDEOS

TAKE THAT & PARTY

BMG Video
Released: 7 December 1992

TAKE THAT – THE PARTY: LIVE AT WEMBLEY

BMG Video

Released: 1 November 1993

EVERYTHING CHANGES
BMG Video
Released: 18 July 1994

TAKE THAT: LIVE IN BERLIN
BMG Video

Released: 15 May 1995
HOMETOWN – LIVE AT THE GMEX
BMG Video
Released: 14 August 1995

NOBODY ELSE – THE MOVIE
BMG Video
Released: 20 November 1995

TAKE THAT – GREATEST HITS
BMG Video
Released: 25 March 1996

PART 2:
GARY BARLOW: 1996–99

SINGLES

FOREVER LOVE
RCA Records
UK Release: 8 July 1996

Peak Position: 1 (for one week)
CD Single (74321 38796 2):
Limited CD Single [with outer sleeve] (74321 39792 2):
Forever Love / I Miss It All / Forever Love (Instrumental)

LOVE WON'T WAIT
RCA Records
UK Release: 28 April 1997
Peak Position: 1 (for one week)
CD Single #1 (74321 47084 2):
Love Won't Wait (Radio Edit) / Love Won't Wait (Junior
Vasquez Mix) /
Meaning Of A Love Song / Always
CD Single #2 (74321 47083 2):
Love Won't Wait (Radio Edit) / Cuddly Toy (Lush Vocal Radio
Edit) / Cuddly Toy (Full On Retro Vocal) / Cuddly Toy (Dumb
& Funky Dub)

SO HELP ME GIRL
RCA Records
UK Release: 14 July 1997
Peak Position: 11
CD Single #1 (74321 50120 2):

So Help Me Girl / Million To One / Offer My Peace / So Help
Me Girl (C Swing Mix)
CD Single #2 (74321 50121 2):
So Help Me Girl / So Help Me Girl (Peter Mokran Mix) /
Interview

OPEN ROAD
RCA Records
UK Release: 3 November 1997
Peak Position: 7
Cassette Single (74321 51819 4):
Open Road / Back for Good (Live for BBC Radio 1) / Open
Road (Mr Pink Mix)
CD Single #1 (74321 51819 2):
Open Road (Rose + Foster Mix) / Open Road (Mr Pink Mix) /
Hang On In There, Baby (Live for BBC Radio 1) / So Help Me
Girl (Live for BBC Radio 1)
CD Single #2 (74321 51829 2):
Open Road (Rose + Foster Mix) / Open Road (Mr Pink Mix) /
Back for Good (Live for BBC Radio 1) / Open Road (Live for
BBC Radio 1)

STRONGER
RCA Records
UK Release: 5 July 1999
Peak Position: 16
CD Single #1 (74321 68200 2):
Stronger (Metro Edit) / Stronger (Metro Extended Mix) /
Wondering
CD Single #2 [Enhanced] (74321 68619 2):
Stronger (Metro Edit) / Looking for Change / Wondering /
Stronger (Metro Extended Mix) / Stronger (Video)

FOR ALL THAT YOU WANT
RCA Records
UK Release: 27 September 1999

Peak Position: 24
CD Single #1 (74321 70101 2):
For All That You Want / Say It / Part Of My Life
CD Single #2 [Enhanced]:
For All That You Want / Say It / The Only One / Part Of My
Life / For All That You Want (Video)

LIE TO ME
RCA Records
Scheduled UK Release: 6 December 1999 (but cancelled)
CD Single:
Lie To Me / I Hate It This Way / Put Your Trust In Me

ALBUMS

OPEN ROAD
RCA / BMG UK
UK Release: 26 May 1997
Peak Position: 1 (for one week)
CD (74321 41720 2):
Love Won't Wait / So Help Me Girl / My Commitment / Hang
On In There, Baby / Are You Ready Now / Everything I Ever
Wanted / I Fall So Deep / Lay Down For Love / Forever Love /
Never Knew / Open Road / Always

TWELVE MONTHS, ELEVEN DAYS
RCA Records
UK Release: 11 October 1999
Peak Position: 35
CD [Enhanced] (74321 70218 2):

For All That You Want / Arms Around Me / Lie to Me / Fast Car / Stronger / All That I've Given Away / Wondering / Don't Need a Reason / Before You Turn Away / Walk / Nothing Feels the Same / Yesterday's Girl [plus promo videos for Stronger and For All That You Want]

VIDEOS

GARY BARLOW: OPEN BOOK
BMG Video
Released: 16 March 1998

PART 3:
TAKE THAT: 2005–11

SINGLES

PATIENCE
Polydor Records
UK Release: 13 November 2006
Peak Position: 1 (for four weeks)
CD Single (171 483-2):
Patience / Beautiful Morning
Enhanced CD Single (171 717-6):
Patience / Beautiful Morning / Trouble With Me / Patience (Video)
SHINE
Polydor Records
UK Release: 26 February 2007
Peak Position: 1 (for two weeks)
CD Single (172 429-4):

Shine / Trouble With Me
Enhanced CD Single (172 6063-4):
Shine / Trouble With Me / Patience / Shine (Video)

I'D WAIT FOR LIFE
Polydor Records
UK Release: 18 June 2007
Peak Position: 17
CD Single (173 717-4):
I'd Wait for Life / We All Fall Down / Shine (BBC Radio 2 Live
and Exclusive) / Back for Good (BBC Radio 2 Live
and Exclusive)

RULE THE WORLD
Polydor Records
UK Release: 22 October 2007
Peak Position: 2
CD Single (174 628-5):
Rule the World (Radio Edit) / Stay Together

GREATEST DAY
Polydor Records
UK Release: 24 November 2008
Peak Position: 1 (for one week)
CD Single (178 744-5):
Greatest Day / Sleepwalking
Enhanced CD Single:
Greatest Day / Sleepwalking / Here / Greatest Day (Video)

UP ALL NIGHT

Polydor Records
UK Release: 2 March 2009
Peak Position: 14
CD Single (179 696-4):
Up All Night / 84

SAID IT ALL

Polydor Records
UK Release: 15 June 2009
Peak Position: 9
CD Single (270 871-7):
Said It All / Throwing Stones

THE FLOOD

Polydor Records
UK Release: 8 November 2010
Peak Position: 2
CD Single (275 598-5):
The Flood / The Flood (Instrumental)
DVD Single (275 708-6):
The Flood (Video) / The Flood (Behind the Scenes)

KIDZ

Polydor Records
UK Release: 22 February 2011
Peak Position: 28
CD Single (276 456-1):
Kidz / Rocket Ship
Also download with extra exclusive track: Kidz [Live from the BRITs]

LOVE LOVE
Polydor Records
Download Single
UK Release: 11 May 2011
Peak Position: 15

ALBUMS

NEVER FORGET: THE ULTIMATE COLLECTION
Sony BMG Music
UK Release Date: 14 November 2005
Peak Position: 2
CD (82876748522):
Never Forget / Back for Good / How Deep is Your Love / Pray /
Relight My Fire / Everything Changes / Babe / Sure / It Only
Takes a Minute / A Million Love Songs / Could It Be Magic /
Why Can't I Wake Up With You? / Love Ain't Here Anymore / I
Found Heaven / Promises / Once You've Tasted Love / Pray
(Live in Berlin) / Relight My Fire (Element Remix) / Today I've
Lost You

BEAUTIFUL WORLD
Polydor Records
UK Release Date: 27 November 2006
Peak Position: 1 (for a total of eight weeks)
CD (171 572-1):
Reach Out / Patience / Beautiful World / Hold On / Like I Never
Loved You At All / Shine / I'd Wait for Life / Ain't No Sense in
Love / What You Believe In / Mancunian Way / Wooden Boat /
Butterfly [hidden track]

THE CIRCUS
Polydor Records
UK Release Date: 1 December 2008
Peak Position: 1 (for five weeks)
CD (179 199-0):
The Garden / Greatest Day / Hello / Said It All / Julie / The
Circus / How Did It Come to
This / Up All Night / What is Love / You / Hold Up a Light /
Here / She Said [hidden track]

**THE GREATEST DAY: TAKE THAT PRESENT THE
CIRCUS LIVE**
Polydor Records
UK Release Date: 30 November 2009
Peak Position: 3
Double CD (272 356-0):
[Disc 1] Greatest Day / Hello / Pray / Back for Good / The
Garden / Shine / Up All Night / How Did It Come to This /
The Circus / What is Love / Said It All / Never Forget /
Patience / Relight My Fire / Hold Up a Light / Rule the World
[Disc 2 – *In Session at Abbey Road*] The Garden / How Did It
Come to This / Greatest Day / Up All Night / Patience / What
is Love / The Circus / Shine / Rule the World / Julie / Said It
All

PROGRESS
Polydor Records
UK Release Date: 15 November 2010
Peak Position: 1 (for six weeks)
CD (274 847-4):

The Flood / SOS / Wait / Kidz / Pretty Things / Happy Now / Underground Machine / What Do You Want From Me? / Affirmation / Eight Letters / Flowerbed [hidden track]

PROGRESSED
Polydor Records
UK Release Date: 13 June 2011
Peak Position: 1 (for one week)
Double CD (277 495-1):
[Reissue of PROGRESS with bonus disc containing eight extra tracks]
Disc 1 [Progress]: The Flood / SOS / Wait / Kidz / Pretty Things / Happy Now / Underground Machine / What Do You Want From Me? / Affirmation / Eight Letters / Flowerbed [hidden track]
Disc 2 [Progressed]: When We Were Young / Man / Love Love / The Day the Work is Done / Beautiful / Don't Say Goodbye / Aliens / Wonderful World

PROGRESS LIVE [LIVE ALBUM]
Polydor Records
UK Release Date: 28 November 2011
Peak Position: 12
Double CD (278 740-1):
TAKE THAT: Rule the World / Greatest Day / Hold Up a Light / Patience / Shine /
ROBBIE WILLIAMS: Let Me Entertain You / Rock DJ / Come Undone / Feel / Angels /
TAKE THAT: The Flood / SOS / Underground Machine / Kidz / Pretty Things / When They Were Young (incl. Medley of A

Million Love Songs / Babe / Everything Changes) / Back for
Good / Pray / Love Love / Never Forget / No Regrets – Relight
My Fire / Eight Letters

DVDs

NEVER FORGET – THE ULTIMATE COLLECTION
Sony BMG
Released: 14 November 2005

TAKE THAT – FOR THE RECORD
Sony BMG
Released: 24 April 2006

TAKE THAT: THE ULTIMATE TOUR
Universal Music
Released: 6 November 2006

BEAUTIFUL WORLD – LIVE
Universal Music
Released: 25 February 2008

TAKE THAT PRESENT: THE CIRCUS LIVE
Universal Music
Released: 23 November 2009

LOOK BACK DON'T STARE: A FILM ABOUT PROGRESS
Polydor/Universal Music
Released: 6 December 2010

PROGRESS – LIVE
Polydor/Universal Music
Released: 21 November 2011

PART 4:
MISCELLANEOUS RECORDINGS 2010–12

SINGLES

HELPING HAITI
EVERYBODY HURTS
Syco Records
UK Release Date: 7 February 2010
Peak Position: 1 (for two weeks)
CD Single (88697661102):
Everybody Hurts / Everybody Hurts (Alternative Mix)

ROBBIE WILLIAMS & GARY BARLOW
SHAME
Virgin Records
UK Release Date: 4 October 2010
Peak Position: 2
CD Single (VSCDT2016):
Shame / The Queen

THE COLLECTIVE
TEARDROP
Future Records/Island Records
UK Release Date: 13 November 2011
Peak Position: 24

CD Single (GBUV71101391):
Teardrop / Teardrop (R1 Remix) / Teardrop (Wideboys Remix) /
Teardrop (Lonsdale Boys Club Remix)
Featured performers: Chipmunk, Dot Rotten, Ed Sheeran, Ms.
Dynamite, Mz Bratt, Tulisa Contostavlos, Rizzle Kicks, Tinchy
Stryder, Wretch 32

GARY BARLOW & THE COMMONWEALTH BAND FEATURING THE MILITARY WIVES
SING
Decca Records
UK Release Date: 28 May 2012
Peak Position: 1 (for one week)
CD Single (GBUM71202976):
Sing / Sing

ALBUMS

GARY BARLOW
SING
Decca Records
UK Release Date: 25 May 2012
Peak Position: 1 (for three weeks)
CD (370 235-8):
Sing (featuring Military Wives) / Sing / Here Comes the Sun /
Amazing Grace (feat. Hayley Westenra) / Stronger as One
(featuring Laura Wright) / Land of Hope and Glory (featuring
Alfie Boe and Military Wives) / God Save the Queen (featuring
Laura Wright)

DVDs

GARY BARLOW – ON HER MAJESTY'S SERVICE
Polydor
Released: 25 June 2012

GARY BARLOW: LIVE
Universal Music
Released: 4 March 2013

PART 5:
GARY BARLOW 2013 –14

SINGLES

LET ME GO
Polydor Records
CD Single: GBUM71306083
Download
UK Release: 17 November 2013
UK Peak Position: 2

FACE TO FACE (with Sir Elton John)
Polydor Records (download only)
UK Release: 20 January 2014
Peak Position: 80
Face to Face/Face to Face (Instrumental)

SINCE I SAW YOU LAST
Polydor Records (download only)
UK Release: 14 April 2014
Peak Position: 129

ALBUMS

SINCE I SAW YOU LAST
Polydor Records
UK Release: 25 November 2013
Peak Position: 2
CD: 3757644
Requiem / Let Me Go / Jump / Face to Face / God / Small Town
Girls / 6th Avenue /
We Like to Love / Since I Saw You Last / This House / Dying
Inside / More Than Life

DVDs

SINCE YOU SAW HIM LAST
Universal Music
Released: 30 June 2014 [scheduled release date]

PART 6:
MISCELLANEOUS RECORDINGS (AS GUEST ARTIST):

ELTON JOHN
SONGS FROM THE WEST COAST
Rocket Records/Mercury Records
UK Release: 1 October 2001
Peak Position: 2
CD (586 330-2):
Features on backing vocals on 'This Train Don't Stop Here
Anymore'

JEFF WAYNE
JEFF WAYNE'S WAR OF THE WORLDS – THE NEW
GENERATION
Sony BMG Records
UK Release Date: 26 November 2012
Peak Position: 13
Double CD (88691922572):
Features on three tracks:
'Eve of the War' (Jeff Wayne featuring Liam Neeson and Gary
Barlow), 'Forever Autumn' (Jeff Wayne featuring Liam Neeson
and Gary Barlow), 'Dead London (Part 2)' (Jeff Wayne featuring
Liam Neeson and Gary Barlow)

AGNETHA FÄLTSKOG
A
Universal Records: CD: 0602537321841
UK Release Date: 13 May 2013
Peak Postion: 6
Features on one track: 'I Should've Followed You Home' (also
songwriter)

PART 7:
SELECTIVE RECORDINGS FEATURING GARY BARLOW
AS SONGWRITER

VANESSA AMOROSI
CHANGE
Universal Music: CD: 066 893-2
Released: 2002
Co-writer of one track: 'True to Yourself', with Andrew Murray,
Sylvia Smith, Jane Vaughan

ATOMIC KITTEN
LADIES NIGHT
Innocent/Virgin: CD: 0724359562223
Released: 2003
Co-writer of three tracks:
'Always Be My Baby', with Eliot Kennedy, Tim Woodcock and
Liz McClarnon; 'I Won't Be There', with Natasha Hamilton,
Eliot Kennedy and Tim Woodcock; 'Somebody Like Me', with
Natasha Hamilton, Eliot Kennedy, Tim Woodcock

JOHN BARROWMAN
MUSIC MUSIC MUSIC
Sony Music: CD: 88697339902
Released: 2008
Co-writer of one track: 'What About Us?', with Chris Braide

DAME SHIRLEY BASSEY
THE PERFORMANCE
Geffen Records: CD: 00602527207803
Released: 2009
Writer of one track: 'This Time'

BLUE
ALL RISE
Innocent/Virgin Records: CD: 7243 8 11415 0 2
Released: 2001
Co-writer of one track: 'Girl I'll Never Understand', with Tim
Woodcock

BLUE
ONE LOVE
Virgin Records: CD: 7243 5 43943 2 4
Released: 2002
Co-writer of one track: 'Supersexual', with Eliot Kennedy,
Duncan James, Lee Ryan, Simon Webbe, Anthony Costa, Tim
Woodcock

BLUE
GUILTY
Virgin Records: CD: 7243 5 95620 2 5
Released: 2003
Co-writer of two tracks:
'Guilty', with Eliot Kennedy, Tim Woodcock, Duncan James;
'Taste It', with Duncan James, Eliot Kennedy, Tim Woodcock

BRITANNIA HIGH
ORIGINAL SOUNDTRACK
Fascination Records: CD: 1784024
Released: 2008
Co-writer of six tracks:
'Start of Something', with Eliot Kennedy and Andy Hill;
'Missing Person', with Eliot Kennedy and Gary Baker; 'Best of
Me', with Eliot Kennedy, Gary Baker and James Bourne; 'What
Good is Love?', with Stephen Lipson and Chris Braide; 'Do it All
Over Again', with Eliot Kennedy and Ina Wroldsen; 'Without
You', with Eliot Kennedy and Lucie Silvas

MATT CARDLE
LETTERS
Syco Music: CD: 88697843592
Released: 2011
Writer of one track: 'Run for Your Life';
Co-writer of one track: 'All for Nothing', with Eg White and
Matt Cardle

CHARLOTTE CHURCH
TISSUES AND ISSUES
Sony BMG Music: CD: 5203462
Released: 2005
Co-writer of one track: 'Easy Way Out', with Charlotte Church
and Eliot Kennedy

MARCUS COLLINS
MARCUS COLLINS
RCA/Syco/Sony Music: CD: 88691946862
Released: 2012
Writer of one track: 'Feel Like I Feel'

ALESHA DIXON
THE ALESHA SHOW – ENCORE
Asylum/Warner Music: CD: 5051865666523
Released: 2009
Co-writer of one track: 'To Love Again', with Alesha Dixon,
John Shanks

LARA FABIAN
A WONDERFUL LIFE
Columbia: CD: COL5151672
Released: 2004
Co-writer of three tracks:
'No Big Deal', with Tim Woodcock, Eliot Kennedy, Lara Fabian and Rick Allison; 'Intoxicated', with Lara Fabian; 'Conquered', with Eliot Kennedy and Rick Allison

DELTA GOODREM
INNOCENT EYES
Epic Records: CD: 5109512
Released: 2003
Co-writer of six tracks: 'Not Me, Not I', with Kara DioGuardi, Delta Goodrem, Eliot Kennedy, Jarrad Rogers; 'Throw It Away', with Cathy Dennis and Eliot Kennedy; 'Butterfly', with John Shanks, Howard Donald; 'My Big Mistake', with Delta Goodrem, Eliot Kennedy, Tim Woodcock; 'Running Away', with Delta Goodrem, Eliot Kennedy, Tim Woodcock; 'Longer', with Delta Goodrem, Eliot Kennedy, Tim Woodcock

DELTA GOODREM
MISTAKEN IDENTITY
Epic Records: CD: 5189155
Released: 2004
Co-writer of one track: 'A Little Too Late', with Eliot Kennedy, Delta Goodrem

GRAHAM GOULDMAN
AND ANOTHER THING
For Your Love Records
CD (FYL CD 14)
Released: 2000
Co-writer of one track: 'Walkin' Away', with Graham Gouldman

HUMAN NATURE
HUMAN NATURE
Columbia Australia: CD: 5011882000
Released: 2000
Co-writer of one track: 'It's Gonna Be a Long Night', with
Andrew Tierney and Michael Tierney

KATHERINE JENKINS
REJOICE
Universal Classics and Jazz: CD: 476 620-0
Released: 2007
Co-writer of two tracks:
'Shout in Silence', with Andy Hill; 'Viva Tonight', with Andy
Hill

PETER KAY (AS GERALDINE MCQUEEN)
THE WINNERS SONG
Polydor Records: CD Single: 178 942-1
Released: 2008
Co-writer of one track: 'The Winners Song', with Peter Kay

PETER KAY (AS GERALDINE MCQUEEN)
ONCE UPON A CHRISTMAS SONG
Polydor Records: CD Single: 179 398-0
Released: 2008
Co-writer of one track: 'Once Upon a Christmas Song', with
Peter Kay

MICHELLE MCMANUS
THE MEANING OF LOVE
19 Recordings: CD: 82876 590662
Released: 2004
Writer of one track: 'I'll Never Know'

LEE MEAD
LEE MEAD
Polydor Records: CD: 1753349
Released: 2007
Co-writer of one track: 'When I Need You the Most', with
Jorgen Elofsson and Wayne Hector

MONROSE
TEMPTATION
Warner Music Germany: CD: 5051011 8689 2 4
Released: 2006
Co-writer of one track: '2 of a Kind', with Eliot Kennedy and
Tim Woodcock

N-DUBZ
AGAINST ALL ODDS
All Around the World: CD: 0602527252292

Released: 2009
Co-writer of one track: 'No One Knows', with N-Dubz

DONNY OSMOND
WHAT I MEANT TO SAY
Decca Records: CD: 986 3139
Released: 2004
Co-writer of nine tracks:
'Breeze on By', with Donny Osmond, Bobby Womack, Eliot
Kennedy; 'Keep Her in Mind', with Donny Osmond, Eliot
Kennedy, Tim Woodcock; 'In It for Love', with Donny Osmond,
Eliot Kennedy, Delaire Peterson, Paul Peterson, Richard
Peterson; 'My Perfect Rhyme', with Donny Osmond, Eliot
Kennedy; 'What I Meant to Say', with Donny Osmond, Eliot
Kennedy; 'Whenever You're in Trouble', with Donny Osmond,
Eliot Kennedy; 'Shoulda' Known Better', with Donny Osmond,
Eliot Kennedy; 'Insecurity', with Donny Osmond, Wayne Hector,
Eliot Kennedy; 'Christmas Time', with Donny Osmond and Eliot
Kennedy

MARK OWEN
IN YOUR OWN TIME
Island Records/Universal Music: CD: 0602498658598
Released: 2003
Co-writer of three tracks:
'Four Minute Warning', with Eliot Kennedy and Mark Owen; 'If
You Weren't Leaving Me', with Mark Owen, Eliot Kennedy and
Tim Woodcock; 'Turn the Light On', with Mark Owen and Eliot
Kennedy

ELAINE PAIGE
ELAINE PAIGE & FRIENDS
Rhino Records: CD: 5249828742
Released: 2010
Co-writer of one track: 'It's Only Life', with Tim Rice

RONAN PARKE
RONAN PARKE
Simco Records: CD: 0886979526020
Released: 2011
Writer of one track: 'Stronger Than I Am'

AMY STUDT
FALSE SMILES
Polydor Records: CD: 980107-4
Released: 2003
Co-writer of one track: 'Testify', with Amy Studt, Eliot Kennedy,
Tim Woodcock

RUSSELL WATSON
AMORE MUSICA
Decca Records: CD: B0004439-02
Released: 2004
Co-writer of one track: 'The Alchemist' (Russell Watson
featuring Lara Fabian), with Eliot Kennedy

WESTLIFE
GREATEST HITS
RCA Records: Double CD: 88691903272
Released: 2011
Co-writer of one track: 'Lighthouse', with John Shanks

ROBBIE WILLIAMS

IN AND OUT OF CONSCIOUSNESS: GREATEST HITS
1990–2010

Chrysalis/EMI Records: Double CD: CDVD3082

Released: 2010

Co-writer of two new tracks:

'Shame', with Robbie Williams (also performer); 'Heart and I',
with Robbie Williams

ROBBIE WILLIAMS

TAKE THE CROWN

Island Records/Universal Music: CD: 3716807

Released: 2012

Co-writer of two tracks:

'Candy', with Robbie Williams and Terje Olsen

'Different', with Robbie Williams and Jacknife Lee

ROBBIE WILLIAMS

SWINGS BOTH WAYS

Island Records/Universal Music: CD: 3756151

Released: 2013

Co-writer of one track: 'Wedding Bells', with Robbie Williams.
This track only appears on the Deluxe Edition
of the album.